# PERVERSE MIDRASH

# PERVERSE MIDRASH

## OSCAR WILDE, ANDRÉ GIDE, AND CENSORSHIP OF BIBLICAL DRAMA

KATHERINE BROWN DOWNEY

Continuum

New York    London

Copyright © 2004 by Katherine Brown Downey

The Continuum International Publishing Group, 15 East 26th Street, New York, NY 10010

The Continuum International Publishing Group Ltd, The Tower Building, 11 York Road, London SE1 7NX

Cover art: Salome by Beardsley, Fogg Art Museum, Cambridge, Mass./SuperStock

Bible translations in this book are from the New Jerusalem Bible (NJB) and the King James Version (KJV).

Cover design: Lee Singer

Library of Congress Cataloging-in-Publication Data

Downey, Katherine Brown.
Perverse Midrash : Oscar Wilde, André Gide, and censorship of biblical drama / Katherine Brown Downey.
    p. cm.
Includes bibliographical references and index.
ISBN 0-8264-1622-5 (pbk.)—ISBN 0-8264-1621-7 (hardcover)
1. Wilde, Oscar, 1854–1900. Salomé. 2. Salome (Biblical figure)—In literature. 3. Wilde, Oscar, 1854–1900—Censorship. 4. Gide, André, 1869–1951—Censorship. 5. Saul, King of Israel—In literature. 6. Gide, André, 1869–1951. Saül. 7. Bible plays—History and criticism. 8. Bible plays—Censorship. 9. Religion and literature. 10. Bible—In literature. 11. Theater—Censorship. I. Title.
PR5820.S23D69 2004
822'.8—dc22
                    2004013141

Printed in the United States of America

04 05 06 07 08 09              10 9 8 7 6 5 4 3 2 1

DEDICATED

IN MEMORY OF
STEVEN JAY COLVIN,
WHOSE FAITH INSPIRED ME,

AND

IN ABIDING LOVE FOR
MARK TREGER,
WHOSE COURAGE SUSTAINED ME,

TO

THE FUTURE WE SHARE IN
AUSTIN RAE DOWNEY,
WHOSE PATIENCE HUMBLES ME

# CONTENTS

# ACKNOWLEDGMENTS

To laugh often and much;
To win the respect of intelligent people and affection of a child;
To earn the appreciation of honest critics,
And endure the betrayal of false friends;
To appreciate beauty;
To find the best in others;
To leave the world a bit better whether by a healthy child,
A garden patch, or a redeemed social condition;
To know that even one life has breathed easier
Because you have lived. . . . This is to have succeeded.

*Ralph Waldo Emerson*

I think of myself as a student of Jeffrey Perl in every sense of the word. Not only was his four-semester course on the history of aesthetics and taste the core of my program at the University of Texas at Dallas, but the many hours he and I spent talking about first Gide and then Wilde—why they wrote *Saül* and *Salomé*, and then the conundrum we discovered—were scholarly training in themselves. It is largely through Professor Perl's good questions and raised eyebrows that this book developed. And because he approached the reading of every iteration of each chapter with the same attention he gives a work for publication, the manuscript took shape in great part as the result of his careful editing. Asking Jeffrey Perl to direct my doctoral dissertation was the best decision I made as a graduate student, and working closely with him was one of the most enlarging experiences of my life. That the dissertation eventually became this book is due largely to the many ready and kind suggestions "JP" emailed to me from his new home at Bar Ilan University.

John Holbert of Perkins School of Theology, Southern Methodist University, taught me biblical Hebrew. Each week for nearly three years I enjoyed the luxuries of his office: his library that became an exam-field reading list, the comfortable chair where I riddled through first a Hebrew primer and then the book of Samuel, his generous attentions to whatever thoughts or whims I had, and the personal homily that reflected his passion for this literature. My approach to reading the Bible I have gleaned from Professor Holbert. So also my faith, for it is not possible to have been in his presence for so long, to have been the grateful recipient of such great and unconditional generosity, without reflecting on the ground of his being. Truly John taught me the language of God.

Early in my graduate school career, I was fortunate to have won the loving attentions of Zsuzsanna Ozsvath, who brings to her teaching and scholarship the awareness of the extreme privilege we academics enjoy. I hope that I will never forget the moment that began the first meeting of her Novel of Ideas course when she paused to savor and revere the experience before us of opening a great work of literature. I savored my graduate school experience, and I hope always to cherish the special privilege of study as I have continued to enjoy the gift of Zsuzsi's friendship.

I learned the rigors of critical scholarship from Michael Wilson, with whom I read Oscar Wilde and Sigmund Freud for the first time with adult supervision. Michael supervised my reading with an attentive eye for my facile, flaccid, or feeble attempts to lay claim to a particular interpretive point of view. Always challenging, always terse in his criticism, always sensitive to intellectual bricolage, Michael is a teacher in the grand Socratic tradition. I have desired and feared his criticism, and I am grateful for the time and attention he put into some of the most penetrating comment on my work and for his continued encouragement of my scholarly career.

The development of the central argument of the book was much facilitated by the comments on the manuscript that I received from Bonnie Marranca of *Performing Arts Journal*, who gave me great counsel on sources and has seen more performances of *Salomé* around the world than anyone I know, and who in her being lives the union of spirituality and drama that I think the nineteenth-century theatre reformers had in mind; from Alex Argyros of UT Dallas who exhibits an enthusiasm for experimental theatre that is infectious and whose comments were fresh, provocative, and offered with kindness and genuine interest; and from Deborah Moreland, now of the Hockaday School, who was colleague, critic, fellow supplicant, and good friend throughout the whole of the writing process, and whose keen eye and forthrightness I deeply valued.

My research was conducted with surprising facility at several libraries and through the able assistance of the interlibrary loan department of the UT Dallas library. I gratefully acknowledge the generosity of the Fondren, Hamon, and Bridwell libraries at SMU where I enjoyed so many hours of quiet research and reading, and which made available to me so many materials I would have traveled great distances to see otherwise. The Harry Ransom Humanities Research Center at the University of Texas in

Austin is one of the loveliest archives to visit, and the staff go out of their way to make research there comfortable and productive. The Performing Arts Library at the New York Public Library is, on the other hand, one of the most exciting places to conduct research. Holding authentic performance materials, elbow to elbow with actors and writers, was quite an exhilarating experience, second only to turning the pages of Wilde's manuscript of *Salomé*.

Henry Carrigan has been gracious from our first phone call when he advised me that my manuscript was a finalist for the Trinity Press International Prize for New and Emerging Scholars, and that Continnum might like to publish it. Always responsive, always encouraging, and always promoting new ideas, Henry must be one of the most unusual editors in this field. His suggestions, as well as those of Ryan Masteller and their extraordinarily capable staff, consistently improved on what I had written (and rewritten many times!) such that the clarity of expression is largely their doing. Of course, any unclarity of thought is my own.

My students at UT Dallas and in the Open Door Class at Greenland Hills United Methodist Church, with whom I have shared *Salomé, Saül,* and my way of reading the Bible, have eagerly and cheerfully shared with me their insights and provocative comments and have encouraged me as a teacher and as a scholar. My friends and family have been supportive even when they did not fully understand what I was doing. Special thanks to Cindy Sailor and Beverly Scott who helped me wrestle with so much, to Kim Neal and Tracy Wallace who literally walked me through my arguments, and to my husband of fifteen years, Mark Treger, who not only made this possible, but also persuaded me that I could do it, and that furthermore it was worth doing.

# PROLOGUE: "HALF BIBLICAL, HALF PORNOGRAPHIC"

Oscar Wilde was in Paris in the fall of 1891, forming friendships with the people who would become his greatest advocates and sources of support (Stuart Merrill, Adolph Retté, Pierre Louÿs, and so on), when he met the fifteen-years-younger André Gide. In a series of lunches and dinners over three weeks, the two spent a great deal of intensive time together.[1] Wilde was drafting *Salomé* that fall. Apparently having started it in London, he worked on it again while in Paris and completed it shortly after his return to London in December.[2] It seems likely that he and Gide discussed it, as

---

1. This time was to be of great importance to the impressionable Gide, as the story goes; Gide excised his journal pages that covered this period. In Wilde scholarship, this narrative serves as a brief episode to demonstrate Wilde's influence in Paris, whereas in Gide scholarship, the story represents a seminal moment in Gide's life. For the standard narrative of their meeting, see, for instance, Ellmann (1985), Dollimore (1991), and Fryer (1997). All of the details in my account here derive from such standard narratives. It is the details' arrangement that prompts new questions.

2. These phases correspond with the extant manuscripts, about which there is some disagreement as to the order of composition. In my opinion, the manuscript now in the Bodmer Library in Geneva is the first draft, the one at the Harry Ransom Humanities Research Center (HRC) at the University of Texas in Austin is second, and the two notebooks now in the Rosenbach Foundation Museum in Philadelphia are the third. In the HRC manuscript, the first one-third or so of the play is written out as if it had been copied, while the rest reflects original writing with notes and scratch-outs. It also is missing speeches and certain details (such as the list of precious goods Herod offers Salomé) and includes notes only as to what in general should appear there. It seems to me that Wilde filled these in when he composed the third draft. It is not clear, however, whether it was the second or the third draft that he sent to Louÿs to peruse, nor whose hand corrected Wilde's French in the HRC manuscript. Every Wilde scholar seems to have an opinion on this. A minority suggest that Gide was that editor.

Wilde talked with many people about his play. He had expected *Salomé* to be produced in London in the summer of 1892 with Sarah Bernhardt in the title role as part of her summer season, but two weeks into rehearsals, Wilde's play was banned by the English examiner of plays, who declared it "half biblical, half pornographic."

The examiner, E. F. S. Pigott, was actually enforcing a proscription against public performance of biblical material that had originated more than three centuries earlier. The sixteenth-century legislation against the public production of passion and cycle plays, first in Paris and then in London and other European cities, followed a period when European communities had been producing large-scale dramatizations of key biblical narratives as major local events. Suddenly these communities—actors, writers, producers, audiences, church, and state—regulated those performances out of existence. There apparently was a broad consensus that this was the correct thing to do, and the consensus persisted until the end of the nineteenth century, when it seems, for reasons never explored, to have broken apart. The breakdown is evident in studies of theatre and censorship written at the time, in newspaper articles defending and challenging the proscription, and in biblical plays for the public stage by significant literary figures. Wilde was outraged, but to no avail. He threatened to renounce his British citizenship, claimed that the French never would have greeted a religious play with such derision, and published *Salomé* in French simultaneously in London and Paris in February 1893. An English translation followed in August.

Meanwhile, Gide had conceived his play *Saül* by 1894, shortly before he met Wilde for the second time in Algeria. Wilde was vacationing there with Alfred Douglas, and Gide reported that when he had checked into a hotel and then seen that Wilde and Douglas also were registered there, he checked himself out. But encountering Wilde again was not to be avoided, and Gide never was able to explain his fear of it; he ran into Wilde later in the city. They talked over dinner, and later, having recognized and articulated Gide's desires, Wilde arranged a tryst for Gide with a young Algerian boy. Though this was not Gide's first homosexual encounter, nonetheless it proved to be a formative event in his life and in his writing.

Wilde returned from Africa to litigation and imprisonment in England, and Gide to Paris to write works replete with images from his desert experience. In February 1896, Lugné-Poe produced *Salomé* in Paris at the Théâtre de l'Oeuvre. The production was intended as a gesture of support for Wilde by those in his and Gide's circle. When he was released from prison in 1897, Wilde settled into exile in France, and Gide reported visiting him several times. *Saül* was the first of Gide's works to interest Wilde, who talked of composing another biblical play, this one about Judas. Both of them had projected books that would demonstrate that authentic Christian faith was in opposition to that of its orthodox adherents.

Gide composed *Saül* in the summer of 1897 and spring of 1898 and hoped, in vain, to produce it soon afterward.[3] Wilde died in November 1900 without having seen either his *Salomé* or Gide's *Saül* performed, without having written the other biblical plays he had talked about with Gide, and without having read or seen the other biblical plays that Gide would write.[4] What were these two men—known more for their aesthetic and philosophical principles than for their religious concerns—trying to accomplish by writing biblical plays? Although they took shocking liberties with the biblical accounts, Wilde and Gide do not appear to be ridiculing scripture. What, then, *are* these plays?

Wilde's *Salomé* and Gide's *Saül* have been considered critically in the traditional contexts of authorial oeuvre,[5] biography,[6] or "thought."[7] And for this reason, these plays have been treated with only rather embarrassed respect, dealt with at all because of the importance of their

---

3. Gide published the play in 1903, then thought it would be produced in 1904 by the Théâtre Antoine with Edouard de Max in the title role. It was not produced until 1922, when Jacques Copeau included it in his June repertoire at the Théâtre de Vieux Colombier (with music by Arthur Honegger).

4. *Le Retour de l'enfant prodigue* (1907) and *Bethsabé* (1910).

5. On Wilde's *oeuvre*, see, for instance, Cohen (1978) and Bird (1977); on Gide's, see Hytier (1962), Yoshii (1992), and Claude (1992).

6. The traditional approach via authorial biography especially characterizes Gide scholarship. See, for instance, Thomas (1950) and McLaren (1953) on Gide's psychological development, and Lerner (1980) and Pollard (1991) on his homosexuality.

7. Most *Salomé* scholarship contextualizes the work in either a grand artistic tradition or in the author's thought. See, for instance, Nassaar (1974) for the play as interpreting literary decadence, and Kohl (1989) for a delineation of the myriad artistic, musical, and literary influences on Wilde's play. Eilmann's "Overtures to *Salomé*" (1985) pursues a thesis similar to that in his biography of Wilde: that the key to understanding Wilde is the influence of Ruskin and Pater on him. Among studies of *Salomé* that consider the play in its cultural context, see Powell (1990), focusing on the question of why Wilde wrote it in French; Kuryluk (1987), studying the play in the context of the *fin de siècle* fascination with the grotto (and thus the grotesque) as a symbol for the unconscious; and Hoare (1997), making use of the Maud Allen case against *The Vigilante* editor for libelous remarks concerning her performance in the English premier of Wilde's *Salomé* as a prism for examining larger cultural issues. My approach is closest to that of Eltis, in that he considers Wilde's work as a product of its culture and its discourses. Eltis, however, does not treat *Salomé*, as he does not see it as "set in and specifically criticizing nineteenth-century society" (1996, 5). This is because he does not consider the religious atmosphere of the time and the discourses it produced; rather, he is interested in Wilde's feminist, anarchist, and socialist concerns.

authors.[8] That Wilde and Gide made use of biblical material seems to discomfit their critics; that they did so at a time when biblical drama was prohibited has rarely been addressed. Rather, traditional critical treatments seek to smooth over the plays' aberrant qualities, situating them in phases of their authors' moral or literary development. This study takes them seriously as aberrations and investigates Wilde's and Gide's claims that these plays are works of faith by considering them as participating in the history of biblical drama.[9] While the church produced liturgical and other adaptations of biblical material, most biblical drama has been of secular origin. Censorship of biblical drama on the public stage, as legal protection of the Bible from public affront (or of the public from biblical affront) reflects an uneasy relation among the church, the state, the artist, and the public. Situating Wilde's and Gide's plays in the history of biblical drama, then, will illuminate them in a new way, as works with a peculiar function that is overlooked when they are considered solely in the contexts of authorial oeuvre or biography.

Performance of biblical material is a tradition older than the Bible itself, if indeed many of its narratives originated in oral performances, as scholars today believe. The Gospels, for instance, reflect the influence of both midrash and a tradition of pageants in which first-century Christians reenacted key events.[10] While commonly associated with its highest form,

---

8. Brée (1963), for instance, observes that Gide took "great liberties in his treatment of the biblical story" and concludes that he merely infused it with his own concerns. Consequently, "in *Saul* Gide has all the elements of an original and exciting play, which fails to come off largely because he was unable to handle the theme of sexual inversion" (110). Brée sees all of Gide's drama as dealing with the character discovering another hidden self within him, and thus, though it is quite clear that *Saül* embarrasses Brée, she concludes, "Yet *Saul* is not a negligible play" (116).

9. Although the history of biblical drama does not comprise one neat narrative, see Roston (1968) or Philomène (1978) for a sampling of the standardized approach.

10. That Gospel is a form of midrash is commonly accepted, but see also Kermode (1979), who makes the related observation that "the evangelists used methods continuous with those by which, before the establishment of the canon, ancient texts were revised and adapted to eliminate or make acceptable what had come to be unintelligible or to give offense. The practice is known as midrash" (81). This understanding of midrash is particularly germane to my argument. Other recent Gospel scholarship has recovered Mark as the finest example of its genre (as opposed to the traditional view of Mark as a primitive work authored by a not very skilled writer of Greek) and suggests that the Gospel of Mark's dramatic quality may be a result of the genre's derivation from an earlier tradition of dramatic reenactment. It may be that in the decades between the death of Jesus and the writing of

achieved in the Middle Ages, midrash as a narrative performance that fills gaps and smoothes aberrations in the biblical text characterizes both the Old and New Testaments. So also does reenactment, as instanced by Jesus' instruction to his disciples to commemorate the Last Supper ("Do this in remembrance of me"), an echo of Moses' instruction to Israel to commemorate the Passover.[11] Like the Passover seder, the eucharist was a reenactment of God's saving activity. By the fourth century, at the latest, ceremonial reenactments of this sort had become part of the celebrations of the church on feast days, according to the Roman noblewoman Egeria.[12] These early performances seem to have functioned as mythmaking, church-forming, doctrine-establishing efforts that preserved the memory of key events and their interpretations, the commemoration of which ultimately became part of Christian orthodoxy.[13] Dramatic biblical performances did not arise spontaneously and originally in the form of the medieval mystery plays. In fact, the relationship between the Bible and drama is older and more continuous. For whatever the impulse is to perform biblical events, it has been preserved through centuries of composition.

The Latin liturgical dramas that seem to have originated in the ninth century flourished through the Middle Ages. By the twelfth century, a distinctly vernacular and lay biblical drama had emerged; these plays were "among the outstanding cultural monuments of medieval Europe" (Muir

---

Mark, early followers of "the way" remembered the final events of his life and death by revisiting key Jerusalem sites and retelling the stories there in a pageant anticipating the stations of the cross. See, for instance, Rhoads and Michie (1982).

11. While this study focuses on the biblical drama of Christian Western Europe, Judaism has a parallel history, perhaps beginning with this originary moment of reenactment. From the Purim plays dramatizing the events in Esther to celebrate that festival to the modern Hebrew drama of Eretz Israel, which influenced the development of the language and identity that would come to be significant to the modern nation, biblical drama has been just as much a product of Jewish popular culture as it was in Western Europe. In Eastern Europe, however, the representational impulse seems to have been expressed in iconography rather than drama.

12. Though no evidence exists of biblical drama between these fourth-century celebrations and the ninth-century Latin liturgical plays performed by Benedictine communities (the earliest record of biblical drama as a form), it seems likely that there was some sort of drama then as well.

13. By the fourth century, the canon of scripture also had been formed. Ehrman (1993) argues that a product of the period of intense rivalry among various groups of Christians advocating divergent ways of understanding their religion, the ante-Nicene age, was an orthodoxy that ironically changed the original meaning of some scriptural texts to support its theology. Merely one way of understanding Christianity, it had routed the opposition, co-opted for itself the designation "orthodoxy," and marginalized the rival parties as "heresies." These representatives of an "incipient orthodoxy" altered New Testament texts during this time of dispute, making them say what they had come to mean, thereby "corrupting" these texts for theological reasons.

1995, 1).[14] While it once was thought that these lay vernacular plays developed out of the earlier Latin liturgical drama, it is now apparent that they were a genre that combined popular art and piety and represented an independent dramatic tradition. Produced in Catholic Europe by whole communities comprising neighborhood groups, trade guilds, and religious confraternities as public spectacles, these plays differed from the tales of chivalry and courtly love portrayed in court and castle masques and considered inappropriate for the merchant and popular classes. Whether this lay vernacular drama ever had been under ecclesiastical aegis, the church certainly had lost control of it by the sixteenth century. The composers of these mysteries, moralities, and saints plays did not limit themselves to simple adaptations of biblical stories, but freely altered them, adding characters, emotions, commentaries, and debates to create works reflecting a freedom of thought and personal interpretation that would not survive the religious reforms of the sixteenth century.[15] These large-scale expressions of popular culture suddenly were prohibited by the church and the state, which now pursued a rather more political than religious agenda.

This prohibition was largely a product of the turmoil of the Protestant Reformation and the Catholic Counter-Reformation. Hardly a popular movement, the Protestant Reformation in England was an extremely painful imposition of a new religion by the Crown onto the English people necessitated by the king's rejection of papal authority. To effect this thoroughly political separation from the Roman church, England—its sovereign and its people—had to become Protestant, and quickly.

One of the many tools for accomplishing this was the biblical play, a popular medium for expressing and teaching ideas, now enlisted by the Crown to counter papist sentiments and tradition. These "polemical plays" were characterized by homiletic didacticism, moralizing, and satire, combining a biblical narrative with a morality subplot and adding

---

14. See Muir (1995) for a detailed survey of the six centuries of medieval plays for which there is evidence in Western Europe.

15. Medieval drama comprises mysteries, also known as passion plays; moralities; and saints plays. Mysteries were probably the earliest, based on biblical narratives and hence of the most interest to the present study. Moralities and saints plays drew primarily on extrabiblical material, the former usually of an allegorical nature to illustrate a teaching point (*Everyman* is the most famous of these), and the latter portraying the life and miracles of a particular saint of the church, often performed on the feast day of the saint. The medieval cycles, also called pageants, consisted of numerous mystery plays, and in their fully developed form, by about the fourteenth century, required thirty or more hours to perform. These cycles are of the greatest interest to scholars of medieval drama today.

abstract figures who comment on the action. This became the format for biblical political satire and the Protestant propaganda perhaps best represented in the work of John Bale.[16] A zealous reformer who hated the papists and felt called by his apocalyptic expectations to engage in the battle against the Antichrist (Rome), Bale rather ironically used as his weapon a medieval Catholic literary form, thereby constructing a powerful antidote to the popular mystery plays. The transition from Catholicism to Protestantism in England was hardly a smooth one. During the brief moments when the Crown was again Catholic, Bale and his friends had to go into exile while Catholic polemical plays were condoned or encouraged. The Puritan legislation against the production of *all* plays has obscured the issues of the original controversy. In general, the plays of this period mirror the history of the Reformation in England.

Whereas in the sixteenth century biblical drama was regulated because of its relationship to the interests of the Crown, by the seventeenth century it became a threat to the authority of the church and was relegated first to private performance and then to the even more private personal reading. On the Continent, humanist dramas, which combined classical form with religious teachings, were composed as "school plays" to be performed privately by schoolchildren.[17] The greatest composer of these school plays was Racine, and the finest biblical drama of this period was commissioned by Mme de Maintenon, consort to Louis XIV, for the school she had established near Versailles at Saint-Cyr for the daughters of impecunious nobles.[18] Production of these plays, however, moved from

---

16. In Bale's play *On the Threefold Law of God*, the three Laws (of Nature, Moses, and Christ) are set against the six Vices, costumed for ready identification, each costume representing some office of the Roman church. Identifying three historical periods during which each of these Laws was operative, Bale also specified a pair of corrupting Vices most active in each. In the final act, the archenemy of Revelation is destroyed, clearly identified as the Roman Church, and the Vices of the moment are its representatives. Three other major Protestant writers of this period were Thomas Sylley, Ralph Radcliffe, and Nicholas Udall. See Blackburn (1971) for the plays of this period.

17. Written by both Protestants and Catholics, in either case usually by clerics, the plays were defended as true history (as opposed to the pagan subjects of classical drama) with special moral benefits, and their production was supported by Erasmus, Luther, Melancthon, and Calvin. The key feature of these humanist plays, however, was that as school plays, they were intended for private performance and therefore did not violate the proscription of biblical drama on the public stage. See the chapters titled "Amateur Religious Plays" and "Religious Plays, 1673–1700" in Lancaster (1936) for a detailed discussion of the plays of this period.

18. Because people of the time considered Latin to be for boys, these plays had to be presented in the vernacular to meet the peculiar demands of a girls' school, to provide sufficient roles for girls, and to serve an educational function. Racine selected the subject of Esther for his first Saint-Cyr play, perhaps because of its straightforward theme of the triumph of female virtue over male vice. Lancaster

Saint-Cyr to the court and ultimately to the Comédie Française, under the protective approval of Louis XIV and Mme de Maintenon. This endorsement of biblical plays was not, however, without controversy. Although Racine's *Esther* had been designed for the edification of girls, it was said to endanger their morals. This private school play that had gone public, then, became a political work subject to public discourse and its restrictions. The appropriate medium for the religious play, concludes the Abbé D'Aubignac in his *Projet pour le rétablissement du theatre*, is the published book, for a biblical play is better read than performed. In a book, the reader does not have to encounter the actor and his unconvincing portrayal of the miracles, nor deal with the inevitable undermining of biblical authority that would follow. According to D'Aubignac, the theatre is unfit to handle religious truth, which properly resides within the magisterium of the church and in the believer's private devotions. Thus did biblical drama become closeted, and it remained so until the nineteenth century.

These "closet dramas"[19] of the late seventeenth, eighteenth, and nineteenth centuries, perhaps best represented by Milton's *Paradise Lost*, were largely poetic epics intended for pious domestic reading.[20] In the eighteenth century, however, musical adaptations of biblical narratives, chiefly those of Handel, revived performance of biblical material without offending the censor, perhaps because, although they were dramatizations of sacred themes, they were combined with the solemnity of church music to create a quasireligious experience consistent with worship. When in the nineteenth century the romantic poets challenged the Enlightenment confidence in an orderly world created and administered by a rational

---

suggests that it also had the value of illustrating the benefits to the state of the king's having a pious and intelligent consort (I, 293). Racine adapted the biblical narrative to produce a play with a more pious Esther than her biblical predecessor, with a fairy-tale plot about a beautiful princess being saved by a king from an ogre, and with action whose biblical sex and violence was greatly tempered. For an audience of schoolgirls who were to take from it a moral lesson, at a time when the fairy tale was beginning to be popular, this portrayal of Esther was appropriate.

19. Roston (1968) terms this "drama without a stage." Thus it is drama without the problematic part, the public medium.

20. Though *Paradise Lost* was composed not as a drama, but as an epic, Milton had argued earlier in his life against the Puritan claim that the theatre was inherently immoral, and he had opposed its abolition. Nevertheless, it is abundantly clear from the preface justifying his choice of dramatic form (on the authority of St. Paul, for instance) that not only did Milton feel the need to defend it, but he also was opposed to the play's performance: "Division into Act and Scene referring chiefly to the Stage (to which this work was never intended) is here omitted." For *Samson Agonistes*, Milton adopted Attic tragedy as a model and adhered to Aristotelian rules, betraying his respect for Greek drama.

God, Byron's *Cain* perhaps best represented the later closet drama.[21] As poetic drama, however, this challenge was safely enclosed between book covers. The closet dramas of these centuries reflect both the historical impulse to dramatize biblical events and the peculiar cultural need to contain that impulse by relegating them to the private realm.

⚜

Over the three hundred years since the original proscription of the performance of biblical plays, censorship became increasingly restrictive, first regulating them, then making them private, and ultimately eliminating them entirely in favor of reading. In the sixteenth century, when the issue was largely political, prohibitions were primarily against New Testament material; in the seventeenth century, the church deemed all biblical material unsuitable for the theatre; and by the nineteenth century, the English examiner of plays had banned Apocryphal, Josephus, and Herod dramas. In the late nineteenth century, even biblical references in otherwise non-biblical plays were banned—metaphorical references to the raising of Lazarus, for instance—as was the physical presence of the Bible on the stage as a prop. Even dramas that had not been technically subject to the censor's examination—those written before 1737, in a foreign language, or presented musically—were prohibited by him in the months immediately preceding the planned production of Wilde's *Salomé*. This increasing restriction over three hundred years, culminating in the absolute prohibition from the public stage of anything even vaguely suggesting a biblical source, is the context in which Wilde and Gide wrote their biblical dramas, the background against which *Salomé* and *Saül* must be understood in order to see them as the remarkable cultural products they were—biblical plays that had come out of the closet.

Why did the English censor ban the biblical play—or more accurately, why, by the end of the nineteenth century, had biblical material become banned from the public stage? Why had it been prohibited for more than three hundred years, and why was the prohibition even more restrictive in

---

21. Widespread interest existed at that time in the story of the first murder. Roston (1968) identifies seventeen plays between 1822 and 1877 on this theme (198) and argues that the Romantics' questioning of an orderly world predisposed them to sympathize with the errant human and to view with distrust any scriptural portrayal of God as merciful and benevolent (199).

the nineteenth than in the sixteenth century? Those who have reflected on these questions have not offered very satisfactory explanations, ranging from political anger to bad taste.[22] They express concerns about producers making money on performances, biblical material being distorted for some other purpose, and audiences identifying with the characters. But they fail to explain why any of these so-called abuses or perversions would present a problem. What was the worst that could happen? What were they really afraid of? Whatever it was, certainly Wilde's Salomé dancing on stage with the severed head of John the Baptist between her legs, or Gide's Saül driven crazy by his love for the young David, would have provoked it. Indeed, in the fracas that followed the banning of Salomé, there was quite a bit of public speculation about the play and the effect it could have had on the public. But because the play had not been performed, speculation on its content could be based only upon the material in the Bible. This popular speculation reflects a fear of perversion *in* the Bible as well as a perversion *of* it, and it is this, I have come to believe, that underlies the history of censorship of the Bible on stage.

In the "play" that follows—and I use this metaphor in the sense of both a *pièce* comprising monologue and dialogue and a *jeu de mots*—I pursue the argument that Wilde's and Gide's plays are the religious works their authors claimed them to be. First I examine *fin de siècle* cultural discourses relevant to biblical drama, pairing biblical critics and theatre reformers to uncover a common impulse underlying both their reforming efforts. This impulse also drives the plays, which I argue are anxious reconciliations of these fundamentally irreconcilable movements. Then I bring literary historians and defenders of stage censorship into dialogic relationship and examine their discourses to unveil the fear underlying and repressed by that censorship. *Salomé* and *Saül* are treated as products of these discourses and manifestations of that fear, Wilde's play embodying the articulated concerns of the censorship's defenders, and Gide's play manifesting their repressed fear. But they also are products of the discourses about biblical criticism and theatre reform and thus are spiritual or religious works, albeit unorthodox ones. Finally, I consider the plays as phenomena in a cultural psychodrama, manifesting repressed fears and effecting a period of aphasia to follow. There I also define a literary genre

---

22. Roston and Philomène are the only two scholars to have studied modern biblical drama as a genre, and both see Wilde's *Salomé* as merely iconoclastic, "tearing down the scriptural heroes from their pedestals, presenting the innocent as villains, and acquitting the guilty" (Philomène 1978, 5).

with a peculiar cultural function, a genre I call "perverse midrash."[23] Thus I contend that E. F. S. Pigott, the examiner of plays who banned *Salomé* in the summer of 1892, was only partly correct when he dismissed the play as "half biblical, half pornographic." *Salomé* and *Saül* are both thoroughly perverse and entirely biblical. They are perverse midrashim.

23. Jeffrey Perl coined this term in 1995 during a conversation about Gide's biblical plays.

# ACT I

# Cultural Dialogues

# Scene 1
# *NOSTOS* AND *SHAVAH*: RECOVERING SPIRITUAL ORIGINS

## THE BIBLE AND THE THEATRE

Biblical drama consists of two components: biblical content and dramatic medium. Both of these components were understood in the nineteenth century to be powerful and dangerous in the wrong hands. The content of the Bible was sacred for many and served both devotional and didactic purposes, while the physical book was an icon for cultural and religious tradition, to be treated with reverence and respect.[1] The public stage was the most powerful cultural medium because of its ability to arouse feelings and action in an audience.[2] The advocates of biblical drama argued that if it treated its material with reverence and respect, and was intended for devotional or morally didactic ends, it could be a powerful agent for good. Its opponents, however, questioned the feasibility of this argument on both grounds, claiming that it was inevitable that the Bible would be held up to public ridicule and that such behavior would undermine the moral fiber of the country. This chapter focuses on several movements

---

1. A particularly relevant example at the time was the prohibition in England of the Bible as a stage prop.

2. That the nineteenth-century riots in Paris started in theatres was frequently held up as a prime reason to regulate theatre activity there. Another point commonly made about the power of the stage was that there is a difference between the impact of narrating in a novel that a woman got up out of her bath and of portraying this on the stage.

that addressed the components of biblical drama, biblical content, and dramatic medium. Understanding the impulses driving these movements may lead to a better understanding of the peculiar *fin de siècle* interest in biblical drama.

Biblical interpretation by the end of the nineteenth century had been revolutionized by the German "historical" or "higher" criticism, which was becoming well known even outside of the academy. A challenge to many traditional notions about the authorship, dating, and uniqueness of the biblical texts, this kind of scholarship was motivated by concern that readers could not understand the Bible and interpret its meaning adequately, given the historical and cultural distance between the nineteenth century and either the period of the events reported or the subsequent period of narrating them. These scholars sought to recover the original historical and cultural contexts in order to understand what the biblical texts had meant. In so doing, they hoped to restore to the modern reading of the Bible the original spiritual experience underlying it.

William Robertson Smith was the scholar most responsible for making this scholarship generally known to English readers. That his work was effective is evident in the subsequent ecclesiastical defense of historical criticism made known to the English public by Frederic W. Farrar, and in the efforts of the most successful British novelist of the time, Mary (Mrs. Humphry) Ward. A related movement within biblical criticism of the time, that of treating the Bible "as literature," was fathered by the literature professor Richard Green Moulton. Working independently, all of these individuals—biblical scholar, cleric, novelist, and literary scholar—argued that the Bible had become deadened by centuries of treatment as inspired and infallible. They sought to return to its origins in order to recover something that had been lost—the spiritual experience—and restore this to modern reading.

Theatre in the nineteenth century had largely devolved to frivolous farces and bedroom comedies, in addition to the persistent seventeenth-century classics, or so argued the numerous writers and directors who sought reform of the public stage. The reformers pointed to the silly and even obscene situations in these comedies and called for more serious drama that would address ideas of importance. Not surprisingly, perhaps, many of these dramatists sought a return to the theatre's origins, when drama was an agent of religious experience and the public stage its medium. One of the most outspoken movements in this vein was that of *symboliste* drama, which tried to restore seriousness and transcendence to the stage by returning to the ritual origins of drama and the symbolic language of the ineffable. A related movement to reform the theatre, similarly motivated, was the revival and re-production in the nineteenth century of the medieval mystery plays of England and France, which had disappeared in the sixteenth century. These two movements differed, the one trying to innovate by returning to ancient ritual and myth, the other trying to reform by reviving a body of successfully spiritual work, but both manifested an underlying impulse to recover a lost experience of transcendence and restore it to the modern theatre. Though the products of these movements were not approved for the public stage,[3] all of these reformers intended to return to an earlier communal spiritual experience and re-create it for the modern public.

Jeffrey Perl (1984) characterizes this impulse to return, recover, and restore as an ideology (*"nostos"* in his shorthand) that informs a variety of historical theories of the nineteenth and twentieth centuries. He argues that this *nostos* is the determinant of modernism that has "been the least acknowledged and studied" (29), and that one reason for this is its "extraordinary complexity, unevenness, inconsistency, and unsystematic character" (35). Perl has identified two general types of historical thinking, which he calls Burckhardtian and theodicean. In the thought of Jacob Burckhardt, the period between the original and its restoration is vastly inferior.[4] In the theodicean thought of theorists such as Heine and Arnold, a dialectic between periods of materialism and idealism synthesizes to produce a unified cultural sensibility. But these two types of historical thinking interacted, and further kinds of return and responses to the return compound the complication. Perl outlines a typology of these returns in *The Tradition of Return: The Implicit History of Modern Literature*. The processes of return manifest in the various movements within biblical criticism and drama are complex, but common to them all is the impulse to return to an originary moment in order to recover a lost spirituality, however defined or understood, and restore it to modern life.

The restoration phase of the process—or rather, the popularization of the fruits of the return—seems to have been most problematic. Here

---

3. The reasons for this censorship are developed in the next chapter, "Unveiling Fears: Literary History as Guardian of Culture."

4. In Perl's parlance, if the first original period may be called "A" and the third period of restoration "A'," then the middle period is "B." This model he calls, informally, "bumpkin history."

"popularization" consists principally of making these fruits known to the public, availing the public of the spiritual experience that had been recovered, and creating in the public an interest in it. Who is this public whose interests are commanded by these movements? It is not necessary to define this public, but simply to recognize that one exists for these movements. All of these movements have a public in mind that has the resources and facility to embrace their products (education, leisure, money), a disposition to do so (shared cultural values or the potential to share them), and the ability to resist authority in the guise of the church, the academy, or the state.

A commonplace of the theatre is that the stage is a force for renewal and action—that it does not reflect change, but creates it. The *fin de siècle* theatre reformers sought to change not just the drama, but also modern life by restoring to it this lost spirituality. Their medium for accomplishing this was the public stage, and hence the alarm of what one might call the "guardians of the status quo." Similarly, neither the efforts nor even the products of the biblical scholars themselves, but rather the attempts to make known to the general public these results, caused the consternation evident in the church's dismissal of theologians sympathetic to the new scholarship and in the crisis of faith it inspired among believers. The reformers' popularizing efforts were key to the movements to change the *fin de siècle* view of the Bible and the stage.

## BIBLICAL CRITICISM AND POPULARIZATION

By the 1890s, William Robertson Smith had made known the German biblical scholarship of the previous century to readers of English. Having studied as a young man in Germany under Wellhausen, Kuenen, and Rothe, Robertson Smith not only benefited from these men's research, but also contributed significantly to the field himself.[5] Associated with the Free Church in Scotland, Robertson Smith was dismissed in 1881 from his position at its college in Aberdeen for his unorthodox views, which he had published not in exclusively scholarly journals, but in places where they might be accessible to "the ordinary English reader who is familiar with the Bible and accustomed to consecutive thought" (1908, x). Robertson Smith's most significant work, both in scholarly contribution

---

5. Rogerson (1990) demonstrates that contrary to the prevailing view of Robertson Smith's work, he was not just a purveyor of others' ideas, but a contributor to the field.

and in popularization of this scholarship, consists of the *Encyclopaedia Britannica*, whose ninth edition he edited and for which he wrote more than fifty articles; public lectures in Aberdeen, Edinburgh, and Glasgow, which were immediately published and became "one of the greatest known literary successes in the department of theology" (1919, vii); and several reviews of major works in the field of biblical criticism and of the progress of this scholarship in general, often adaptations of public lectures.

The most notorious of all Robertson Smith's work, and ultimately the cause of his dismissal from Aberdeen, was his *Encyclopaedia Britannica* article "Bible," first published in 1875 and reprinted until at least 1900 along with the entire ninth edition.[6] This article, printed before Wellhausen had published his famous source theory, advanced both of Robertson Smith's key ideas: that three documentary sources existed for the Hexateuch (the "Levitico-Elohist document," "Jehovistic narrative," and a "Northern Israel author") plus deuteronomic editing; and that the Levitical law and priesthood were of late date, postexilic, and in no way dating from the time of Moses and the "first legislation" or from the time of the prophets and the "deuteronomic legislation." From both of these positions, Robertson Smith argued for the prophetic experience as the originary spiritual moment and for the later law and priesthood as conservative, "unspiritual," and therefore not authoritative. Similarly, in the New Testament, Robertson Smith dismissed all nonapostolic writing as false, recognizing as genuine only that which reflected direct experience with Christ. Arguing that Jesus had also viewed the prophets as authoritative, Robertson Smith could observe a continuous line of original prophetic experience running through the Old Testament and into the New. Starting and ending with the premise that the Bible is not revelation itself, but the written record of it, Robertson Smith sought to recover this original experience of revelation for the modern reader.

That this article—fourteen pages in extremely small print on rather large paper—challenged principal teachings of the church regarding the inspiration and infallibility of the Bible, as well as the foundations of the church's claim to authority, and did so within the authoritative binding of the *Encyclopaedia Britannica*, was apparently more than the church could tolerate. Robertson Smith's efforts in the 1870s and 1880s to make known

---

6. The ninth edition of the *Encyclopaedia Britannica* was recognized as one of the finest and was published for at least twenty-five years. The 1900 edition with the Revised American Supplement contains all of Robertson Smith's articles.

to the general public the historical critical scholarship on the Bible cost him his position at Aberdeen. He went on to Cambridge, not as a theologian, but as an Arabist and expert in Semitic languages. But by then he had already published his major work in biblical criticism, a work that had entered the public domain and become enormously popular.

Robertson Smith's *Encyclopaedia Britannica* entry "Bible" is written from a believing Christian perspective. Though Robertson Smith studied ancient Judaism for most of his life, he was no advocate of its postbiblical manifestation, and he was even less enthusiastic about Islam. Nor was he sympathetic with nonbelieving biblical critics. The first paragraph of the article summarizes his position as a believer: that the Bible comprises "the sacred writings of Christendom" and that they are "made up of a number of independent records, which set before us the gradual development of the religion of revelation." The article provides an account of the historical and literary conditions that gave rise to the Bible, noting that its "development is divided into two great periods by the manifestation and historical work of Christ. In its pre-Christian stage the religion of revelation is represented as a *covenant* between the spiritual God and His chosen people the Hebrews. In accordance with this . . . Jesus speaks of the new dispensation founded in His death as a new *covenant*," hence its Old and New Testaments (1900a, 634).

Of its fourteen pages, the article devotes seven to the Old Testament, four to the New, and four to a discussion of manuscript history. Though this allocation of space seems proportionate to the amount of biblical material each testament comprises, it also may reflect Robertson Smith's much greater interest in the Old Testament, and even more important, his attempt to separate "spiritual" from "unspiritual" texts and historical periods.

He divides the "pre-Christian stage" into two periods, one of religious productivity and the other of subsequent stagnation and conservative tradition. The work of the prophets, beginning with Moses, characterizes the first period; the priesthood, beginning during the Babylonian exile, characterizes the second. Throughout his discussion of the Old Testament, Robertson Smith refers to "the struggle between spiritual and unspiritual religion," which in the early period is the struggle with other indigenous religions: "the true and spiritual religion which the prophets and likeminded priests maintained at once against heathenism and against unspiritual worship of Jehovah as a mere national deity without moral attributes . . ." (635). This "period of prophetic inspiration" predated the establishment of ritual law and the sacred ordinances, the outline of which Robertson Smith perceived in the last chapters of Ezekiel, which sketch the era of captivity. The period following, characterized by the canonization of the writings from the earlier period and the establishment of the priesthood, produced material that is less authoritative and spiritual than that which the "prophets generally spoke under the immediate influence of the Spirit" (639). While "in all ages a priesthood is conservative, not creative; . . . sometimes [priests] even appear as the opponents of the prophetic party, whose progressive ideas are distasteful to their natural conservatism and aristocratic instincts" (634).[7] Therefore, biblical material generated in the earlier period is deemed "spiritual" and original, but that from the later period is not.

A key point in Robertson Smith's discussion of prophecy, the prophets, and the prophetic writings is that "prophecy" is not prediction, but communication from God. What the prophets wrote, however, was surely secondary to what they had said, so what we have now is "no doubt, greatly abridged" (639). Furthermore, "there is no reason to think that a prophet ever received a revelation which was not spoken directly and pointedly to his own time" (640). The prophetic writing in the Old Testament, then, is specific to its own time and only a secondary record of the actual prophecy, whereas the experience recorded in the text is originary, authoritative, and "spiritual." It is to this originary experience that Robertson Smith wants to return, and it is what he understands to be the foundation of true faith. This is accomplished for him through the criticism of the Bible's account, with supplementary research on its context, in order to glimpse that originary experience it records. The category of the "spiritual" includes, then, the period of prophecy, the Genesis through Kings narrative, the Jehovistic narrative, Deuteronomic law, brief poems, psalms indubitably Davidic, Proverbs (except chapters 1–9), Job (except Elihu's speech), and the earlier prophets. All of this is characterized by having emanated from direct spiritual experience.

Following the "unspiritual" period of Levitical law, the priesthood, postbiblical law, and apocalyptic expectation came "the manifestation of God in Christ crucified, risen, and soon to return in glory" (642). It was with these "unspiritual" products that Jesus "had openly joined issue" and

---

7. One can see how Robertson Smith upset the church with statements like this. And no doubt he would have been pleased by J. W. Rogerson's reference to his dismissal, along with F. D. Maurice's from Kings College and W. M. L. deWette's from the University of Berlin, as resulting from his "prophetic voice."

"saw the commandment of God annulled." Furthermore, Robertson Smith argues, "it was His part not to destroy but to fill up into spiritual completeness the teaching of the old dispensation and herein He attached himself directly to the prophetic conception of the law in Deuteronomy" (642). Like the prophets of the Old Testament who had recorded their direct experiences with revelation, so those who in the New Testament had had direct experience with the revelation of Christ were the most authoritative.

Robertson Smith's language here shifts from "spiritual" as the essential criterion to "genuine," as opposed to "a considerable portion of the New Testament [that] is made up of writings not directly apostolical"—that is, not genuine or spiritual (643). Those he considers genuine are "the main books of the *Apostolicon*, the Acts, thirteen epistles of Paul, 1st Peter, 1st John, and the Apocalypse." Other material "of quite recent date [is] not of prophetic or apostolic authority" (645), and "a main problem of New Testament criticism is to determine the relation of these writings, especially of the gospels, to apostolic teaching and tradition" (643). As with the Old Testament, he also divides the New into two periods, one of earlier spiritual authenticity and the other of later conservatism.

With his emphasis on returning to the originary experiences underlying their written record (and his call for the criticism that facilitates that encounter), along with his conviction as a Christian believer that this return is necessary to an authentic faith, Robertson Smith describes a Burckhardtian *nostos*, in which the earlier prophetic age was eclipsed by the later inferior age of conservatism, dogma, and institutional hierarchy. This inferior age, however, was succeeded by the life of Christ, which was then followed by another inferior period. "In a word, the Church was speedily cut off from all historical appreciation of Revelation and Redemption, became unable to grasp in their fullness the deepest teachings of the Gospel, and was thrown back on an unhistorical intellectualism, that found its expression in neonomian theology and an allegorical exegesis" (1912, 213). Thus "the mediaeval Church, understanding by God's Word an intellectual revelation, looked in Scripture for that alone, and where no intellectual mysteries appeared, saw only, as Luther complains, bare dead histories. . . . Not so the Reformers" (228).

The Protestant Reformation is for Robertson Smith the end of that second inferior "B" period and marks the recovery of the prophetic spirit that had been lost. Modern criticism must continue "the same principle that the Reformation applied" and use the fruits of scholarship as Luther did in his time to "study the contemporary history, and learn how things stood in the land; how men's minds were bent, what designs of war or peace they had in hand, and, above all, their attitude to God, the Prophet, and religion" (230). What Robertson Smith advocates is a historically informed reading of the Bible that permits access to what was originary, the ancient direct spiritual experience, the revelation that is the foundation of spiritual religion. This is the way to restore to modernity that prophetic spirit, the spirituality that centuries of traditional reading and church dogma had deadened.

The biblical scholar, then, is one who "strives to enter into sympathy with [the ancient author's] thoughts, and to understand the thoughts as part of the life of the thinker and of his time" (1908, 17). By studying the historical context, the surrounding cultures and their documents, and the development of the Bible's and other related languages, the biblical scholar may be able to read the text with greater understanding of the conditions of its production and therefore discern the underlying experience that it intends to record. The scholar participates in the ongoing Reformation by setting aside the dogmatizing and doctrinal efforts of the church hierarchy—which had moved so far away from its sources—and returning to the documents and experiences themselves. As Robertson Smith said in the preface to one of his published lecture series, in which he laments the inaccessibility of modern biblical study to the general reader, "There is a religious as well as an historical gain in learning to read every part of the Bible in its original and natural sense" (1919, liv). He calls on the biblical scholar to do this great work. At a time when schools of theology were abolishing the study of Hebrew and biblical criticism out of fear that it would lead to the adoption of dangerous and unsound views, and when the church was concerned with staying the development of this liberal thought (Rogerson 1990, 68–69), Robertson Smith lectured about and published the results of his study in such a way as to make them accessible to the average thinking reader of English.

For more than a hundred years, scholars have regarded Robertson Smith as merely a popularizer of the German higher criticism; only recently have his contributions to biblical scholarship been recognized.[8]

---

8. Robertson Smith seems to be enjoying a resurgence of interest in his work, recognized by at least two scholars as original and not merely popularizing. See the introduction in Day (1995), a publication of the hitherto unpublished and even unknown texts of these series, and the chapters on Smith in Rogerson (1990).

But he also has been regarded as the principal popularizer of this scholarship, the one most dedicated to and successful at making it known to the general public. The nature of his work is a reflection of this dedication—encyclopedia articles, nonscholarly books, public lectures—and the reception of that work is an indication of its success. The encyclopedia articles were reprinted for decades, and in the preface to the 1895 republication of Robertson Smith's *The Prophets of Israel*, Rev. T. K. Cheyne, professor of interpretation of holy scripture at Oxford and canon of Rochester, reports that this work was "on its first appearance, eagerly bought and as eagerly read" (vii). Audiences of hundreds and even thousands attended the lectures.[9] Robertson Smith himself articulates both his project and his success: "I have striven to make my exposition essentially popular in the legitimate sense of that word. . . ." He also observes that "the sustained interest with which this large audience followed the attempt to lay before them an outline of the problems, the methods, and the results of Old Testament Criticism is sufficient proof that they did not find modern Biblical Science the repulsive and unreal thing which it is often represented to be" (1908, x).

Perhaps another testament to the success of Robertson Smith's project is the published defense of historical criticism by a representative of the church. In 1885, Frederic W. Farrar, late fellow of Trinity College at Cambridge, archdeacon and canon of Westminster, and chaplain in ordinary to the queen, gave a series of Bampton Lectures titled "History of Interpretation" to the University of Oxford. This lecture series was apologetic in intent, designed to defend the cause of Christianity by drawing attention to the inevitable change in the conditions of criticism, showing that there is in the teachings of scripture "a grandeur which secures for them transcendent authority," and robbing of their force the objections "of infidels and freethinkers to the historic details or moral imperfections of particular narratives of the Old Testament" (Farrar 1886, x). Farrar quoted a Professor Drummond, who wrote in an *Expositor* article, "Contributions of Science to Christianity," published in February 1885: "There are things in the Old Testament cast in the teeth of the apologist by sceptics [*sic*], to which he has simply no answer. These are the things,

---

9. See the appendix to Day (1995), in which he has reprinted the press reports of these lectures, delivered in 1890 and 1891. All accounts report that attendance was large. Robertson Smith himself writes that "the average attendance on the course in the two cities [Edinburgh and Glasgow] was not less than eighteen hundred" (1908, ix).

the miserable things, the masses have laid hold of" (xi). Whether or not this last is hyperbole, certainly the results of biblical criticism had been made public enough, and one of the responses to it had been a crisis of faith. Even if this more accurately was the view of a vocal few, still the perception of it as a "mass" movement prompted clerical response. And it is perhaps telling that the response provided was to defend historical criticism as a legitimate development in the progress of interpretation.

Farrar's thesis in these lectures and in the book he published from them, which until recently was the only history of biblical interpretation,[10] is that biblical exegesis is an evolutionary process. Nearly quoting Robertson Smith, without attribution,[11] Farrar asserts that "the Bible is not so much a revelation as the record of a revelation." And the history of exegesis is one of false suppositions being slowly and progressively corrected. Furthermore, "the last Revision of the Bible has once more reminded us that many passages and hundreds of expressions which have been implicitly accepted by generations, and quoted as the very word of God, were in fact the erroneous translations of imperfect readings" (xiv). Clearly borrowing ideas popularized by Robertson Smith, Farrar's thesis also reflects the rapid change in worldview in the nineteenth century as a result of new scientific advances. As J. R. Moore points out in an article about Darwin, the view of the world in the first half of the century as consisting of a static nature created by God, a static society of inequality, a moral order of rules from the Bible and the church, and the hope in the world after death, was supplanted at the *fin de siècle* by a view of the world as evolving, of society as progressing, of morals as coming from scientific professionals, and of hope directed at an improved world.[12]

Though Farrar reformulates the findings of historical criticism that Robertson Smith had popularized, in a historical model of progress and evolution distinctly different from Robertson Smith's *nostos*, his thought on this is a little more complex than it might appear at first. The series of lectures consists of studies of seven periods of interpretation: Rabbinic, Alexandrian, Patristic, Scholastic, Reformation, Post-Reformation, and Modern. Farrar makes caustic and deprecatory comments about the

---

10. In 1993, the first volume of *An Introduction to the History of Exegesis*, edited by Bertrand de Margerie, was published. In his introduction, the editor acknowledges Farrar's work.

11. Farrar's history does not mention Robertson Smith, perhaps reflecting his reputation as a popularizer of historical criticism rather than a contributor.

12. This is cited and discussed by Rogerson (1990) in his chapter introducing Robertson Smith.

periods before that of the Reformers, using phrases such as "decadence of knowledge" and "deepening misinterpretation." But for him the Reformation "revived the studies which alone render possible a sound interpretation, and shook itself free . . . from the errors of tradition, and the trammels of bondage" (15–16). The Post-Reformation period, however, forced the whole Bible to speak the language of accepted formulae in accordance with dogmatic systems. "To this day men repeat the vague and extravagant assertions of seventeenth-century divines, which furnish no assistance and solve no difficulty, and which can only be maintained in detail by an accumulation of special pleas" (27). Farrar provides many examples of misinterpretations and points to some of the horrible results they led to, the evils perpetrated in the Bible's name. Thus, despite his thesis of progress, Farrar also sees periods of authentic and false interpretation.

In his lecture on the Modern period, Farrar observes that the Church of England has always lagged behind the rest of the world in religious scholarship and had actively resisted the conclusions of "the anathematized German theology." Citing Coleridge's explication of German theology to the English, and pointing to the "spirit that animated English teachers" such as Matthew Arnold, Farrar mentions only one biblical scholar in England, Frederic Denison Maurice, who had been dismissed from Kings College in London in 1854 for making quite moderate use of historical criticism. But although this work was originally met with derision, Farrar says, it has now been taken into the church and its exponents are "among its saints for it" (424). Furthermore, "it is by means of those very investigations that the Bible has triumphed over keen ridicule, over charges of fiction, over naturalist explanations, over mythical theories, over destructive criticism" (424). The sense of historic continuity, presumably continuity with the Reformation, was "kindled once more by the Evangelical revival" and the "progressive learning, science and culture of the age" (424). Farrar concludes that the model for interpretation is Christ himself and the way he engaged with the standard school of interpretation in his time (434–36).

Farrar wrote a later book,[13] titled *The Bible: Its Meaning and Supremacy* (1897), in which he addresses the fears expressed to him by the masses

---

13. Farrar was a prolific writer on biblical criticism and the issues of his day. His publications include commentaries on individual books of the Bible: *The Book of Daniel* (1895), *The Epistle of Paul the Apostle to the Hebrews* (1912), *The Gospel According to Luke with Maps* (1893), *First and Second Book of Kings* (1893, 1894), and *Minor Prophets* (1890); expositions on biblical criticism: *Exposition*

influenced by the writings of freethinkers who "seem to think that if they hold up to ridicule this or that narrative, almost invariably of the Old Testament, they have demonstrated the futility of the Christian religion" (7). Farrar explains that there was "scarcely one argument which did not cease to be valid when it was shown that no doctrine about Biblical inerrancy has ever formed any necessary part of the faith of Christendom" (8). His book addresses these fears and answers questions about the meaning of the findings of higher criticism to the faithful. Just a survey of several of the chapter titles provides the gist of Farrar's argument: "The Bible is not one homogeneous book but a gradually collected canon"; "The Bible represents the remains of a much wider literature"; "The Bible is not homogeneous in its morality"; "'Verbal Diction' is an untrue and unspiritual hypothesis"; "The Bible contains the Word of God"; "Dangerous results of the 'supernatural dictation' theory"; "The Bible not the only source from which we can learn of God"; "Misinterpretation of Scripture: true and false views of Scripture."

Throughout his responses to each of these issues, Farrar adopts two parallel tones. One is of reassurance: there is nothing to fear from higher criticism; it reinforces the faith. The other is of admonishment: rejecting the findings of higher criticism is to reject the progress of revelation. Echoing Robertson Smith, Farrar asserts:

> One of the most urgent duties of good men in the present day is the simplification of religion into its primitive and essential elements. . . . It has suffered . . . most of all from the confusions, corruptions, and ignorance which during the Dark Ages, and under the sway of the mediaeval Papacy, invaded the God-given liberty of Christians; quenched, or tried to quench, the light which came from Heaven;

---

of the Bible (1904), *Messages of the Books* (1885), and *Texts Explained* (1899); collections of sermons: *Eternal Hope* (Westminster Abbey 1878), *Fall of Man* (University of Cambridge 1876), *Lord's Prayer* (Westminster Abbey 1893), *St. Paul at Athens: Spiritual Christianity in Relation to Some Aspects of Modern Thought* (1878), *Silence and the Voices of God* (1874), *Theism and Christianity* (Christian Evidence Society 1878), *True Religion* (1899), *The Voice from Sinai: The Eternal Bases of the Moral Law* (Westminster Abbey 1892), and *Witness of History to Christ* (University of Cambridge 1872); histories: *Early Days of Christianity* (1882), *Herods* (1898), *Life and Work of St Paul* (1879), *Life of the Fathers* (1889), *Life of Christ* (1874), and *Solomon: His Life and Times* (1880); treatises on Christian life: *Seekers after God* (1898), *Sin and Its Conquerors* (1897), and *Social and Present Day Questions* (1891); a discussion of Christian literature: *Great Books* (1898); and *Inspiration: A Clerical Symposium on "In What Sense and within What Limits Is the Bible the Word of God?"* (1885). This list of Farrar's work is only representative and not exhaustive.

subjected free human souls to the cruel, degraded, and effeminating bondage of ignorant teachers; and utterly marred the truth and beautiful simplicity of the primeval Gospel. An unprogressive Christianity will be of necessity a stagnant and corrupt Christianity. (14)

Lest his readers worry, Farrar assures them that "I do not deviate in the smallest particular from the definite teaching of the Church of England." As Dean of Canterbury now, he might even be understood as representing the church to his flock. Combining the tones of reassurance and admonishment, Farrar concludes his chapter on higher criticism: "I know that it will not be easy for some readers to abandon their former views on these subjects. . . . Let them take to heart the warning of Scripture that 'a sluggard' may 'be wiser in his own conceit than seven men who can render a reason'" (130).

True religion, for Farrar, is simplified, primitive, and essential, embodying the return to the primeval gospel that occurred during the enlightenment of the Reformation, before which the darkness of medieval papacy had quenched the light of the original revelation. So the man (and I use this word advisedly) of faith must try to return to these origins by participating in the Reformation liberation, resisting the effeminization of merely accepting old (that is papal, and therefore wrong) interpretations as authoritative teaching, and progressing with the faith and its revelation. Modern biblical criticism is a continuation of that Reformation enlightenment and a way to return to those primeval origins that are the foundation of true religion. Like Robertson Smith, Farrar identifies the periods of revelation and reformation as free of the errors of tradition, and the task of the modern period as being the return to their essentials and recovery of their truth. But perhaps betraying his clerical status, Farrar is more interested in the authentic practice of religion and interpretation of scripture than he is in recovering originary experience. Returning to the primitive essentials of religion for Farrar means relocating authority from tradition to enlightened scholarship, which does, however, seek that moment of revelation. Spiritual experience for Farrar is authentic interpretation of scripture that is achieved by returning via biblical criticism to an understanding of its original meaning. Thus is he able to implement both a *nostos* of return and of progress.

In Farrar's last chapter on the supremacy of the Bible, he lists and quotes a "cloud of witnesses to the glory and supremacy of the Holy Scriptures" (245), a lengthy compilation of clerical, scholarly, scientific, literary, philosophical, and political luminaries who had commented on the value of the Bible. He might have included Mrs. Humphry Ward, author of twenty-five novels "of ideas." Mary Ward was raised at Oxford during the time of both the Tractarian and the reactionary movements. As Matthew Arnold's niece, she spent a good deal of her life at the Arnold family estate in Westmorland. Both Oxford and Westmorland figure in her novels, Oxford as a place of learning and intellectual debate, and Westmorland as a place of antiquated and "primitive" belief. While at Oxford, where her father was a tutor, Ward taught herself German in order to pursue research on early church history, and in the process, she read the major works of the new German historical criticism of the Bible. *Robert Elsmere*, published in 1888, was Ward's most successful novel, fictionalizing her own experience of the impact of this criticism on faith. Ward was clear in her intentions to make known to the public the results of this scholarship and the salvific effect it might ultimately have on a faith consistent with modern life.

It sprang into my mind that the only way to show England what was in truth going on in its midst, was to try and express it concretely,— in terms of actual life and conduct. Who and what were the persons who had either provoked the present unsettlement of religion, or were suffering under its effects? What was their history? How had their thoughts and doubts come to be? and what was the effect of them on conduct? (xxiv)[14]

*Robert Elsmere* appeared at a particular time when its arguments resonated with the thoughts of a great many people. "Its enemies and its friends agree in attributing to it a certain wide popular influence. It has been much written about, and a good deal preached against," Ward wrote twenty-one years later.

The three-volume novel focuses on an Anglican parson trained at Oxford and exposed to the liberal ideas and thinkers of his day. He is a man of both action and ideas, committed to both church work and scholarship. After taking his orders, he accepts a post in southern rural England, but not before marrying the daughter of a northern evangelical clergyman who has retained all of her father's Puritan leanings. Elsmere

---

14. Ward references are to the 1909 edition of *Robert Elsmere*, for which she wrote an extensive introduction to the novel. This is part of a complete collection of her works, now viewed as the standard.

befriends a great English critic, an early follower of Newman who later became an atheist and historian of "testimony," and through this friendship gradually absorbs the historical scholarship on the Bible and its implications. Though quite happy in his marriage and work, Elsmere's intellectual exploration ultimately creates in him a crisis of doubt. He realizes that he no longer believes in the supernatural features of Christian dogma—the incarnation, the resurrection—and that he cannot continue to serve as a representative of the church, which requires these beliefs. Elsmere leaves his orders and relocates his family to London, in the process inflicting considerable pain on his Puritan wife. In London, he explores the avenues available to the nonbelieving man of faith. Intellectual society is stimulating but not ultimately satisfying. Affiliation with the Broad Church movement he quickly finds hypocritical. Partnership with a Unitarian seeking to improve the lives of urban tradesmen and their families is satisfying, but it leaves him with a deep desire for religious worship. Building on the foundation of his need to work among the disenfranchised, Elsmere makes use of his society connections to finance his establishment in a working-class neighborhood of the New Brotherhood, an organization to educate and ultimately restore faith to this community of nonbelievers. Compelled by the vision of a new church, Elsmere, always physically weak, drives himself to the point of terminal illness, all the while dealing with the discomfort of his wife's dissenting view of his new faith.

While all the factions in the religious debate of the mid-nineteenth century are represented in the novel, its argument centers on the work of Roger Wendover, the squire of the southern land where Elsmere is parson. Wendover has worked for fifty years on a history of testimony, in which he argues:

> Testimony like every other human product has *developed*. Man's power of apprehending and recording what he sees and hears has grown from less to more, from weaker to stronger, like any other of his faculties, just as the reasoning powers of the cave-dweller have developed into the reasoning powers of a Kant. What one wants is the ordered proof of this, and it can be got from history and experience. (2:41)

Biblical testimony also is conditioned by its historical context and cannot have a validity for the mind of the nineteenth century, "when in truth [biblical narratives] are the imperfect, half-childish products of the mind of the first century, of quite insignificant or indirect value to the historian of fact, of enormous value to the historian of *testimony* and its varieties" (2:41). The mind of the first century believed in the supernatural and expressed its experience in supernatural terms. For the nineteenth-century man, believing with Hume that "miracles do not happen," confidence in the biblical witness as historical and true is not possible. The incarnation and resurrection are supernatural fictions. But—and this is really the crux of Ward's argument against both defenders of tradition and nonbelieving skeptics—faith is not dependent on dogma. In fact, if the dogma is removed, it is possible to return to the original context and content of faith, and the articles of that faith may be expressed in these affirmations: "In Thee, O Eternal, have I put my trust," and "This do in remembrance of me" (2:509). With the church's insistence on subscription to the thirty-nine articles, it is hypocritical for one who does not believe in them to remain within that church, so Ward advocates leaving it and devoting oneself to Christian service.[15]

Although Ward calls for a return to predogmatic Christianity, her ideology is firmly based on theodicean progress. This dialectic is played out in the novel in numerous ways. Northern England represents the past, preindustrial and characterized by simple faith; southern England, the world of modern knowledge and doubt; and London, the synthesis of faith and knowledge (Peterson 1976, 139–40). Elsmere's wife represents dogma, Roger Wendover thought, and Elsmere a synthesis of the two. The good works of Puritanism and the intellectualizing of secularism synthesize into a rational faith of doing and thinking, of improving and exploring the world. Just as Judaism evolved into Christianity, so will Christianity be supplanted by a new faith.

Near the end of his life, Elsmere tells his dearest friend that he has admonished a Broad Church clergyman:

> It was borne in on me to tell him that it is all owing to him and his brethren that we are in the muddle we are in to-day. Miracle is to our time what the law was to the early Christians. We *must* make up our minds about it one way or the other. And if we decide to throw it over as Paul threw over the law, then we must *fight* as he did. . . . The ground must be cleared; then may come the rebuilding. (2: 555)

---

15. Ward changes her view on this later, as is evident in *The Case of Richard Meynell* (1911), a sequel to *Robert Elsmere* in which Elsmere's heir and Meynell work for change within the church instead of leaving it.

The new faith will have given up miracles just as Christianity gave up the Torah. Archibald Tait had observed that "the great evil is—that the liberals are deficient in religion and the religious are deficient in liberality" (quoted in Peterson 1976, 136). Ward solves the problem by offering her uncle's dialectic: the destruction of orthodoxy by modern rationalism must be followed by a new synthesis that provides a reasonable religion for nineteenth-century men and women (136–37). This reasonable religion is constructed from what can be recovered of the original moments of faith, before dogma encrusted them in superstition and myth.

In all of Ward's writings about faith and biblical criticism—and this includes at least five novels, several articles, and pamphlets[16]—she tries to show that what was denounced as unbelief by the church was merely a particular way of judging a series of documents and events of history, and that this way of reading might lead to a faith inviolable to modern science. Ward felt called to make this faith available to the average layperson, and in "The New Reformation," published the following year in *The Nineteenth Century*,[17] Ward says:

> For my own part I believe that we in England, with regard to this German study of Christianity, are now at the beginning of an epoch of *popularisation*. The books which record it have been studied in England, Scotland, and America with increasing eagerness during the last fifteen years by a small class; in the next fifteen years we shall probably see their contents reproduced in English form and penetrating public opinion in a new and surprising way. (2:587)

Echoing Robertson Smith on the subject of his project, she continues:

---

16. Ward's writings include novels of faith: *History of David Grieve* (1892), *Helbeck of Bannisdale* (1898), *Eleanor* (1900), and *The Case of Richard Meynell* (1911); articles on issues of faith: "M. Renan's Autobiography" (1883), "The Literature of Introspection: Amiel's *Journal Intime*" (1884), "Review of *Marius the Epicurean* by Walter Pater" (1885), "The New Reformation: A Dialogue" (1889), "A New Book on the Gospels" (1890), "The Apostles' Creed: A Translation and Introduction" (1893); pamphlets: *A Morning in the Bodleian* (1871) and *Unbelief and Sin* (1881); and nonfiction books: *Towards the Goal* (1917) and *A Writer's Recollections* (1918). Ward also wrote on literature and other issues of the day, plus twenty other novels.

17. In this dialogue between a High Churchman and a student of German criticism, Ward mentions the Manchester Church Congress in which Robertson Smith and Cheyne participated, and she even quotes them. Later she refers to Archdeacon Farrar as making appeals to all sections of Christians to close their ranks, not against each other, but against "the scepticism [*sic*] rampant" among the cultivated class and against the religious indifference of democracy.

A minimum of readers among us read German, and translations only affect a small and mostly professional stratum of opinion. But when we get our own English lives of Christ and histories of the primitive Church, written on German principles in the tone and speech familiar to the English world, then will come the struggle. (2:587–88)

Over and over again, Ward explains to her public that the biblical critics were not attacking the Christian witness, but seeking to understand it, to "translate" it from the world of first-century thought to that of the nineteenth century. Quoting Taine on the German philosophic genius as the equivalent to the Renaissance and Classical periods, Ward believed she was participating in a "new reformation" in which the Christian problem was first and foremost a literary problem that ought to be handled as such.

Like Robertson Smith, Ward dismisses the centuries of dogma encrusting the original experience behind the biblical account, though she seems to have taken it a step further by requiring that the first-century perspective apparent in that account be "translated" into the nineteenth-century worldview, thereby pointing to the Bible itself as the origin of that encrusting dogma. Distinguishing between belief and faith, Ward claims that unbelief (in encrusting dogma) may lead to faith, a faith that is true to its original moments and is defined by trust and remembrance rather than by belief in the supernatural. Church, for Ward, as the institutionalization of faith, is where ideas should be explored and scholarship popularized, while it is also where work on behalf of the disenfranchised should be conducted. Thus trust in God and remembrance of Jesus' good works are those original moments of faith to be recovered by biblical criticism and made known to nonbelievers by the likes of Robert Elsmere and Mrs. Humphry Ward. Like Farrar, Ward is passionately interested in the progress of biblical interpretation, but like Robertson Smith, she is just as concerned with returning to spiritual origins to bring back something that is lost, in her case a faith that is not dependent on belief.

Just a few years before Ward's novel appeared, the revision of the Authorized Version had been published, and in its preface, the Bible is referred to as "an English classic." David Norton, in his recent and comprehensive *History of the Bible as Literature* (1993), even coined the term "AVolatry" to convey the excessive devotion of the English reading public to the Authorized Version. Descriptions of the Bible "as a classic" (Le Roy Halsey) and "as a composition" (Byron and Shelley) reflect an approach in which the Bible as religion is set aside. Norton observes that as "a new phrase for a new phase," the Bible as literature "signals an awareness of this narrowed focus that is rarely to be found in discussion prior to the middle of the nineteenth century" (262). An example of this is *Passages of the Bible Chosen for their Literary Beauty and Interest*, first published in 1895 by J. G. Frazer, author of the better-known *Golden Bough*. In his preface to this anthology of biblical passages, Frazer observes that the English version was a great classic in the language but had not been so read. Read by the religious for guidance and comfort, by scholars to analyze it and discuss its authorship and date, and by historians for its facts illustrative of other subjects, the Bible had not been read for "the enjoyment which as pure literature it is fitted to afford" (Frazer 1909, v).

The phrase "the Bible as literature" was first used by Matthew Arnold, who had argued for the Bible as a literary and cultural work.[18] As a school inspector, Arnold prepared a revision of Isaiah for classroom use, in the preface of which he observes: "The Bible is for the child in an elementary school almost his only contact with poetry and philosophy. . . . All who value the Bible may rest assured that thus to know and possess the Bible is the most certain way to extend the power and efficacy of the Bible" (quoted in Norton 1993, 274). Thus Arnold combined the Bible as literature with the Bible as religion, prompting Norton to comment that "in Arnold there is a sense that the Bible as religion is a disguise for the Bible as literature" (274).[19] But "the Bible as literature" as both an expression and a significant movement was not really established until Richard Green Moulton became its most energetic popularizer. Moulton produced a syllabus titled *The Literary Study of the Bible* and used the same title for his 1895 publication of a study of the Bible's leading forms of literature. Also in that year, he began publishing *The Modern Reader's Bible* in twenty-one volumes. It was eventually collected into one volume that became enormously popular, remaining in print until the 1950s. Moulton also published an anthology of essays titled *The Bible as Literature* in 1899 and *A Short Introduction to the Literature of the Bible* in 1901. As "the father of modern literary study of the Bible," Moulton is the most quoted of its nineteenth-century literary critics (Norton 1993, 277). He anticipates the work of such late-twentieth-century scholars as Robert Alter,

---

18. Arnold argued for the Bible's importance to culture in *Culture and Anarchy* (1869) and *Literature and Dogma* (1873) and for its importance as a literary work in *God and the Bible* (1875).

19. The first half of Norton's comment, "Whereas in America the Bible as literature became a disguise for the Bible as religion," refers to the "Bible as literature" movement here, which is beyond the scope of this book but is key to a study of this movement in general.

Meir Sternberg, and Harold Bloom in arguing, as they all do, that the literary study of the Bible is something new.[20]

Moulton distinguishes his study of the Bible as literature from the higher criticism, for the "literary investigation stops short at the question *what* we have in the text of the Bible, without examining *how* it has come to us" (1895, vi). Moulton goes on to say that the higher criticism's "province is distinct from that which I lay down for myself in this book. The higher criticism is mainly an historical analysis; I confine myself to literary investigation. . . . I think the distinction of the two treatments is of considerable practical importance; since the historical analysis must, in the nature of things, divide students into hostile camps, while, as it appears to me, the literary appreciation of Scripture is a common ground upon which opposing schools may meet" (v). But Moulton also acknowledges his debt to the major recent works of biblical criticism and its popularizers, who have "placed the best results of modern investigation within easy reach of the ordinary reader" (x). Moulton, however, focuses on the literary form of the biblical text: "The underlying axiom of my work is that a clear grasp of the outer literary form is an essential guide to the inner matter and spirit" (viii). And here we come to the point at which, despite Moulton's protestations, the Bible as literature and higher criticism meet. For like Robertson Smith, Farrar, and Ward, Moulton is concerned with recovering that spirit, and his "experience has uniformly confirmed what I have called above the foundation axiom of my work—that an increased apprehension of outer literary form is a sure way of deepening spiritual effect" (x).

One of Moulton's key ways to accomplish this is by re-presenting the Bible in a format conducive to reading it as if for the first time and to interpreting it on its own. The problem is that ordinary versions of the Bible "present a double divergence from the sacred original: first, that they give no indication of the varieties of literary form and structure that distinguish different parts of the Bible; secondly, that they impress upon the whole another structure that does not belong to it, but was the creation of

---

20. For instance, Alter says in his preface to *The World of Biblical Literature*, "When I was first drawn to work on this subject, in the mid-1970s, the notion that one could understand the Bible in serious, even rigorous, terms as literature was still relatively new, and the attempts to do so, with a few notable exceptions, were rather fumbling" (1992, ix). This is typical of the scholarship beginning in the 1970s and continuing through the present in which the tools of literary criticism have been applied to the biblical text. Still, it is difficult to believe that Alter and his cohorts were unaware of Moulton's painstaking analyses.

mediaeval commentators. In the face of obstacles like these it is indeed difficult to apply the principle that the Bible should be its own interpreter" (1907, vii). Frazer makes a similar observation, commenting that "the passages of greatest literary beauty and interest are scattered up and down it, imbedded, often at rare intervals, in a great mass of other matter which . . . possesses only subordinate value as literature" (1909, vi). Frazer's anthology disengages "these gems" from their setting and re-presents them in a continuous series. Moulton's solution to the same problem is to repackage the whole Authorized Version according to literary form and to use the devices of modern printing to indicate structure to the eye of the reader. His premise is that "the revelation which is the basis of our modern religion has been made in the form of literature: grasp of its literary structure is the true starting-point for spiritual interpretation" (1907, vii). So recovery of the literary form will facilitate the reader's apprehension of the biblical text and its meaning as it was originally intended. And Moulton feels that in this enterprise, he is serving a popular need: "I believe that many have a longing to get to the sacred texts at first hand, to fling their minds, without any intervening medium of interpretation, directly upon the original literature, and appreciate it, each reader for himself, in all its freshness. One thing only is required for such a purpose—the arrangement of the materials in a rational order: and this is what the present edition attempts" (1497).[21]

In an echo of Robertson Smith, Moulton claims, "The literary study of the Bible has no more important task than that of describing Prophecy from the literary point of view" (1899, 39). Moulton argues that the starting point of all literature was the ballad dance, combining verse, music, and imitative gesture. From this point, and considering these three directions, he traces the development of all types of literature.[22] Robertson Smith, however, disapproves of this sort of "classification of poetic effects

---

21. Though it is beyond the scope of this book to consider this repackaged Bible in more detail, it is worth noting that Moulton started a movement that was perpetuated by others, including James Moffat and Ernest Sutherland Bates, who came up with their own versions. In his introduction, Bates asserts that "little can be done to revive the reading of the Bible so long as it is presented in the traditional manner" (1936, viii). The new presentation arranges the books by time and subject matter, and omits genealogies, repetitions, "the whole of Chronicles, the minor Epistles, and similar unimportant passages throughout, to the end that the Bible may be read as living literature" (cover advertisement).

22. Moulton traces the development of literature from poetry to epic, lyric, and drama; and from prose to history, philosophy, and rhetoric. Epic and history are descriptive, drama and rhetoric presentative, and lyric and philosophy reflective. Moulton also includes a detailed chart to illustrate this model of literary development (1899, 108).

according to the principles of rhetoric," favoring as "true criticism" what he calls "the unfolding of the living forces which moved the poet's soul." Still, to "enjoy a poem is to share the emotion that inspired the author" (1912, 405). But prophecy, for Moulton, is the one exception to his classification of the literature of the Bible, for, he argues, prophecy is not a universal literature, but rather a distinctive genre "not of form but of spirit." "Biblical Prophecy, in a sense that belongs to no other class of literature, presents itself as an actual Divine message" (1899, 112). Robertson Smith makes a similar argument that Hebrew prophecy was a unique phenomenon not comparable to Hellenic or other Semitic variations.[23] While methods of revelation are found in all ancient religions, "no other religion presents anything precisely analogous to prophecy" (1900b, 820). Both Robertson Smith and Moulton, then, point to prophecy as unique, spiritual, and originary, and both sought to read it for its original sense.

Thus in the work of Robertson Smith, Farrar, Ward, and Moulton, there is a common impulse, a desire to be able to read the biblical text to recover the original and spiritual experience underlying it. Each also endeavors to popularize both this activity and his or her particular approaches to accomplishing it, whether historical or literary. From these published works, it is apparent that the movement to popularize the reading of the Bible for its original sense was widespread, encompassing for instance these four writers of quite different vocational and intellectual backgrounds. That their efforts were well received seems apparent from how quickly their works were purchased, how many reprintings and editions they enjoyed, and the number of people who attended lectures and asked questions. Each of these writers also seems to have felt in some way embattled or alone, and they all comment on negative reactions to their efforts to make the scholarship known and resistance to their perpetuation of the Reformation placement of the Bible into the hands of a reading public.

Rejecting any interpretive intermediary—ecclesiastical authority or interpretive tradition—these writers emphasize not only the individual's own ability to read and understand, but also the lay and communal origins of the biblical text itself. Defending a rearrangement of its material, Moulton and his followers point to the collective nature of the Bible's

---

23. See Robertson Smith's article "Prophet" in the *Encyclopaedia Britannica*, where he takes pains to distinguish the Greek etymological origin of the English word from the Hebrew *nabi*: "In actual usage the idea conveyed by the word prophet has never quite corresponded with its historical prototype" (1900b, 814).

origins. For Robertson Smith, "Prophecy itself may from one point of view be regarded simply as the brightest efflorescence of the lay element in the religion of Israel . . . and the popular literature of the nation; for in the Hebrew commonwealth popular literature had not yet sunk to represent the lowest impulses of national life" (1900a, 635). This literary diffusion of spiritual ideas was not the effort of priests, whose work he sees as representing those low nationalist impulses, but of the believing community. In each case, then, these writers are seeking a return to the ancient origins of the Bible in order to recover the spiritual experience underlying its texts—revelation, original meaning, predogmatic faith, and the union of form and spirit—and restore this experience to a modern reading.

## *SYMBOLISTE* THEATRE AND REFORM

In his discussion of prophecy as a literary genre unique to Hebrew literature, Moulton makes the intriguing observations that "prophecy in one of its aspects . . . [is] the philosophy of history erected into a drama" and that this body of biblical literature served for the ancient Israelites the role that drama had in classical literature (1899, 364). Though the Hebrew people had strong dramatic impulses, he argues, they did not produce any theatre or dramatic literature. Hebrew prophecy—"the most highly wrought and spiritual of literary forms"—is distinctive and may be regarded as an extension of drama (380–81). This last observation serves as a suitable transition to a discussion of the nineteenth-century movements to reform the theatre, for it was to the ancient ritual origins of the drama that some of these reformers advocated a return. That Moulton essentially equates the classical ritual drama with Hebrew prophecy serves to reinforce the common impulse underlying all of these movements.

In the introduction to his study of the English theatre in the 1890s, Kerry Powell (1990, 1–3) points out that our notions about the character of the theatre in that era have been influenced by the plays that have survived. Because most plays of the time were not published in any form, we today have a completely skewed understanding of turn-of-the-century theatre. "Today the English theatre of the 1890s has been reduced to the plays of Wilde and Shaw, the influence of Ibsen, and—to a far lesser extent—certain works by Pinero and Jones. But for its patrons the *fin-de-siècle* drama bore scant resemblance to the highly selective recollection of it in the twentieth century. . . . Most plays of the period, even prominent ones, disappeared utterly with the final performance" (3).[24] We need then to take seriously the critical comments on the theatre in both England and France that proliferated in this period, for they are among our only clues to the nature of the theatre in the nineteenth century. We might discern two general lines of criticism, one arguing that the theatre was a dangerous and immoral place, to be avoided by God-fearing Christians, and the other criticizing the theatre for having lost its spiritual center and having devolved to mostly shallow and lowbrow entertainment. Both lines of criticism take issue with the theatre's failure as a site for serious engagement with ideas, and with its general titillation of the public.

An early example of the first line of criticism is Robert Kaye Greville's *The Drama Brought to the Test of Scripture and Found Wanting* (1830), a 130-page diatribe against theatregoing. Greville argues that the nature of the theatre and its manifestation in his time are opposed to scriptural values. A particularly interesting line of his argument tackles the claim that "the British theatre is derived from the Spiritual Drama" (50). Greville asserts that the dramatic representation of religious subjects introduced in the fourth century, to counteract "the pernicious effects of ordinary drama," became corrupted under the popes and "tended greatly to diminish respect for the holy mysteries of religion, and to turn into ridicule every thing sacred. Nothing but the grossest superstition could have tolerated them as religious spectacles" (51). Continuing his history of medieval drama, Greville further claims that "by gradually mixing profane matters with religion, they [medieval playwrights] at length, however, disgusted the people; and in 1548, they were only permitted to perform on condition of excluding the mysteries of religion."[25] He concludes sarcastically, "Thus may our modern drama be distinctly traced to a religious origin" (53).

In dismissing the spiritual origins of the modern theatre, perhaps Greville was responding in part to the claims of some that theatre had declined from its spiritually pure origins to its modern decayed state. The French theatre critic Francisque Sarcey, in an essay titled "La Décadence

---

24. See Powell (1990), who seeks to recapture the vanished and essential context of Wilde's theatrical career in order to demonstrate that his writing derived from these largely forgotten plays. In contrast with Bloom's theory of poetic influence, Powell argues that Wilde was contending not with the greatest of the dead, but with the living. Wilde's writing required this contemporary influence, and his later writing suffered from not being so engaged. Wilde's play *Salomé* is one of his most strongly influenced works.

25. See the next chapter, "Unveiling Fears: Literary History as Guardian of Culture," for a detailed explication of the argument Greville refers to here.

du théâtre," notes the sheer number of brochures dating from 1768 through 1880 variously titled *Causes of the Decadence of the Theatre*.[26] The sense that the theatre had declined from an earlier and purer age seems to have prevailed. This is the condition George Bernard Shaw refers to in the preface to his collection of theatre reviews written for the *Saturday Review*. "Weariness of the theatre is the prevailing note of London critics. Only the ablest critics believe that the theatre is really important" (1931, viii). Greville argues that the impulse to reform the theatre, to return to its spiritual origins and recover and restore what had been lost, was a faulty effort because the nature of theatre itself was opposed to spiritual principles. There were no spiritual origins for theatre to return to, and Christians should not attend it at all.

Greville and Robertson Smith seem to agree that "spiritual" refers to an originary moment of revelation, a historical event of genuine transcendence reported in scripture. "Spiritual" for Greville is both Christian and scriptural, and so for him pre-Christian drama is inherently unspiritual. But although Robertson Smith might concur with Greville's identification of all "ordinary" drama as "unspiritual," he will not, as Greville does, merely equate scriptural with spiritual. Some scripture is and other scripture is not "spiritual." Greville acknowledges the existence of "dramatic representation of religious subjects" but dismisses them as papist corruptions. So "spiritual" for him is also, apparently, Protestant. Farrar's confidence in the Reformation as having revived and freed interpretation "from the errors of tradition, and the trammels of bondage," indicates that he likely would agree with Greville that Protestantism had recovered the authentic and true—the spiritual—from the decadent and false. As for Robertson Smith and Farrar, for Greville "spiritual" refers to particular moments in Judeo-Christian history. Ward, however, goes even further than these English Protestants when she separates "spiritual" from supernatural. For her the events of the Christian story were clearly and intrinsically historical, occurring in the natural world and not as supernatural intrusions into it. "Spiritual" is a quality applied interpretively to these events, a hermeneutic, a way in which they are understood. Nonetheless,

---

26. Sarcey has only disdain for this view, noting that M de Sacy, the author of one of these brochures, titled *Rapport au Sénat sur la décadence de l'art dramatique*, "had never in his life set foot in a theatre" ("n'avait de sa vie mis le pied dans un théâtre"), and "the truth is that art, that of the theatre as well as the others, will be renewed without ceasing" ("La vérité est que l'art, celui du théâtre comme les autres, va se renouvelant sans cesse"). (1900–1902, 186–87). Translations from the French in this chapter are my own.

for Ward, as for Robertson Smith, Farrar, and Greville, spiritual events occurred within Judeo-Christian history and were reported, and therefore may be glimpsed, in the Bible.

For those interested in the future of the theatre, reforming it also meant returning to spiritual origins and principles, but these predate Christian history and dogma. For them, "spiritual" was not exclusively a Christian or Judeo-Christian domain. Furthermore, just as Moulton claims that there is a continuity between the form and content of prophecy that is essential to this most spiritual of literary genres, reformers of the theatre would argue that drama is where spiritual experience, its form and content, originated, and that this union of form and content is itself originary. Not merely a historical moment of revelation to be glimpsed through the intermediary of scripture, the spiritual to these reformers is an immediate experience of transcendence available any time drama's spiritual form and content are recovered.

Those concerned with recovering the stage for the serious engagement of ideas, however, often despaired of the feasibility of their project. They called for "literary" and "poetic" work and distinguished themselves from "the melodramatists and farce writers" of the day (Powell 1990, 5). Powell observes that, for these reformers, "to write for the popular stage was to risk the loss of artistic prestige, even at a time when theatres attracted increasingly fashionable audiences and held out to dramatists the prospect of wealth" (5). Even to be associated with the stage rather than with literature was suspect. The innovator of the French stage, Jacques Copeau, in his report of meeting the English innovator Gordon Craig, quotes him as saying of Copeau, "Well. You have much of a literary man. You are not of the theatre." And Copeau responds to his reader, "Indeed, I come to the theatre via literature; I started my theatrical career through a disgust for base theatrical productions and values, prompted by a literary morality" (Copeau 15, September 14, 1915).[27]

André Antoine, founder of Théâtre Libre and father of the new theatre movement in Paris, despairs of London as an appropriate place for any new theatre: "The environment . . . hardly strikes me as suitable for a

---

27. My source for Copeau's comments on the theatre is a collection edited and translated by Rudlin and Paul (1990), an anthology that draws not only on the four published volumes of Copeau's *Registres*, but also on two unpublished volumes prepared by his heirs and several independent sources, making it an unusually rich resource of otherwise unavailable materials. The quoted Copeau comment is in the Rudlin and Paul translation. The frontispiece of this collection is a 1920 sketch by Berthold Mahn titled *Jacques Copeau lisant 'Saül' à André Gide*. References include the anthology page number and the essay title or date.

literary movement. The English theatre subsists on ephemeral works, facile but simple, sufficient only for a public interested in superficial distractions" (Antoine, December 16, 1890).[28] And Copeau observes: "Theatre has fallen so low in France that everyone must become aware of it and at least discuss it. Current production has become so insipid that even the most paltry novelty finds an audience to welcome it as revitalising" (26, *Cahier No. 2*). Copeau complains about the fickle public, lazy critics, directors concerned with making money, and authors caring only about being produced and inventing characters with specific actors in mind, saying, "There has been a shifting mediocrity in the theatre." Although "public taste is no longer exclusively concerned with frivolous plays," he continues, "thought has been lowered to meet it" (105, *L'Ermitage*, February 15, 1905).

Copeau asks: "How can this frivolous theatre recover its meaningfulness? . . . How can this literary theatre, low or refined, be restored to the simple, forceful and naive life which would give it back its social *raison d'être* and its popular importance?" (164, speech in Buenos Aires, July 7, 1929).[29] Previous efforts to change had failed: "It is certainly not change that we need . . . but a serious return to principles. . . . I always believed that our 'chapel' . . . could not honestly be described as anything but a renewal or, even better, a preparation. Renewal of dramatic feeling through an understanding of the masterworks, and a renewed contact with the great technical traditions" (26–27, *Cahier No. 2*). This invocation of a return to first principles and of the theatre as a site of religious experience became a common reformist's call. Shaw comments that the theatre "is as important as the Church was in the Middle Ages and much more important than the Church was in London in the years under review. A theatre to me is a place where two or three are gathered together" (Shaw 1931, viii). Charles Morice, in an article about the aims of the new Théâtre d'Art in Paris, declares that the theatre is the church of the future (Jasper 1947, 97). Copeau argues that "it is the theatre's imperative objective to

---

28. My source for Antoine's comments on the theatre is a 1964 translation by Carolson of Antoine's *Mes Souvenirs sur le Théâtre-Libre*. Though Antoine claims to have assembled his *souvenirs* from his journal notes, he reconstructed them long after the events the journal relates, and his work has been demonstrated by the translator to be full of errors. Thus I have resorted to the translator's corrected text rather than to Antoine's original, and the quoted Antoine comment is in the Carolson translation.

29. This "literary theatre" to which Copeau refers consists of the "low" *realiste* movement, which adapted Emile Zola's novels to the stage, and the "refined" poetic work of *symboliste* drama. Copeau observes that "realism gave our vision precision and colour" (*L'Ermitage*, February 1905).

rediscover its function and its natural vocation" and that "the theatre will not rediscover its grandeur until it ceases being an exploitation and becomes a ceremony" (27, "Is a Dramatic Renovation Possible?" Brussels lecture, 1926).

This return to ceremonial or religious origins arrives in either of two historic moments: ancient classical ritual drama or the medieval mystery plays. Copeau, imagining a new popular theatre rooted in both, claims:

> There was a time when an entire people would prepare itself through meditation and self-purification to await an annual theatrical celebration presided over by a god. All the rites, meant to inspire man's feeling of civic dignity, would serve as a preface and accompaniment to the contest of the tragic poets. . . . The forms of the performances were so powerful that they touched the spectator to the very core. . . . Why did these spectacles hold such a far-flung attraction for an entire region? Because they produced images and expressed ideas based on popular forms and sources from which an entire people could learn and receive spiritual nourishment. . . . These two examples from the distant past, antiquity and the Middle Ages, are the indispensable preface to all development of popular theatre. They illustrate two forms of dramatic presentation which originate in the moral life of the people and which also influence it. (186, *Le Théâtre Populaire*, 1941)

And making explicit the intentions of his call for a return to these origins, Copeau exhorts, "What is it we want? In a word, we want to return the theatre to its religious character, its sacred rites, its original purity" (198, lecture to the New York Drama League, 1918). *Symboliste* drama attempted to do just that, and in doing so, it embraced both sites of return in its work.

Although *symbolisme* has been a subject of abiding interest among scholars of modern literature for some time, the scholarship on *symboliste* drama consists of only half a dozen works[30] and mostly agrees that it originated with Charles Baudelaire's "Correspondances," Edgar Allan Poe's "Philosophy of Composition," and Stéphane Mallarmé's theatrical theory of poetry. Taking Mallarmé's poems "Hérodiade" and "L'Après

---

30. Knowles (1967), Jasper (1947), Balakian (1977, 1982), Marie (1973), Block (1963), and Deak (1993).

Midi d'un Faune" to be fragments of theatrical pieces seminal to *symboliste* drama through their influence on Van Lerberghe and Maeterlinck, these scholars argue that Mallarmé conceived of his poetry as an act of performance. Mallarmé's writing about *symboliste* poetry, then, is understood to be a theory of theatre that was implemented by those he influenced, particularly those associated with Lugné-Poe and the Théâtre de l'Oeuvre.

The elements of Baudelaire's poem "Correspondances" had become the components of doctrine: the unity of creation, the materiality and spirituality of the creature, the correspondence between the material and the spiritual through the symbol, and the correspondence among diverse sensations through synesthesia. Mallarmé refers to the word as a spiritual instrument: "Unlike a facile and representative everyday fiction, as the crowd treats it, the word—which is, after all, dream and song, found in the poet,—by necessity constitutes an art consecrated to fictions, its potential" (Michaud 1947, 26, preface to *Traité du Verbe* by R. Ghil, 1885).[31] And he refers to the theatre as "sacre d'un des actes de la Civilisation" and "un fait spirituel" (27, *Richard Wagner*, 1886). Théodore de Banville suggests that to create a new theatre consecrated to the word, to poetry, the system of official theatres should be circumvented and the model of the popular theatre embraced. With a close identification between artists and audience, minimal financial and material needs, actors who were half amateur and half professional, and a small appreciative audience, it was Banville's idea for the new theatre that was taken up by Lugné-Poe and later Copeau in their efforts to implement a *symboliste* theory of theatre (Deak 1993, 20).

---

31. Quoted material translated from "Au contraire d'une fiction de numéraire facile et représentatif, comme le traite d'abord la foule, le parler qui est, après tout, rêve et chant, retrouve chez le poète, par nécessité constitutive d'un art consacré aux fictions, sa virtualité." My source for this and other nineteenth-century writing on *symbolisme* is an anthology by Michaud titled *La Doctrine Symboliste: Documents* (1947), in which he has collected in one place the major texts of this movement. "If it is relatively easy to understand the work of symbolist poets, at least the greatest among them, it is much more difficult to obtain first-hand information about their doctrine. It might then be desirable to complement this with a study of the symbolist movement [. . .] putting together the core of the texts that contain the doctrine" ("S'il est relativement facile de connaître les oeuvres des poètes symbolistes, du moins des plus grands d'entre eux, il est beaucoup plus malaisé d'avoir des informations de première main concernant leur doctrine. . . . Il pouvait donc sembler souhaitable qu'en complément d'une étude sur l'histoire du mouvement symboliste [published simultaneously under the title *Message Poétique du Symbolisme*] fût réuni l'essentiel des textes qui en contiennent la doctrine") (7). References include the page number in Michaud.

In a manifesto of *symboliste* literature, *La Littérature de tout à l'heure* (1889), Charles Morice discusses the nature of its project:

> We shall also visit the school of ancient cults, extracting from all the mines the piece of eternal gold which their greed has guarded; and when the joy of faith shatters the enthusiasm of our spirits, we will celebrate this mystical joy with sacrifices and celebrations of art. . . . This joy, which can smile upon the soul sometimes in a way that adds to brilliant gayity, nonetheless remains serious: its path is only toward the Absolute, its pasture is only that of eternity. (Michaud 1947, 40)[32]

Morice is clear that this is a spiritual movement, one that is interested in returning to ancient origins and recovering the religious sense; it is a return to simple origins and it is accomplished through art:

> While waiting for Science to put an end to Mysticism, the intuitions of dreams precede Science, celebrating that still future but already definitive alliance of the religious sense and the scientific sense in a celebration that exalts the very human desire for a coming together of all human powers by a return to their original simplicity. This return to simplicity is the core of Art. (42)[33]

"Art returns to its origins, and as it was a whole in the beginning, here it returns to the original Unity, where are Music, Painting, and Poetry." (102).[34] This one unified art is manifest in theatre: "The theatre—that no doubt, if this civilisation doesn't go to pieces too soon, will fulfill the rites of aesthetic religion—belongs to the Poet first of all."[35] This is as it should

---

32. Translated from "Nous irons à l'école aussi des Cultes antiques, extrayant de toutes les mines la parcelle d'or éternel que nous gardait encore leur sein avare; et quand la joie de la foi ébranlera d'enthousiasme nos âmes, nous célèbrerons cette joie mystique par les Sacrifices et les Fêtes de l'Art. . . . Cette joie, qui peut parfois sourire à l'esprit en son sens complémentaire et à la brillante gaîté, pourtant reste d'essence grave: sa voie n'est que vers l'Absolu, sa pâture n'est que d'Eternité."

33. Translated from "En attendant que la Science ait décidément conclu au Mysticisme, les intuitions du Rêve y devancent la Science, y célèbrent cette encore future et déjà définitive alliance du Sens Religieux et du Sense scientifique dans une fête esthétique où s'exalte le désir trés humain d'un réunion de toutes les puissances humaines par un retour à l'originelle simplicité. Ce retour à la simplicité, c'est tout l'Art."

34. Translated from "L'Art remonte à ses origines et, comme au commencement il était un, voici qu'il rentre dans l'originelle voie de l'Unité, où la Musique, la Peinture et la Poésie."

35. Translated from "Le théâtre, où sans doute, si cette civilisation ne s'effondre pas trop tôt, s'accomplira le rite de la Religion esthétique, appartient au Poète d'abord."

be, however, and not as it is: "But how dare speak of the theatre! This art is lost, inspite of the talent of the writers whose efforts I have noted. Nonetheless, to it is promised the supreme celebration."[36] Not the theatre of the present but of the "tout à l'heure," it will effect the perfect synthesis of the disparate arts and thereby create the synesthesia of Baudelaire's doctrine. In recovering "a poetry of the original man" ("une poésie de l'homme originel") and expressing it in the language of the symbol, "La Literature de Tout a l'heure' is synthetic: it dreams of suggesting every man by 'tout l'art." (103).[37]

For these *symbolistes*, the *spirituel* derived from their understanding that creation comprised both matter and spirit, form and content, and that these had been separated and must be reunited. "Spiritual," then, was a quality of one of the two components of creation, and not, as it was for the biblical critics, a quality of certain historical events. In the realm of the *spirituel* were symbol, poetry, purity, simplicity, unity, and ceremony. Spiritual transcendence of the material, the goal of *symboliste* drama, was effected through the poetic symbol, pure, simple, and one that was expressed in the ceremony, the drama. This is what Mallarmé meant when he called the word a spiritual instrument and the theatre "a spiritual act,"[38] for not only might transcendence be accomplished through them, but form and content, matter and spirit, would be reunited by the symbol in drama. The material, then, was a necessary part of creation and agent of the spiritual experience, whereas for the biblical critics, the spiritual occurred only in spite of the material. So while the biblical critics returned to spiritual origins as a historical event, an isolated moment during which the spiritual penetrated the material, the theatre reformers advocated a return to ancient principles and to the unity of creation in order to recover the spiritual infused in the material as an experience continually available.

---

36. Translated from "Mais comment oser parler du théâtre! Cet art, malgré le talent dont l'honorent les écrivains de qui je constatais les beaux efforts, est perdu. C'est à lui pourtant qu'est promise la Fête suprême."

37. Translated from "La Littérature de Tout à l'heure est synthétique: elle rêve de suggérer tout l'homme par tout l'art."

38. See Perl's 1985 monograph on Stéphane Mallarmé for an explication of Mallarmé on the "word" as absent. "The Word depends for its existence on words" (Perl 1985, 1577). Perl's adoption of Mallarmé's life as relevant context for understanding his art produces an intriguingly fresh perspective on this seminal artist whose own words originated the trend toward dissociating the work of art from the artist's life. Recovering this context permits an interpretation of his works as products of their cultural moment and Mallarmé himself as the "greatest poet of a transitional century" (1593).

The dramatist most responsible for effecting the *symboliste* dreams of a synesthetic theatre was Lugné-Poe.[39] As an acolyte in the Catholic Church, he was in awe of its elaborate ritual, and as a young student at Condorcet, where many *symboliste* poets had gone to school, he was exposed very early to the theatre and to the new movements in it.[40] Influenced by the *symboliste* poets and aided by his similarly influenced friends, Lugné-Poe enacted Mallarmé's ideas on theatre—harmony of artists, music, and rhythmic verse—in drama that truly attempted the synthesis of the arts and the synesthesia of experience. He actively sought new material from the *symboliste* poets. "A hundred, a thousand times it is better to be on the side of the poets!" (217).[41] It is perfectly representative of Lugné-Poe that he was the first to produce Oscar Wilde's *Salomé* in 1893. Enamored with Wilde's play, friendly with those who had helped Wilde with its French text, and ever the advocate of the struggling artist in trouble, Lugné-Poe recognized *Salomé* as worthy of the attention of his company, Théâtre de l'Oeuvre.[42] Certainly one of *symbolisme*'s hardest-working exponents, he was also responsible for continuing and broadening the reform of theatre in France that Antoine initiated. In all his efforts, though, Lugné-Poe also tried to re-create in the theatre the kind of awe he had experienced as an acolyte in the mass, and to bring new ways of expressing the ineffable to the stage.

W. B. Yeats, another exponent of *symboliste* drama, carefully explicates the connection between art and spirituality in his essays on good and evil, "for [art] entangles, in complex colours and forms, a part of the Divine Essence" (Yeats 1961, 148, "Symbolism in Painting," 1898).[43] The art of the

---

39. Aurélien-François Lugné was born in 1869, the same year as André Gide. He added the name Poe from a branch of his family and claimed to be related to Edgar Allan Poe.

40. Trained as an actor at both the Conservatoire and in Antoine's Théâtre-Libre, Lugné-Poe embodied simultaneously these fundamentally different approaches to both theatre and acting. He calls Antoine and the Théâtre-Libre his "tremplin" and titled the first of his three volumes of *La Parade: Souvenirs et impressions de théâtre* "The Fool of the Springboard" ("Le Sot du Tremplin"). To explain this: "The springboard of the theatre is a constant sacrifice which permits us to last without too many exterior marks of having become obsolete" ("Le tremplin use l'homme aussi bien que son élan. Le tremplin du théâtre est un constant sacrifice, qui nous permet de durer sans trop de stigmates extérieurs de caductié") (Lugné-Poe 1930, 53).

41. Translated from "Cent fois, mille fois, il vaut mieux encore être avec les poètes!"

42. He also did all that was in his power to protect Wilde's rights in France and registered the play with the Société des Auteurs et Compositeurs. See Jasper (1947) for more detail on Lugné-Poe and the Théâtre de l'Oeuvre. Jasper had access to Lugné-Poe, his wife, Suzanne Després, Maeterlinck, and Ludmilla Pitöef.

43. My discussion of Yeats's writing about *symboliste* drama draws on two collections of his essays: *Essays and Introductions* (1961) and *Uncollected Prose by W. B. Yeats*, edited by Frayne and Johnson (1970). References also include the essay title and date.

turn of the century—Wagner's operas, Villiers de l'Isle-Adam's plays, Beardsley's drawings, Verlaine's poetry, Maeterlinck's plays—differs "from the religious art of Giotto and his disciples in having accepted all symbolisms . . . and in having accepted all the Divine Intellect, its anger and its pity, its waking and its sleep, its love and its lust, for the substance of their art" (149). As during the Renaissance, the artists of the turn of the century "have sought for no new thing, it may be, but only to understand and to copy the pure inspiration of early times" (155, "The Symbolism of Poetry," 1900). But referring to "the new sacred book, of which all the arts, as somebody has said, are beginning to dream,"[44] Yeats asks, "How can the arts overcome the slow dying of men's hearts that we call the progress of the world, and lay their hands upon men's heart-strings again, without becoming the garment of religion as in old times?" (162–63). If theatre had become the garment of religion—that is, the garment that covered the nakedness of men's hearts, the deeper, more primal and sacred substance— then it must return to its sacred origins: "The theatre began in ritual, and it cannot come to its greatness again without recalling words to their ancient sovereignty" (170, "The Theatre," May 1899). Throughout his writing about the theatre, Yeats refers to what is available as "the theatre of commerce," and to the plays he proposes as "remote, spiritual, and ideal" (166). These will be of interest to those "people who read books and ceased to go to the theatre" (Frayne and Johnson 1970, 141, "The Irish Literary Theatre," January 1899). Yeats blames not the playwrights, but the audiences, for this theatre of commerce:

> A common opinion is that the poetic drama has come to an end, because modern poets have no dramatic power. . . . I find it easier to believe that audiences, who have learned, as I think, from the life of crowded cities to live upon the surface of life, and actors and managers, who study to please them, have changed, than that imagination, which is the voice of what is eternal in man, has changed. (1961, 166–67)

So the project, and for Yeats it was the establishment of the Irish Literary Theatre, was to restore the communal ritual of ancient drama and to produce plays that gradually educate the public. Quoting Victor Hugo's observation that in the theatre, the mob becomes a people, Yeats comments that

---

44. That "somebody" may have been Morice, Moréas, or more likely Mallarmé, whose "Livre" seems to be a conception of this unified and sacred canon of art.

"though this could be perfectly true only of ancient times when the theatre was a part of the ceremonial of religion, I have some hope that, if we have enough success to go on from year to year, we may help to bring a little ideal thought into the common thought of our times" (Frayne and Johnson 1970, 141). It is the calling of the descendants of the ancient priesthood to "spread their religion everywhere, and make their Art the Art of the people" (168).

Like Yeats, Copeau too was interested in educating the public on the theatre's function and nature, establishing a school alongside his theatre. His school, however, also trained young actors. The "theatre artist" who would be his school's product would not be the "great personality," the actor; rather, "there is only one great personality, one great individual who has the right to dominate the stage: that is the poet; and through him the dramatic work itself" (Copeau 11, lecture notes about the school, 1917). Copeau's theatre training involved movement, physical exercise, strength and flexibility training, voice development, breathing, and a host of other techniques to produce an actor who could adequately embody the poet's work and evoke the effect in the audience that the poet intended. Copeau understood his task to be to train actors to become the dramatic instruments of these poets, and his theory of staging further served this task:

Theatre's call for poetry is essentially a call for freedom. . . . This is where poetic truth is opposed to the lies of Realism, whence emerge spiritual reality, true creativity, and the real gift of life. But in order for it to develop all its inspirations, it must not collide with material obstacles, complications, and heaviness. We must give the poet what Mallarmé called 'the uncluttered stage open to fictions.' (111, Buenos Aires 1938)

As for the poet:

The new cry of the Poets breaks a silence which was beginning to weigh on us. They are proclaiming the supremacy of verse drama or, as they call it, idealistic theatre. They differentiate—at last!—between the body and the soul. They want to address themselves to the soul. . . . They will be the seers and the apostles. . . . They will move the Isle of Patmos to the Théâtre des Bouffes-Parisiens." (103, *L'Ermitage*, February 15, 1905)

Poets who had left the stage or who had never come close to it could begin thinking about honoring it. "Whence came this renewal, this refreshening? Simply from the fact that we had returned to the ancient laws of theatre and to its original traditions" (111).

All of these *symboliste* dramatists, then, sought a return to a time when drama *was* ritual, and its language poetry, the symbolic expression of, and invocation of, the ineffable. In an ancient time when the spiritual and the material were properly understood as inextricable components of creation, the poet was the high priest and the actor his word made flesh.[45] It was not, however, only the classical period to which these dramatists looked, but also to the only period in Christian history in which they saw these same principles operating, the Middle Ages. Copeau's new popular theatre would be based not just on the Greek dithyramb, but also on the medieval mystery play as the other primal source: "In art an inner strength is renewed as it was by the giant in the myth—by a periodic return to primal sources, to the maternal lap" (186, *Le Théâtre Populaire*). Both the ancient Greek and the medieval European communal theatre were that lap. Copeau especially revered the collaborative nature of the ancient and medieval drama, and he believed in the possibility of renewal of the theatre as a sacred public event through the melding of Greek tragedy and medieval church ritual. "My aim is to propitiate, to exalt the work, and for that purpose to form a brotherhood of artists who will be its servants" (11, lecture notes about the school, 1917). This brotherhood would be modeled on the medieval monastic orders. The chorus was another venue of collaboration, and its function was to preserve "the serenity of philosophy, of contemplation, of prayer, of invocation—that serenity which, on stage, eludes mankind brutalised by destiny, by events, by passion, struggling with one another or with themselves or with the gods. In its words and in its songs, experience, tradition, the wisdom of the ages and of man abound, and the voice of the poet is heard" (167).[46] But Copeau's emphasis was always on returning to the primal experience:

---

45. See *Shelley's Defence of Poetry* (Winstanley 1911) for Shelley's explication of these principles. "In the infancy of society every author is necessarily a poet, because language itself is poetry, and "poets . . . are the institutors of laws, and the founders of civil society, and the inventors of the arts of life, and the teachers, who draw into a certain propinquity with the beautiful and true, that partial apprehension of the agencies of the invisible world which is called religion" (8).

46. For *Miracle du Pain Doré*, a play based on his research into medieval staging, Copeau used the monodic and polyphonic repertoire of the fourteenth and fifteenth centuries, as well as other songs composed by the chorus master of Dijon Cathedral, to create the serene experience he had described.

If the popular theatre is to undergo a healthy birth and live its own life, it must live through this entire developmental experience for itself. It must take its point of departure from the soil, drink at the source, discover and gradually assimilate the laws of dramatic creation, composition, and performance. . . . Let its tragedy begin with choral chants. Let its comedy begin with gatherings and festivals, embellished with songs and Ioca farces, inspired by the images of characters known in the area. . . . At least they will have grown out of the people for whom they were made, they will have been renewed, refreshed at the very source, and will have developed organically, naturally. (194)

Copeau is here describing the theatre of ancient Greece and of medieval Europe and advocating it for the popular theatre of his day.

Even before Copeau, there was a renewal of interest in the medieval *mystères* in Paris, and many writers experimented with new plays based on their themes and techniques. The critic Jules Lemaître concludes that a revival of religious drama was taking place in the Paris theatre of the 1890s, especially evident in the various modern versions of mystery plays that had become so popular.[47] Although he observes that most of these represented a "piety without faith," he finds the plays on Christian themes performed in marginal theatres to be of authentic religious inspiration. These include the puppet plays of Maurice Boucher performed at the Petit Théâtre de la Galerie Vivienne, the shadow theatre of the Chat Noir, and several ambitious and large-scale "passion" plays. In response to the acclaim he received for his first puppet play, *Tobie*, Boucher writes that puppets were more effective than actors because "it is certain that the best actor would never know how to portray with such simplicity and strength these mystical gallic scenes with more piquant effect" (Henderson 1971, 124).[48] This, plus the complicity created between the characters and the audience by their explaining the action, was understood to be characteristic of the mystery plays, and these modern versions were enthusiastically received. A note in *Art et Critique* (April 1890) comments, "The only theatre doing anything artistic just has to be a theatre of marionettes!"

---

47. In the preface to his *Annales du Théâtre* for 1892.

48. Translated from "il est bien certain que jamais, au grand jamais, un acteur, le plus grand fût-il, ne saurait rendre avec autant de simplicité et de force ces scènes mystiques et gauloises du plus piquant effet."

(124).[49] Well known among the shadow theatre productions was Henri Rivière's *La Marche à l'Etoile*, a nativity play consisting of a series of images and tableaux projected as silhouettes, accompanied by a text set to music in the form of an oratorio. The dramatic impression apparently heightened the overall effect, and the peculiar relation between simplicity and grandeur seems to have been a highly valued feature of these modern mysteries.

The more ambitious and large-scale "passion" plays of Charles Grandmougin and Edmond Haraucourt, performed in the period leading up to Holy Week, also were received favorably by progressive reviewers. Grandmougin had produced an earlier play, *Caïn*, in 1890 at Théâtre Mixte, but *Le Christ*, performed at the Théâtre Moderne in 1892, was one of the successes of the season (117). Sarah Bernhardt and two other players recited *La Passion* by Edmond Haraucourt on Good Friday in 1890 at the Cirque d'Hiver. Actors performed it in full again to enthusiastic audiences the next two years at the Théâtre d'Application. Théâtre de la Rose Croix founder Joséphin Péladan, devoted to *symboliste* drama and intimately associated with the Rosicrucian movement, produced *Le Fils des Etoiles* during Holy Week in 1892 and 1893. Clearly these theatre innovators and their supportive audiences were interested in these modern religious plays based on the medieval mystery plays' themes and techniques. Evoking simple faith, spiritual grandeur, and the tragic power of the Christian story, these modern plays were something different from the entertainment of the commercial and official theatres.

The most famous of the passion plays is the one performed in Oberammergau, Germany, every ten years. By 1870, it had become all the rage among English travelers abroad. This "relic of the Middle Ages" (Elliott 1989, 26) was so successful that dramatists interested in producing religious plays sought out its ingredients of success. These included the sense that the production was not acted, but lived. The actors had to have lived after the example of Christ in order to qualify for the leading parts. The conduct of the audience as if they were in church was another ingredient, including reverence and the absence of applause. The reverent peasantry who produced the play was a further element, a primitive people devoted to performing this play, as legend had it, as a gift in gratitude for

---

49. As Henderson points out, the success of the puppet plays affected the theatre in general. Maeterlinck, associated with *symboliste* drama and eventually with Lugné-Poe's theatre, originally intended his plays to be performed in a puppet theatre. Alfred Jarry conceived of *Ubu* first as a puppet play, and indeed it was first performed as such.

their rescue in the seventeenth century. And the rustic surroundings added both simplicity and the sense of antiquity and timelessness. But as John R. Elliott has demonstrated, none of these features was in fact medieval, nor was the Oberammergau play itself. Rather, this "medieval relic" was in fact "Victorian gothic," all of its features contrived to appeal to nineteenth-century sensibilities.[50]

Believed to be a true example of folk art and appealing to nineteenth-century ideas of taste and reverence, the Oberammergau play, to which the best of modern German art was once again aspiring, was not just a play, but a total experience. F. W. Farrar, the canon whose apologies for biblical criticism have already been reviewed here, wrote a book about the experience,[51] and allaying the fears of some that perhaps witnessing a play in which Christ appeared was not right, he observed that "the sweet, pure, happy, and deeply religious population of this Tyrolese village" could not approach their task with "anything but the most solemn reverence" (27). So popular was the play that numerous accounts of attending it were published, and there was talk about importing it to England and France. But even more people resisted such a move, including Farrar: "The conscience of Christendom might well cry out in alarm against the hideous profanation of transplanting such a spectacle from its true surroundings in the hearts of a simple, believing peasantry to pollute it into wicked and blasphemous vulgarity by setting it upon the boards of some coarse rendezvous of idlers, or worse, in Paris or in London" (37).

The idea of reviving the mystery plays of the English Middle Ages met with just as much resistance. Though only a few were known at the time, literary historians and religious dramatists had considerable interest in these indigenous and communal works. But in comparison with the Oberammergau play, these English mysteries seemed rustic, violent, profane, and indecent. That they were comparing authentic medieval plays with a nineteenth-century production never occurred to these critics; rather, the English plays were seen as vastly inferior and not worthy of revival.

In 1879, a defrocked Anglican priest started the Church and Stage Guild to foster reconciliation between these traditional enemies and to encourage the production of religious plays. That it had been prohibited in

---

50. See the chapter "Oberammergau and the Victorians" in Elliott 1989 for his discussion of how this came about.

51. *The Passion Play at Oberammergau* (1890).

England for more than three hundred years to perform any biblical or religious work on the public stage was now a topic of much discussion, and Stuart Headlam hoped to make the sacred material for drama and the stage a means of religious expression.[52] In 1900, Headlam disbanded the guild, claiming success manifest in the reintroduction of drama into churches and the nascent movement to revive the English morality and mystery plays (fully realized in the 1920s and 1930s).

Though performing plays in a church had been forbidden since the sixteenth century, the churches, perhaps out of their need for new methods of evangelism, introduced biblical tableaux, as embodied in the medieval plays, to increasing general acceptance in the 1880s and 1890s. The first full-scale play presented in a church was *The Conversion of England* by Rev. Henry Cresswell, performed in 1889 in the Great Hall of Church House in Westminster. In his review of it, Shaw remarks, "It has come at last, the parson has carried the war into the enemy's country" (54–55). Shaw also predicts that soon the medieval passion plays would be performed publicly and to great acclaim. He was wrong; it was another thirty years before these plays received license for public performance. But it is clear that there was a great amount of interest in these plays, that dramatists were eager to return to these medieval religious plays to restore something to the modern stage that had been lost. Overtly a religious effort, all of these manifestations of returns to the medieval plays reflected a serious interest in recovering religious drama for the public stage. The medieval plays were understood to be pure, natural, and popular in context and origin. These dramatists sought to recover a sense of awe through the witness of the events of the Christian story, the techniques of tableaux and symbols, and the reverence that comes with faith in ancient truths. They aimed to restore the stage as a site for religious expression and experience, as well as to restore drama to the Christian story.

The return of all of these innovating dramatists to either ancient classical or medieval Christian origins reflects a common impulse to go back to those origins, to recover lost spirituality and restore it to a modernity they saw diminished by materialism, science, and loss of belief in transcendence. This is the same impulse that motivated the popularizers of biblical criticism, and the same general concern. Both movements sought recovery of the moment when the Word became flesh, however understood, and

---

52. The next chapter discusses the nineteenth-century persistence of the prohibition.

saw this as the central spiritual experience. But though the impulse is the same, some key differences are worth noting, for they make the projects of biblical criticism and theatre reform nearly irreconcilable.

A fairly apparent difference is the biblical critics' view of the Middle Ages as an inferior "B" period of mysticism, popish superstition, and foolish allegorical reading versus the theatre reformers' view of the era as an "A" period of dramatic purity and spiritual appreciation. Whereas the biblical critics sought to eliminate mysticism and revered rationalism and intellectual apprehension of the ancient texts, the dramatists tried to recover the mystical experience for a world they felt was too enamored with science and materialism. Whereas the biblical critics tried to accommodate modern science, the dramatists disdained it. The biblical critics consistently refer to the Reformation as both a period of return to ancient origins and a period of return for moderns. It is the project of the Reformation, they argue, that has been lost and that they seek to resume. The dramatists, however, reflect a more Catholic worldview in their appreciation of the medieval emphases on symbol and mystical experience, perhaps best exemplified by the eucharist itself, and on the intellectual challenge of interpretation of symbols.

It is perhaps not inconsequential that biblical criticism was a predominantly Protestant movement in German and English scholarship, whereas most of the new theatre ideas developed in Catholic France. When the English criticized the theatre, they frequently used the French plays as examples of offensive and immoral theatre, and the French referred just as often to English Puritanism as infertile soil for art.

National tendencies aside, although biblical criticism and theatre reform shared the *nostos* impulse to return to origins to recover lost spirituality, they also differed fundamentally on both the site of that return and the nature of that spiritual experience. Biblical critics looked back to the period of the Hebrew prophets as a time when revelation began and to the life of Christ as the time when it was embodied. The experience they sought to recover was the prophetic one—the experience of being present as revelation was occurring, either through a prophet or in the person of Christ. The dramatists, however, looked back to both ancient Greek ritual drama and medieval Christian mystery plays as times when drama served its original functions as a means of spiritual expression and as a site of spiritual experience. This experience happens to members of the audience and involves the connection between a symbol and its platonically pure origin, the idea. It is an experience of transcendence occurring in the individual through the agency of drama. For biblical critics, the spiritual experience was an encounter with revelation in history; for the dramatist, it was a direct and individual experience with the divine in the real. To put the situation into Matthew Arnold's terms, nineteenth-century biblical criticism enacted a Hebraicist *nostos*, while theatre reform pursued a Hellenist *shavah*.

Later, in the early decades of the twentieth century, these two movements would be harmonized, as evident for instance in Mrs. Humphry Ward's *Eleanor*, which took up the issue of Catholic modernism and celebrated its joining of historical criticism with the mysticism of faith. But at the end of the nineteenth century, biblical criticism and the new theatre represented alternative avenues of spiritual return. Biblical drama, then, encompassing both biblical content and the dramatic medium, embraced two irreconcilably alternative movements. In all situations of ambivalence, anxiety is the natural product, and thus it is perhaps not entirely surprising that biblical drama in the nineteenth century was a problem. Increasingly restricted over three hundred years, biblical plays at the *fin de siècle* had been absolutely prohibited from the public stage, yet some reformers were composing them again. Reconciling the irreconcilable, both effecting and reflecting cultural anxieties, they also provoked a cultural debate that, if examined closely, reveals the fears underlying these anxieties.

## Scene 2
# UNVEILING FEARS: LITERARY HISTORY AS GUARDIAN OF CULTURE

### ACCOUNTING FOR THE MEDIEVAL MYSTERIES

Literary historians in England from the end of the eighteenth century through the first decade of the twentieth were fascinated with the biblical drama of the Middle Ages. Thomas Warton's reference to the medieval plays in his *History of English Poetry* (1797), and his comments about their place in the history of English literature, formed one of the foundations that nineteenth-century historians built upon. So also did William Hone's *Ancient Mysteries Described* (1823), cited heavily for its descriptions and illustrations of these medieval performances. But it was A. W. Ward's thesis in *A History of English Dramatic Literature to the Death of Queen Anne* (1875, 1899) that became the prevalent view: that the ancient source of modern drama was religious ritual. Ward argues that church ritual evolved into biblical drama and that the mass, as the central act of worship in the Western church, comprised the elements of dramatic action. This drama, he continues, had originally been written in Latin and was performed within the church building itself, then gradually came to be written in the vernacular and performed in the public square. Out of the mystery plays of the fifteenth and sixteenth centuries developed modern tragedy, through the transitional phase of the chronicle histories, and comedy, through the transitional phase of the interludes.[1]

The one thing needed was that literary genius should apply itself to this form of literary composition. . . . The great opportunity was therefore consciously seized; and it is no mere phrase to say that in seizing it our first great Elizabethan dramatists addressed themselves to a national task, as men understanding their age, its signs, and its needs. (Ward 1899, 268)

Thus Ward traced the development of English drama from the church to Shakespeare. Until the middle of the twentieth century, scholars understood the medieval mystery plays to be merely "Shakespeare's predecessors."

The most influential scholar to articulate this understanding of the place in English literary history of the mystery plays was E. K. Chambers, author of *The Mediaeval Stage* (1903), which became the definitive and comprehensive summary of what literary historians believed about these plays. Chambers outlines the evolution of the liturgical play, which was complete, he says, by the mid-thirteenth century. From these liturgical origins, he traces a "process of secularization," constituting the move out of the church and into the hands of the laity and the broadening of the plays' "human as distinct from their religious aspect" (1903, 69). The development of secular and comic elements accompanied this "laicization" of the drama. Chambers mentions possible rivalries between clerical and lay actors both wanting to perform the plays, and later, the church's growing discomfort with and eventual opposition to these secularized mysteries.

With Chambers, Hone, and Warton cited in every history of English drama since, their understanding of the mysteries as part of an evolutionary process originating in the church and culminating in Shakespeare became standard. Chambers summarizes and includes the findings of all the

---

1. The interlude was a genre of comedy derived in the sixteenth century from the short farcical entertainment performed between the acts of a medieval mystery or morality play. A mystery play was a dramatization of a biblical account. These plays were organized into cycles, eventually composed of dozens of these mysteries, which together formed a Christian narrative beginning with creation and ending with judgment. Passion plays were those treating the suffering, crucifixion, and resurrection of Christ. Morality plays were generally allegorical dramas, singular in nature, and not based on biblical material. Miracle plays, also known as saints plays, were singular dramas as well, these treating the legend of a saint's life. This chapter focuses mostly on the mysteries, because they are biblical dramas, but the scholarship on them generally treats all of these medieval genres together.

nineteenth-century scholars who preceded him. These scholars' evaluation of the mysteries, however, seems at odds with their fascination with them, for they were unanimous in their estimation of the plays as primitive, vulgar, and riddled with farce and other unspecified "abuses." J. J. Jusserand may summarize this ambivalence best:

> Read as they are, without going back in our minds to times past and taking into account the circumstances of their composition, Mysteries may well be judged a gross, childish, and barbarous production. Still they are worthy of great attention, as showing a side of the soul of our ancestors, who in all this did *their very best*: for those performances were not got up anyhow: they were the result of prolonged care and attention. (1895, 466–67; italics in the original)

Chambers, and the historians before him, had constructed a narrative to account for the medieval mysteries, situating their origins in the church, tracing their evolution from sacred to profane through their movement out of the church and into the public square, indicating the abuses that attended this secularization process, and pointing to these growing abuses as the weight under which the drama finally collapsed, replaced by the far superior and more highly evolved Elizabethan stage.

Until relatively recently, only a few literary historians questioned this nineteenth-century account, and despite their work, it has remained the standard narrative. O. B. Hardison (1965) challenges this view by demonstrating that the manuscript history of the medieval plays does not support the evolutionary thesis of Chambers and his predecessors. Hardison claims that examination of Latin and vernacular plays reveals that "the neat theory of a drama that moves from the church to the church portal, from the church portal to the plaza in front of the church, and from there to movable pageant cars, changing its language from Latin to vernacular in the process, badly needs revision" (ix). Hardison leaves it to later scholars to complete this work of revision, focusing his attention instead on how the prevalent view of the genesis of medieval drama came to be: "Like all other scholars, including the present author, Chambers [and subsequent historians] . . . wrote in accordance with their conceptions of the nature of drama and the normative mode of literary development. . . . Their data are invaluable, but their interpretations of the data rest on assumptions now generally discredited" (vii). And these assumptions were the product of a particular moment in the history of scholarship, during which empirical criticism and the application of Darwin's ideas to cultural study had come into general acceptance. This view could not have been more aptly articulated than by mathematician and biologist Karl Pearson: "A study of the medieval [German] passion-plays will . . . bring before us an intermediate link in the chain of evolution from savagery to liberal faith" (quoted in Hardison 1965, 5). Hardison demonstrates that despite the solid appearance of Chambers's theory and the enormous body of material around it, "it proves to be arbitrary. Buried among the facts and protestations of objectivity are assumptions peculiar to a specific age and group of thinkers" (26).

Ten years later, Robert Potter (1975) picks up Hardison's invitation to revise the prevalent view of medieval drama, particularly the morality genre. He focuses on how the play's historical context "came to be misunderstood by scholars and critics in the eighteenth and nineteenth centuries, and how it was rediscovered and transformed in twentieth-century theater" (5). Similarly, Glynne Wickham (1980) focuses on stagecraft and performance history in order to dismiss the view inherited from nineteenth-century scholarship that these plays were "primitive and being succeeded by the more sophisticated Restoration stage spectacle" (113).

Martin Stevens neatly summarizes the work of these and other recent scholars that counters the nineteenth-century view of medieval drama "as a primitive organism that, as it moved away from its connection with worship, grew into ever more complex and, therefore, more interesting new forms." Stevens points to the single-source and simple-to-complex theory of medieval drama as reflecting the social Darwinism at the turn of the century to account for the assumption "that a literary form, like a biological species, grows organically over the years," when "the facts show otherwise. The Latin church drama did not, through some sort of mutation, develop into the vernacular drama. . . . Instead, the drama of the church existed side by side with the Corpus Christi cycles performed in the heart of the city. The two were different genres—indeed, different art forms" Hardison, Potter, Wickham, and the recent scholarship, the social Darwinist and secular humanist Chambers and his nineteenth-century predecessors, "spiritually removed from their subject," were fundamentally wrong in the way they had interpreted the historical documents available to them. Their faith in evolution and progress had led them to describe a "process of secularization" in which the chief function of the medieval drama was to make the transition from religious ritual to fully realized and mature modern drama (1990, 41–45).

Because recent scholars have been anxious to change the Whiggish[2] view that medieval drama merely leads to Shakespearean or modern drama, they have paid more attention to the nineteenth-century scholars' relationship to that process and its end than they have to the relationship between those scholars and the theoretical religious origins of that drama. In fact, the evolutionary model and secular humanism together make for an inconsistent theory, as Hardison points out. For if the far superior drama of the Renaissance were indeed superior because of its classical sources, as many historians have argued, then there must not have been an evolutionary process originating with the church and culminating in Shakespeare. Hardison and his followers criticize the anticlericalism of Chambers and his age, and they reconcile the evolutionary model with secular humanism by observing Chambers's enthusiasm for the increasing distance of drama from its religious origin, having broken "the bonds of ecclesiastical control" and appealed to a "deep-rooted native instinct," which Hardison identifies as "clearly a pagan instinct" that "triumphs over Christianity in the secularization of the drama" (1965, 15). While all this may be so, I suggest that Chambers and the nineteenth-century scholars were even more conflicted and complicated, and that their claims about medieval drama echo the discourse exactly contemporary with them about the Bible on the modern stage.

Chambers and the other scholars of his day may not have been as enthusiastic about the predisposition to progress as Hardison claims they were. One indication is their repeated reference to abuses in the performance of these plays. They never clearly articulate the nature of these abuses, but obliquely convey them in references to nudity on stage, devils and demons poking fun at the biblical characters, and the introduction of

---

2. Butterfield (1965) argues that historians tend to write from the perspective of a "Protestant, progressive, and whig, and the very model of the 19th century gentleman" (3). In the Whiggish interpretation, history is progress, and thus all study of the past is conducted from the perspective of the present. Whig historians tend to be generalists, and even when specialists correct their errors, these corrections are merely co-opted into the existing Whig narrative. Whereas Butterfield observes that Whiggishness is characteristic of historians in general, I argue that it is rather more characteristic of nineteenth-century historians in particular. But I do agree with Butterfield's historical approach: "Real historical understanding is not achieved by the subordination of the past to the present, but rather by our making the past our present and attempting to see life with the eyes of another century than our own" (16). For "perhaps the greatest of all the lessons of history is this demonstration of the complexity of human change and the unpredictable character of the ultimate consequences of any given act or decision of men" (21).

farcical portions of drama between the more painful narrative segments. These scholars were dealing with a couple of historical problems, only one of which was their interest in tracing the origins of Shakespearean drama. They also had to account for the sudden disappearance of enormously popular and spectacular productions. Most of these scholars seem to have taken pains to explain that the sixteenth-century Tudor ban on religious plays, which was the origin of the three-hundred-year history of theater censorship in England, was called for—in fact, was practically necessary in light of the abuses that were rampant and unchecked by any authority. The fact that most of their narrative histories of English drama did not begin before the establishment of the Christian church, and that their story is one of religious origin, gradual secularization, increasing abuse, and eventual intervention and prohibition, suggests that they were pursuing neither a secular humanist nor an evolutionary agenda as much as they were deeply interested in the process of secularization as abusive and deserving of censure.

William Kelly's compilation of manuscripts from the Borough of Leicester (1865) is a particularly strong example of this. In his preface, a 150-page discussion of the manuscripts' history, Kelly refers to the mysteries' faithful adherence to their biblical source, even to the point of having Adam and Eve naked on stage. Though he cites one critic as saying it was unlikely that this was in fact the case, he responds:

> Still, taking the explicit stage direction, etc., coupled with the habit which had long universally prevailed and which was continued to a much later period, of retiring to rest perfectly naked (several persons sleeping in the same room), and other gross manners of the people, together with the coarse and indecent language frequently put into the mouths of the female characters in the so-called religious plays, the question is still open to considerable doubt whether the earlier commentators were not correct in their opinion. (4)

Further on, Kelly criticizes the apparent nonadherence to the Bible of some vignettes, which drew more on old country life. In a series about three shepherds' offering to the baby Jesus, the knave Trowle declares, "I offer unto thee a payer of my wife's oulde hose." Kelly admonishes the reader: "Such is a specimen of the ancient Mysteries which three or four centuries ago the ministers of religion thought not unworthy of representation in the house of God, and to which our forefathers listened without any sense of impropriety or profanity. We may indeed truly say, '*Tempora mutantur, nos et mutamur in illis*'" (21). But later, referring to incidents in which an actor playing Christ almost died on the crucifix and an actor playing Judas had heart failure while hanging, Kelly comments that "the Scripture narrative was closely adhered to on the stage in this case, so much so as to be not unfrequently attended with danger to the actors" (29). Faithfulness to Scripture, seemingly a virtue, was an absurdity to Kelly and even an abuse of it, whereas the introduction of nonbiblical and especially scurrilous material was merely improper.

In the seventy-page introduction to Alfred W. Pollard's 1890 collection of selections from pre-Elizabethan English plays (1927), the author invites the student of the history of religious thought to reflect on the "meaning of the irreverence and prurience with which the most sacred subjects are occasionally handled" (xxxix). Like Pollard, Katharine Lee Bates (1893; 1921) argues that these plays were "the training-school of the romantic drama . . . preparing the day of the Elizabethan stage, for despite all crudities, prolixities, and absurdities of detail, these English Miracle Cycles are nobly dramatic both in range and spirit." But along with these noble dramas grew comedy, "bringing the theatre at once into collision with the church" (36). And as comedy developed, so also "it was natural, indeed, inevitable that the Miracle Plays . . . be seized upon by these pro-fane imitators, who soon became rivals and supplanters, too often turn-ing what had been illustrated Scripture into scandal and buffoonery" (37). This was natural because of the "rude laughter-loving tastes" of the general public. But, Bates cautions, just because the comic material was coarse, it "should not be taken as proving intentional irreverence on the part of players or of hearers. It points to social rather than moral causes" (48). Whereas Pollard is concerned about the meaning of this irreverence, a "line of investigation well worthy of pursuit" (1890; 1927, xxxix), Bates dismisses it as merely the bad taste of the common people. But both are clear that what they are observing is indeed irreverent.

Bates draws on the conclusions of A. W. Ward's history (1899), which she cites heavily. Ward holds the clergy accountable for this turn of events, when they "allowed the introduction into the religious dramas acted or superintended by them of scenes and characters of a more or less trivial description; . . . when devils and their chief advanced to prominence, and had to be made hideous or contemptible in order to inspire instantaneous antipathy,—the comic element could not fail to assert itself" (43). But again, this was just natural, for "it certainly would not have occurred either to authors or audience that the former were dishonouring the sacred narrative by patching it with rude lappets of their own invention; or that a bit of buffoonery introduced into a religious play implied irreverence towards its holy theme" (63). They simply did not know that these things were improper.

Bates, though, is more than condescendingly sympathetic with the "rude, warm heart of England." She also describes these medieval plays as "a barbaric art, unguided, untaught; and it was a blind faith, bowed in ignorant obedience before the authority of Rome" (1893; 1921, 196–98). The plays had dragged the people out of heathen paganism so that they could grasp the message of God as love, she argues, and the Reformation was needed to push them further toward the spirituality of God. This echoes the derisive conclusion of Thomas Warton, who points out the irony that people could not read the Bible itself but could see it on stage, "disgraced with the grossest improprieties, corrupted with inventions and additions of the most ridiculous kind, sullied with impurities, and expressed in the language and gesticulations of the lowest farce" (1737; 1797, 520). Thank God for the Reformation and its ban on this primitive, vulgar, and irreverent drama.

The observations of these scholars seem hardly to be "spiritually removed from their subject," as Stevens would have them; rather, they seem curiously close to it. For they all sound like apologists for the Reformation censorship, which brought to an end this drama whose origins they situate in the church. If they are critical of the church, it is for its failure to maintain appropriate oversight of these plays and for releasing control of them to lay and eventually commercial leadership. These scholars relate at great length, by description, citation, or selection, just how vulgar these plays were, mentioning over and over again their abuses, though never really articulating what those were. These abuses seem, however, to fall into two categories: those that reflect a too-close adherence to the biblical source, and those that involve the addition of farcical material. Both seem to be characterized by prurience, impropriety, and ridicule. These observations, however, seem to reflect a more than scholarly discomfort with these plays' handling of sacred scripture, as well as a predisposition to a Protestant worldview.

## DEFENDING CENSORSHIP OF THE BIBLE ON STAGE

Apart from historiographical interest, all of this is intriguing because the concerns of these scholars, the nature of their criticisms, and the pattern of their narratives seem to echo the concerns and predictions for a censorless future of those who concurrently were defending the censorship of biblical material on the modern English stage. Whether the public stage in England should be censored at all had been debated numerous times in the second half of the nineteenth century and into the first quarter of the twentieth. The question of biblical material on the stage was, then, merely a subset of the larger censorship issue. But it seems to have generated more heated debate than the general one, perhaps because it raised specific questions of morality and did so in such a way as to clarify the debate for the public. The question of biblical material on stage may, in fact, have functioned as the archetypal case for the censorship debate, organizing the issues and sides. The question raised in the 1890s, in reaction to the banning of *Salomé*, was, "Is it desirable that plays founded upon, or connected with, Biblical history should be introduced upon the English stage?" (Farrar, February 1893, 185). A series of articles in the public press addressed this question, and it is curious to observe the concerns, criticisms, and narrative patterns of this debate.

In February 1893, *New Review* published several essays under the title "The Bible on the Stage." The contribution of F. W. Farrar,[3] an Anglican clergyman, provides a good introduction to the terms of the debate. In his judgment, any attempt to put the Bible on stage should be "most seriously deprecated" (185). The events narrated in the Bible are associated with sacred religious feeling and should not then be "mixed up with questions of literary taste, of journalistic criticism, of the dresses, the appearance, the success or the failure of particular actors" (185). Nor should these narratives be associated with amusement, which necessarily attends plays, for "few plays are liked which do not introduce some comic characters or scenes" (185). But Farrar goes on to observe that the previous fifty years of efforts to purify the stage had been successful, and that as a result, it was exceptional to hear anything immoral or offensive in "our best theatres" (186). Not, however, that Farrar actually would have known this, for he attended the theater only "on the extremely rare occasions" (186). Rather, he has confidence in the censor and the reform movement that had been supported by the clergy and had rescued the stage "from misuse by the world, the flesh, and the devil" to be a "form of recreation which may in itself be elevating and salutary." But even so, if sacred characters were

---

3. This is the same Farrar of the previous chapter, who wrote apologies for the new higher criticism and an appreciation of the Oberammergau Passion Play.

presented in plays "which as a whole could not in any sense be regarded as sacred," this would be a "shocking and positive profanation." Farrar partially excuses the mystery plays as "a means of bringing home religious truths to the imagination of the ignorant" in a time of illiteracy and as "sometimes acted in churches . . . exclusively by clergy or those whom they trained," but even these plays "led to abuses so gross and intolerable that they fell not only into desuetude, but into abhorrence and contempt." Like the literary historians, Farrar never specifies exactly what these abuses were, and we are left to surmise that they had something to do with commercialization and irreverence, with meeting the desires of the audience by introducing comedy. Farrar sees as a syndrome the inevitable process of devolution from the sacred to the profane, from reverence to abhorrence, a process that could be stayed only by precluding its beginning. The introduction of plays in any way associated with the Bible onto the English stage, he concludes, inevitably would result in the kind of abuses evident in the medieval mysteries and in the violation of sacred religious service.

We do not know how Farrar knew about the medieval mystery plays, though we might presume that his knowledge about them came from sources similar to those from which his knowledge of nineteenth-century English theater in general derived. But Farrar seems to express the same understandings and opinions of the medieval mysteries as his literary historian contemporaries. Even his terminology is the same as theirs: "abuses," "comic characters or scenes," "the imagination of the ignorant." Farrar was a clergyman[4] who shared the same view of both the nature of the mysteries and the process of their development from ecclesiastical origins to profane ends. He even suggests that their abuses had led to public abhorrence and contempt. Farrar seems to have envisioned a general outcry against mysteries as contemptible. Like Chambers, Farrar cites abuses and the secularization process—to use Chambers's language—to condemn the medieval mysteries, and he uses this as the basis of his argument against the introduction in the nineteenth century of biblical subjects on stage. Chambers, then, narrated a literary history that at the very least supports the position taken by the clergy on the issue of biblical drama. Whether this was intentional or coincidental, Hardison's criticism of Chambers as anticlerical seems not to hold up here, for Chambers, the

---

4. See the previous chapter for more details on Farrar's career as a High Church clergyman, a prolific writer, and a commentator on contemporary religion.

literary scholar, in 1903 used the same approach and even the same language as Farrar, the clergyman, had used ten years earlier.

The other two writers addressing the question of the Bible on stage in the *New Review* both criticize the variety of view represented by Farrar. Alexandre Dumas *fils* sarcastically challenges the conventionally understood relation between religion and the theatre, suggesting that the theatre might be destined to save the church, and if so, this "would be a truly Christian revenge, for the Church has always done its uttermost to destroy the theatre" (183). Dumas observes that religion was in need of assistance and that theatre spectators in France left performances such as the *March à l'Etoile*, the passion, and the mystical puppets of Boucher "as deeply impressed as if they had really returned from the Holy Land" (183). Then Dumas gets to the point and asserts that the French public would "not have visited the *Salomé* of Oscar Wilde with the condign disapproval which it had received at the hands of the English censor" (183). Dumas thus refers to the event prompting the current debate and contrasts the sensibility of the French public with that of the English censor: the French public that was attending these theater performances, and leaving them inspired, with the English censor at pains to protect the interests of religion; the French public that would not have been shocked by Salome's kissing the severed head of John the Baptist with the English who "applaud Hamlet when he throws Yorick's skull back into the grave with a gesture of disgust" (184). Dumas predicts that the Bible will one day be represented on stage, and that when it is, it will delight the church, "which will look upon the emotion which the public will evince, if the work is well performed, as a return to faith. . . . And the world at large will be grateful when this is done"—when the theater is baptized "at the traditional font of the religious idea" by returning to the mysteries and their pristine religious ideal (184). Dumas further predicts that this movement will originate in France, to the reproach of the "narrow and petty minds" that "will imagine that the time of blatant blasphemy has come" and that will "emphasise on this ground the symptoms of moral degradation of which we have seen several of late years" (184). Someday, "even the English would permit themselves to enjoy *Salomé*—provided it is translated into English" (184). Dumas's view clearly reflects a very different understanding of the nature of the medieval mystery plays from that of the literary historians and Farrar, as well as a confidence in the public and in the theater that none of them would support. He also addresses the real issue, Wilde's banned play, rather than abstractly theorizing about biblical drama. Like Wilde's play, Dumas's view confronted the English censorship by focusing on its greatest fear.

We might conclude that Dumas did indeed zero in on that fear, judging by the reaction in an article titled "The Bible and the Stage" in the February 4, 1893, *Spectator*. Referring to Dumas's "patronising little article in which he declares that he . . . is in favour of going back to mysteries on the stage," the *Spectator* article quotes Dumas specifically about *Salomé* to show "how the introduction of Bible subjects on the stage would work, blending the solemn histories of the Bible with the poor melodramatic tricks of histrionic art, associating, whether in satire or in earnest, the severe austerity of a hermit-prophet with the hysterical passion of a Salomé, and teaching English audiences to expect and desire the morbid shiver which marks the collision of incompatible emotions." The writer asks, "Who, that had seen Salomé kissing the head of John the Baptist, could hear again the brief and bare statement in which Scripture records the scene of the murder, without interpolating in his imagination all that exciting mimicry of grim death and hysteric passion with which the stage had invested it?" The public, this writer implied, would forever focus on the perverse context of John's beheading, and the thrill they had experienced in seeing it enacted, thereby making "the greater conceptions of revealed religion ludicrous or contemptible" by having bound up their imaginations "with the delineation of impure and overwhelming passion" rather than with "the reverence and enthusiasm of the Christian life." Thus representation of this "kiss of the wanton" endangered religion and would "extinguish its highest influence over all but the very best and purest of the believers in its lessons" (1893, 155–56).

The well-known literary critic Henry Arthur Jones was the third contributor to the *New Review* article. In it, he worries about the danger of these dramas to art, rather than to religion. For religion, he says, is like gravitation, never in danger, absurd to try to help, and as impossible to escape. What Jones envisions as a problem is the religious use of the stage, "though doubtless there would be a huge harvest of wealth and popularity to be reaped if by chance our great religious public took to saving their souls through the medium of religious melodrama as they now save them through lithographs of the Crucifixion and serial stories in the *Sunday at Home*" (188). But Jones also can envision the nonreligious use of the great wealth of dramatic material in the Bible and sees "no reason why a drama founded on one of the Biblical themes . . . should not be done at one or two of our best West End theatres; that is, done from artistic motives, and without any suspicion of saving anybody's soul in the matter" (188). For the "English theatre could not possibly make a worse use of the Bible than the sects have done, or misunderstand it so completely" (189).

Predictably, the *Spectator* writer responds to Jones's criticism of English religion as vulgar by focusing on intention, pointing out that at least street preachers, as the archetype of vulgarized religion, did not intend to be "insincere and patronising towards divine revelation," nor would they tamper "in an irreverent spirit with prophecy and inspiration" (1893, 156). This writer had picked up on the same point as Archdeacon Farrar and the literary historians: that the inevitable products of the Bible on stage are abuses—irreverence, holding religion up to ridicule, an "easy-going standard of morality." Noble as the idea of dramatizing sacred history may appear, they all argue, in fact it would always and inevitably be subject to the forces attendant on the stage: the "commonplace idealisms of the multitude," the "histrionic and sentimental" nature of actors, and the likes of Alexandre Dumas *fils* as dramatist and Henry Arthur Jones as critic who were "guided by artistic feeling." Just as the medieval mystery plays had fallen to these forces, so would modern biblical dramas. Defenders of the ban—the *Spectator* writer, Archdeacon Farrar, and apparently the literary historians—appear to have been united in their understanding of the nature of the medieval mysteries and the process of devolution from sacred scripture to secular ridicule, and so they also were in agreement on the need to curtail the modern movement to put the Bible back on stage.

The narrative that situates the origins of the medieval mysteries in church ritual and traces their movement out of the church into the public square, from Latin to the vernacular, from clerical oversight to lay control, and from pure enactment of religious truths to abusive farcical dramatization, ends with the sudden banning of the mysteries in the sixteenth century. But are these the forces to which the medieval mystery plays fell? Because of the nineteenth-century literary historians' Whiggish viewpoint, not much emphasis was put on the precise conditions bringing about the end of the mystery plays. An example of this appears in the last chapter of L. Petit de Julleville's *Les Mystères*, which is suggestively titled "Décadence et fin des mystères." This 1880 book was an influential work and the first of his three-volume study, *L'Histoire du Théâtre en France*, which, like so many other histories, traces the origins of French drama to church liturgy. After more than four hundred pages of discussion of the mystery plays, Julleville finally must account for their disappearance, and this account is so concise that it has been quoted by every literary historian of this subject after him. The "arrêt du Parlement de Paris du 17 novembre 1548" would not have had such a pervasive effect on the rest of the country "if other causes had not seemed to conspire together for the suppression of the mysteries."[5] These were "the attacks of the Protestants, the scruples of the Catholics, the disgust of the lettered, tending toward the same object," which was "odious to Protestants because it altered the Bible" and "became suspect to Catholics because it spoke too much of the Bible and might furnish a new pretext for discussions of dogma" (441–42).[6] Only Chambers summarizes this view more succinctly, for to him the main reason for the decline of the mysteries "need hardly be sought beyond the 'Zeitgeist,'" as they comprised "an institution which had outlived its day" (1903, 180). Until 1946, this view of the end of the mysteries, like that of their origin, remained standard and unquestioned in literary history.

Harold C. Gardiner (1946) challenges the standard narrative of the nineteenth-century literary historians—or rather, he challenges the end of it. Though he never questions their situating the mysteries' origins in church liturgy (in fact, he repeats this part of the narrative numerous times), he does take on their evolutionary assumptions and their dismissal of the plays as mere products of their Zeitgeist: "It has been too long the fashion to consider the history of the drama from the evolutionary point of view, tracing the development of form from preceding more rudimentary form, with the consequent impression that growth of the morality and the secular chronicle play presupposes the antecedent decline of the mystery and miracle" (93). What Gardiner is at pains to demonstrate, and does so quite emphatically, is that the medieval mysteries had not declined in any sense, but were fully developed, extremely popular, and a major component of community life until they were intentionally exterminated by the English government as a major portion of its systematic imposition of Protestantism on a resistant people. The Tudor ban on biblical drama was a radical political move on the part of an extremely sensitive government, newly separated from the church in

---

5. Translated from "si d'autres causes réunies n'avaient semblé conspirer ensemble pour la suppression des mystères." Translations from the French in this chapter are my own.

6. Translated from "les attaques des protestants, les scrupules des catholiques, le dégoût des lettrés tendirent au même objet"; "odieux aux protestants parce qu'il altérait la Bible"; and "devenait suspect aux catholiques parce qu'il parlait trop de la Bible et pouvait fournir un prétexte nouveau aux discussions dogmatiques."

Rome and claiming religious as well as political authority over a people that had weathered more than fifty years of severe religious wars and sudden turnabouts:

> Now, whatever may have been the popular nature of the whole course of Reform in other lands, it is a recognized fact that in England the whole long process, from Henry's break from Rome until the compromise effected by Elizabeth, was one guided, fostered, even imposed from above. The beliefs and feelings of the people at large remained, until well beyond the middle of the sixteenth century Catholic in all essential matters. . . . The religious drama owed its decline in England not to a Reformation spirit which can fairly be conceived as a move of popular disfavor . . . but rather to a Reformation spirit, a Protestant sentiment which seeped down from above, which was imposed upon a people who wished still to cling to their old pageants, not perhaps wholly or even largely because they regarded them with passionate devotion as the last organized remnants of the old faith but at least because they were wedded to them from a love for a venerable tradition.

In fact, "the steady undermining of the old stage was one of the means adopted by authority to shatter contact with the life and thought of former Catholic times" (47–48).

To demonstrate his thesis, Gardiner takes the reader through church edict, government proclamation, and a wealth of economic detail,[7] showing that "the drama, as always, mirrors the times faithfully" (57). As Protestant propaganda, biblical plays were commissioned by the government from Protestant dramatists to ridicule the old Catholic beliefs and practices, especially the eucharist. These were performed in English towns as polemic. Under the tutelage of local government authorities, the traditional mystery plays were edited to tone down Catholic assumptions and to reinforce Protestant ones. But the popular love of these mysteries persisted, so that under Elizabeth they were finally attacked by the government as seditious and banned entirely. Far from the secularization process that Chambers and his predecessors, "more concerned with the origins of the type" (xiii), had described, the move of the mysteries from the church

---

7. The economic detail is presented so as to show that the mysteries' demise was not the result of the trade guilds' balking at their tremendous financial burden.

to the public square was a wholly religious development in keeping with the religious view of a still-medieval people, a view that the nineteenth-century literary historians had failed to appreciate or understand:

> It is worth remarking that the element of religious controversy, of polemical animosity which colored the final years of the religious stage in its miracle and mystery plays, has not ceased to prejudice its memory ever since, so that we find even today a trace of Puritanism still hovering about the whole subject. (xii)

Gardiner quotes the mayor of Chester, who had remarked at a 1906 meeting of the Archeological and Historical Society that although it was desirable to perform the old Corpus Christi cycle, many points "must be treated with great care." He asks why there should be this "apologetic air" to the mayor's remarks. Gardiner traces this attitude to Warton's observation that the medieval mysteries were "disgraced with the grossest improprieties, corrupted with inventions and additions of the most ridiculous kind, sullied with impurities, and expressed in the language and gesticulations of the lowest farce" (xiii). He challenges this prevailing view with documentary evidence and political expedience. That he was a Catholic priest doubtless facilitated his developing a different view of the history of the medieval mysteries. Perhaps that "trace of Puritanism still hovering about the whole subject" also could have been observed in Warton, Ward, Bates, and Chambers.

In challenging the evolutionary assumptions of the narrative constructed by the nineteenth-century literary historians, Gardiner revealed that the fears motivating the sixteenth-century ban on biblical drama were treason, sedition, and the perpetuation of Catholic belief at a time when the church and the state had become one and therefore religious dissent could not be tolerated. Although the evidence for this revelation was available to the nineteenth-century literary historians, it did not fit the narrative they had already constructed to explain the medieval mysteries. This evidence was in fact cited by those who were attacking censorship of the stage in general, and of the Bible on stage in particular. Several histories of censorship in England were published just after the turn of the century and just after the most recent of several government inquiries into the office and practices of the stage examiner. It is immediately apparent from these works that they are examples of polemic against censorship and not mere histories of a government institution. As histories, however, they are at pains to demonstrate that the origins of stage censorship were political, whereas the persistence of it in the nineteenth and twentieth centuries was entirely unrelated. Consistently, these accounts point to the politics of the Tudor ban, using the same evidence that Gardiner employs fifty years later in his challenge to the literary historians.

One such work (G. M. G. 1908) argues that the stage censor had originated in a political situation, was supported later by corrupt ministers, and was still maintained in 1907 despite public taste and the unconstitutionality of the institution. For example, the Tudor censor prosecuted a "lewd play-book," but "the word 'lewd' here . . . is clearly to be understood in the sixteenth-century meaning of generally objectionable and in this case presumably, as seditious" (13–14). The Tudor government had not been concerned with morality or taste, but with politics, and it was therefore sensitive only to works challenging its authority.

In the early eighteenth century, legislation had been proposed by a Quaker on moral grounds to reform the drama, which under the Restoration had become so immoral as to incite popular backlash. The legislation failed, but it was taken up again several years later when various plays openly criticized the corrupt Walpole administration. This legislation, pushed by Walpole himself, remained in effect through the nineteenth century, but by the middle of that century, the censor had become more interested in moral than political issues. G. M. G.'s point is consistent: the censorship of the stage began as a political expedient, it was maintained to protect political corruption, and its defenders at the turn of the century were arguing illogically for this censorship on the basis of this historical precedent, when in fact it was an unconstitutional institution.

Another such work of polemic against censorship followed the 1909 report of the government committee charged with investigating the operation of the censorship, with a clear view to pointing out the absurdity of much of the debate. John Palmer (1913) highlights the unconstitutionality of the censorship, the illogic of deploying its history as its defense, and the absurd way in which it actually functioned, particularly with respect to the Bible on stage. On the legality of the censorship, he observes:

What is most startling about dramatic authors today is that, so far as their property is concerned, they are virtually outside the law. A play may be worth many thousands of pounds on performance; but it is possible for the Lord Chamberlain to destroy it utterly as a commodity by refusing it a licence. He may destroy it on no ascertainable ground, and according to no fixed body of law or tradition; and there is no appeal from his decision. (19)

On the history of the censorship, Palmer clarifies its original purpose:

It does not at first sight seem necessary in a study of Censorship today to go back in history beyond the Theatres Act of 1843. But it so happens that many of the Censor's friends have impudently claimed the historical argument for themselves. To this claim they have not a shadow of right. . . . Theatres and plays were strictly regulated under the Tudors; but this regulation did not rest upon any idea that play-houses should be stigmatised. . . . The point about Tudor Censorship is that it dealt impartially with the theatre, the pulpit, and the press. (20–21)

Palmer explains why no one understood this: "In the latter half of the sixteenth century an attempt was being made to govern England on bureaucratic lines. The story about this attempt is not yet adequately written" (24). Specific to biblical drama, Palmer quotes the transcript of the interrogation of the examiner of plays regarding a biblical play that had been banned: "I have no power, as Examiner of Plays, to make any exception to the rule that Scriptural plays, or plays founded on, or adapted from, the Scriptures, are ineligible for licence in Great Britain" (107). But the examiner could not say when or by whom "the rule" originated, because it had not been written down anywhere. In fact, there was no such rule, and biblical plays were prohibited merely because they "traversed custom." Palmer concludes that the examiner's "conduct as to religion utterly baffles investigation" (107).

That same year, a similar work was published by Frank Fowell and Frank Palmer in response to the 1909 commission report and the 1912 public letter calling for the elimination of the censor. Fowell and Palmer are cited by every subsequent study of censorship, despite the fact that their work clearly is not history, but polemic. Like the others, they resort to a historical argument and argue the same thesis:

It must not be forgotten that the functions of the Master of Revels [sixteenth-century censor] were, even theoretically, very different from those popularly attributed to the modern Censor. It would be idle to claim for him any of that moral anxiety which is supposed to animate his modern prototype. He was, first and foremost, a court official, defending the powers and privileges of the court, guarding the person and authority of the King. (1970, 48)

Fowell and Palmer also had actually read the law, and they say that specific to biblical plays:

> There is nothing whatever in the Act of 1737, or the subsequent one of 1843, to justify the Censor in refusing to consider a play merely because it dealt with a Scriptural theme. . . . The effect of these capricious actions has been to rule out the whole Biblical field from the playwright's scope. . . . It is surely time that the causes of religion should cease sheltering themselves behind so puerile a guard as that of the dramatic Censor. . . . It is not the function of the State to protect any code of thought or morals from the natural fluidity of public opinion. (213)

Throughout the book, Fowell and Palmer point out in great detail how flawed the contemporary operation of the censor was, and how historical claims for its defense were consistently wrong.

While literary historians pointed to the natural demise of the medieval mysteries, and defenders of stage censorship cited abuses as the reason for their coming into general disfavor, evidence clearly was available that the plays still had been extremely popular when they were banned in the sixteenth century, and that the ban had been motivated by the purely political concerns of a government recently separated from the church in Rome and claiming religious authority. The evidence that the fear underlying the sixteenth-century ban of biblical plays was sedition must have been readily available, for those attacking the censorship made free and consistent use of this data.

If this evidence was so available, then why did the literary historians overlook it? Glynne Wickham, in the first study of the medieval plays as performance, concludes that by focusing on stagecraft, he can reveal the glaring inaccuracies in the literary-historical understanding of these plays. And the source of these inaccuracies? "It is becoming increasingly clear that for some four hundred years we have been the dupes of Puritan bigotry where the mediaeval religious stage is concerned" (1980, 8). As another mid-twentieth-century scholar challenging the evolutionary assumptions of the nineteenth century, Wickham demonstrates that these plays were hardly primitive works succeeded by the more sophisticated Restoration stage spectacle: "In short, the builders of the Public Playhouses of Elizabethan England were the direct heirs of a fully developed tradition of stagecraft and not novices in their profession as they have so often been represented" (117). Furthermore, Wickham also thwarts the traditional secularization argument: "Once, however, we concede that the Church, whether Roman Catholic or Reformed, controlled the plays' destiny to the very end, the grounds on which these long-accepted suppositions have been based are exposed as being both flimsy and improbable" (119–20). Wickham, like Gardiner (and citing him often), emphasizes that the plays were always religious and always under church control, though which church that was had changed. Clearly the narrative constructed by the literary historians and employed by the defenders of censorship of the Bible on stage masked fears that neither group sufficiently articulated. And clearly the nineteenth-century fear was not the same as that in the sixteenth century, for sedition seems hardly an issue in Victorian England. But to support their argument, the nineteenth-century defenders of censorship made full use of the sixteenth-century situation—or rather, the sixteenth-century situation as explained to them by their literary historian contemporaries.

But why had this become an issue at the end of the nineteenth century? Why this elaborate theorizing apparently to bolster an opinion about biblical drama at a time when, as Fowell and Palmer put it, "the biblical field had been ruled out from the playwright's scope"? As Wickham explains, "Not until the nineteenth century was any serious interest again likely to be tolerated in Miracle or Morality plays" (xxiii). And in fact, serious interest in these plays arose again in the nineteenth century, perhaps most significantly announced by all of the literary historical scholarship suddenly done on them. Several movements originating at the end of the nineteenth century actively engaged in the project of returning the Bible to the stage. We might assume that it was these that the defenders of censorship had in mind.

The English censor prohibited more plays during the two decades from 1890 to 1910 than in any other period since the censorship began. In the 1850s, the stage examiners had considered loosening the restrictions on biblical plays, but letters from the general public to the censor and to the editorial pages of mainstream newspapers indicate that the public preference was for even more stringent regulation. In 1879, Stewart Headlam, a defrocked Anglican priest and Christian Socialist, founded the Church and Stage Guild to promote religious and social sympathy between the church and stage, publishing annual reports of its progress. By the 1890s, the battle had come to a head. An increasing number of biblical plays were submitted for license, and the examiner of plays often took recourse to his superiors for decisions. When a version of the Oberammergau Passion Play, terrifically popular even among the English travelers to Germany, was proposed in 1895, the request for a license was ultimately denied by Victoria herself.[8]

Despite the lack of public support and state approval, proposals for biblical plays proliferated between 1895 and 1907. Among these were religious spectaculars, modernized psychological studies, and revivals of medieval plays. The spectaculars, such as *Ben Hur* and *Quo Vadis*, combined the popular elements of religion, spectacle, and sex, and eventually found film a superior medium. The psychological studies, in which Christ appeared in modern dress and devoid of his divine nature, continued to be quite popular well into the 1950s, as represented in hundreds of these "modern passion plays," such as *Servant in the House, Greater Love Hath No Man, The Sign of the Cross*, and *Good Friday*. The revived medieval plays came to be recognized by most as serious religious drama, whereas the spectaculars and the psychological studies were called "religious melodramas" by their detractors. Henry Arthur Jones, for instance, caricatures these plays as "Maria the Martyr" and their producers as "Mr. Godly-Slime" (1909, 32). All, however, seem to have been in large part religiously motivated.

Many of these plays were performed, despite being denied a license, in private quarters by private societies established for this purpose. Most popular and influential among these was William Poel's production in

---

8. The examiner of plays, responsible for issuing licenses for public stage performances, reported to the office of the Lord Chamberlain, an office subject to the court. The question of the German passion play was tricky because it had been so thoroughly praised as reverent. The examiner sent the question up to the Lord Chamberlain, who in turn sent it up to the court. Queen Victoria instructed her secretary to tell the Lord Chamberlain that she "entirely concurs in the view that he takes and is very glad that he has acted as he has done in the matter." This letter, dated January 30, 1896, is quoted by Elliott in his chapter on the Oberammergau Passion Play and the Victorians, where he notes as I do the agreement on the matter at even this highest government level. But we do not know the substance of Victoria's objections; she was a Hapsburg, and one might have expected her to be more sympathetic with the German play. The Lord Chamberlain's memo to her, with which she said she concurred, merely asserts that "transplanting the simple Peasants from their native homes where they have been used to perform the Drama as a religious Service to London would entirely alter the whole character of the performance, which must therefore degenerate into a theatrical spectacle" (Elliott 1989, 39). See note 9 on the constitutionality of the Crown's authority on this question.

1901 of *Everyman* in the courtyard of the Charterhouse in London. The production of this early Tudor morality play was sponsored by the Elizabethan Stage Society and reflected in its "stunning pre-Raphaelite beauty" Poel's advocacy of open-stage drama in England (Elliott 1989, 42). It was also exceptional in having a woman play the leading role and in the impersonation of God on stage. Though a private production to a subscription-only audience, *Everyman* was enormously successful, going on to commercial theatres in England, Scotland, and America through the next quarter century. Completely unlike the melodramas and farces that had become the standard fare of the English theatre and the butt of criticism by advocates of serious drama, this medieval drama confronted audiences with "unalleviated seriousness, preaching a doctrine of renunciation and spiritual perfection" (43). And its style was so solemn as to thwart the view that medieval drama was not religious enough. *Everyman* bypassed the censor because of its private production status and because it technically was not subject to license, having been written prior to the 1737 Licensing Act. But perhaps most important, the current censor, when asked by a select parliamentary committee some years later why he had permitted its production, answered that he had never heard of the play and had no idea that God was a character in it. Notices on the play were so generally favorable that its production continued unimpeded by the authorities, though when it moved into commercial theatres, the character of God became the "voice of Adonai" and was kept off stage. With the triumph of *Everyman*, the Church and Stage Guild declared victory and dissolved.

The success of *Everyman* was inspiring to several parties. B. W. Findon (1905) observes, "[Until] recently I never regarded Holy Writ as a hunting-ground for the playwright, but experience has shown that the religious drama is both a possible, and, when treated in a reverent spirit and handled with artistic care, a valuable instrument for good" (708). Performances of *Everyman* or *Ben Hur* "point to the fact that in the Bible and all that appertains to it we have a field of literature which, properly treated, could be made the means of winning to the side of dramatic art those who are now conscientiously opposed to the Stage" (709). Such plays were not only morally elevating, but also popular when "accorded such warm encouragement by the Church," indicating that there was "room for the religious drama." In pursuing his plea, Findon constantly refers to "delicate" or "reverent" treatment of biblical material as the correct standard; "there is no hope for the religious drama if it be approached in a sceptical [*sic*] spirit and treated with mocking contempt" (711). Findon seems to argue against the view, expressed by the *Spectator* writer and Archdeacon Farrar, that the Bible could not be handled on stage with the appropriate reverence. Whereas they had claimed that abuses would be inevitable because of the nature of the theatre, Findon cites the examples of *Ben Hur*, *The Sign of the Cross*, and *Everyman* as evidence that religion and stage can be brought into "social and religious sympathy," as Headlam had put it.

Findon also resorts to the narrative constructed by the literary historians about the origins of medieval drama to support his view of it as inherently religious:

> The drama having owed its birth to religion, it is interesting to trace the course of events which ultimately led to the divorce between church and stage. . . . For centuries the drama lay quiescent, unheeded, amid the silence of the Dark Ages, and then, strange to say, it was again brought to life in direct association with religion. . . . As time went forward, critics were not wanting who took exception to some of the ludicrous inconsistencies of the representations, but the coarseness of the age, the absence of refinement, the low standard of taste, were undoubtedly responsible for much of the vulgarity that attended the performances, and possibly many beautiful truths were masked in hideous inventions. . . . In *Everyman* there was a combination of spirituality and realism which compelled serious attention and effectually removed any disposition towards irreverence. The sentiment of the Church was strong within it, and the impression it made on the senses was akin to that produced by a solemn service held in an ancient cathedral. (711–12)

Findon, like others before him, holds the Puritans responsible for the "unsympathetic attitude of millions of worthy people towards the drama" (712) and calls for an end to the antipathy between the church and the stage. "For nearly three centuries Puritanism has dominated the country and ruled the bulk of the middle classes. . . . Having shown the intimacy that existed between Religion and the Drama in the classic and middle ages . . . we are now free to deal with what may be considered the first steps toward a *rapprochement*, and we come to those arguments which may be advanced to further the union of the Bible with the drama" (713). But Findon is not calling for the elimination of censorship entirely; rather, he says, "The Censor should be strictly enjoined to sanction none but those conceived in the most reverent spirit." These would not permit the Trinity on stage, and he suggests that it be obligatory that all biblical plays "be written as poetical dramas" (715). The censor and the public had nothing to fear from these sufficiently reverent religious plays.

But reverence is not easily measured. In 1907, a group of dramatists and literary critics drafted a public letter demanding an inquiry into the operation of the office of censorship, and in 1909, a select committee heard testimony from theatre managers and examiners of plays on the subject. The result of the inquiry was minimal, with only some relaxation of the prohibitions against biblical material on the public stage and some clarification of the guidelines. These very minor changes prompted numerous publications criticizing the censor and the office of censorship, including Fowell and Palmer's "history" of censorship, which pointed out its political function; John Palmer's argument that the office of censorship was unconstitutional;[9] and a "letter" by Henry Arthur Jones (1909) that was intended to speak for the playgoers, a group unrepresented in the hearings. Jones cites the thousands of unlicensed plays that had been performed with no untoward effect as an example of how an unregulated theatre would operate. Though he does not really offer a way out of the "Censorship Muddle," Jones points out the essential difficulties in implementing moral regulation of the theatre. With reference to the religious melodramas in particular, Jones observes that it was their "wax-doll" morality that failed to impress "serious English playgoers." Meanwhile, "deeply conceived" plays were declared immoral by the censor and banned. This banning, however, only served to advertise these plays, for "moral or immoral, the net result of the Censor's action was that scandal was caused, the Censor was defeated, and the play was performed to increased audiences" (10). The problem was that the censor was called upon to decide

---

9. The office of the examiner of plays had been established by the court under the office of the Lord Chamberlain, but no law ever treated censorship of the stage or established this office. With no law, there were no legally enforceable guidelines or prohibitions. Rather, the exercise of the office, with no legal authority, was completely arbitrary. Its critics repeatedly made this point in the nineteenth century. Palmer observes that this office with no legal sanction was capriciously capable of preventing people from earning their living. A play text that would have had commercial value could be emptied of it for no legally defensible reason and without recourse. It was on these grounds that critics referred to censorship as unconstitutional. But of course, it also gave the Crown final and arbitrary authority over the public stage at a time when the Crown had direct authority over very little else. This whole situation of the Crown's involvement in the censorship of the public stage, though beyond the scope of this chapter, bears more research and might constitute an intriguing microhistorical study of Victoria.

what was moral or immoral, and he was no better than his public, so he sanctioned the moral "wax-doll" and banned the deeply conceived and therefore troubling drama. From Jones, we might determine that what the censor feared were these deeply conceived and morally troubling plays.

The revival of *Everyman* influenced more than the question of the possibility of religious drama. In 1911, the Morality Play Society organized to promote modern performance of medieval plays, and this movement continued to gain momentum through the century, resulting in a whole field of scholarship and research, as well as the large-scale production of the medieval cycles in England, France, and most recently Canada and the United States. At the same time, new dramas that made use of certain medieval dramatic techniques were conceived. This movement to foster drama as religious expression was promoted by the Religious Drama Society and its Canterbury Festival, culminating in T. S. Eliot's *Murder in the Cathedral*, and encouraged by John Masefield, Dorothy Sayers, and Christopher Fry, among numerous other contemporary dramatists. These were "serious" dramas on moral questions, religiously motivated, and they combined modernist aesthetics with medieval stage techniques. By the 1930s, the censor's restrictions on biblical material on stage had loosened, though these plays continued to be performed under private conditions. It was in this climate and context that Oscar Wilde's *Salomé* finally was performed in England, some forty years after it had been banned.

## "ABUSES" AND FEARS

The vaguely articulated abuses mentioned repeatedly by the historians of medieval drama, the changes and ridicule anticipated by the defenders of censorship of the Bible on stage, and the irreverence that promoters of religious drama had cautioned against do not seem to have been evident in most of these dramas. For the revival of the medieval plays apparently was inspired by religious motivations and was attended by a spirit of solemnity, and the new moralities that employed medieval technique but addressed modern problems were equally religiously motivated and serious. Even the religious melodramas, which to the sensibilities of Henry Arthur Jones and other highbrows were abusive of wax-doll morality, were intended to be religiously and morally uplifting. Clearly these groups of plays were not what the censor and his defenders had had in mind, for none of the fears, as unspecific as they were, had manifested in these dramas. Yet the undercurrent of discussion still retained this unspecified fear in its language—the caution against irreverence, the demand for suitable and appropriate material, the need for discretion. What specific fear was all of this veiled language intended to express?

One feature of the medieval plays that the historians consistently pointed out and condemned was the presence of devils, demons, Vices, Satan or Lucifer, and Hellmouth on the stage. Katherine Bates observes: "The handling of the Old Testament subjects was . . . marked by extraordinary freedom. To the vision of the Creation, received as literal history, was persistently added the wild, feudal legend of the Fall of Lucifer" (1921, 171). Bates's choice of words is telling: feudal legend persistently added to the literal history. It is clear that she understands the entire "Fall of Lucifer" narrative to be non-Christian. But the real problem for these historians was that the presence of these devils introduced a comic element to the sacred story, and they found this "buffoonery" offensive and abusive.

A. W. Ward observes that "when devils and their chief advanced to prominence, and had to be made hideous or contemptible in order to inspire instantaneous antipathy,—the comic element could not fail to assert itself," and this would "contribute to give a profane character to what could no longer be regarded as essentially a part of religious worship" (1899, 43). E. K. Chambers, in indicating the transition from religious to secular, points specifically to the incorporation of secular and comic elements as accompanying this laicization:

And in the growth of the devil scenes, from their first beginnings . . . to their importance in the *Adam* or the various treatments of the Fall of Lucifer and the Harrowing of Hell, may we not trace the influence of those masked and blackened demon figures who from all time had been a dear scandal of the Kalends and the Feast of Fools? It is certain that the imps who sallied amongst the spectators and hauled the Fathers off to their limbo of clashed kettles and caldrons must have been an immensely popular feature of the *Adam*. (1903, 91)

Echoing Bates's language, Chambers terms the presence of demons a scandal and then supplies no justification for his conclusion that they must have been popular. J. J. Jusserand explains why they had been added:

Fearing the audience might go to sleep, or perhaps go away, the science and the austere philosophy taught in these plays were enlivened by . . . the gambols of a clown, fool, or buffoon, called Vice. . . . And

often, such is human frailty, the beholders went, remembering nothing but the mad pranks of Vice. It was in their eyes the most important character in the play, and the part was accordingly entrusted to
the best actor. (1985, 491–92)

Bates makes a similar observation, imagining the audience's response to
these demons and their antics:

Although they sometimes gave an impressible man the nightmare,
the average spectator had a lurking affection for the lesser devils. They
were all he had left of the goblins, kobolds, and pixies of his ancestral
heathenism. As for Satan himself, there was a delicious excitement in
viewing the shaggy monster on the pageant scaffold, with God or
Christ at hand to hurl him down presently into hellmouth. Seeing
Satan off the stage might be quite another matter. (1921, 194)

Never indicating how they knew the feelings and reactions of the audiences, these nineteenth-century historians apologize for their medieval
ancestors. Jusserand observes that "a feeling for measure is a product of
civilisation" (1895, 479). Ward explains, "It certainly would not have
occurred either to authors or audience that the former were dishonouring the sacred narrative . . . or that a bit of buffoonery introduced into a
religious play implied irreverence towards its holy theme. . . . Of course
the historic sense—the sense of what is correct—was as completely wanting in these plays as a sense of what was fitting" (1899, 63). The medieval
dramatists could not have known that presenting devils on stage, and
thereby introducing a comic element, was irreverent, unfitting, and
unhistoric—so argue the nineteenth-century historians, who consistently
and repeatedly refer to this abuse as feudal, pagan, and heathen.

It was both the addition of nonbiblical material to the biblical narrative
and the nature of that addition as comic and heathen that made it for
these historians an abuse. Lynette R. Muir (1995) believes that the presence of the devils were integral to the whole play cycle, observing that
when the plays were under attack in the sixteenth century, it was primarily
this feature that was removed so that the plays became more "straight biblical." She theorizes that the devils functioned to distance the audience
from the violence and convey the understanding that God's mercy was
more powerful than man's sinfulness. When the devils were eliminated, a
"theatre of cruelty" replaced the medieval cycles, reflecting a different

attitude to evil. John Wesley Harris (1992) suggests that there must have been "some powerful religious impulse that developed in the society of late medieval Europe and fueled the desire for large-scale dramatic demonstrations of faith. . . . Late medieval man had suddenly become very aware of his sinfulness and his vulnerability" (82). The devil had an active role in this drama, and his work supplemented the biblical material. Historians in the nineteenth century, however, viewed the addition of the devils to the biblical account as merely for comic purposes, which to them constituted an abuse.

In the 1867 work *Les Prophètes du Christ*, "the most important book published up to that time on the drama" (Cargill 1930; 1969, 2), Marius Sepet in Paris hypothesizes that every scene from the medieval plays was a growth from, or even a direct duplication of, material existing in the liturgy of the church. Oscar Cargill, in his fascinating study of this "liturgical theory" of the origin of the medieval mysteries (*Drama and Liturgy*, 1930, 1969), demonstrates that it is simply wrong. Cargill studies the liturgical history of the Middle Ages to determine whether such a theory would be plausible in light of ritual development. By comparing the tropes in the liturgy with those in the drama to observe any relationship between them, Cargill reveals that no generic connection exists between the drama and the liturgy. Although Sepet was not a scholar of medieval culture, his conclusions apparently had remained unchallenged, and Cargill now raises skepticism about a nineteenth-century theory that no one had ever seriously questioned:

> The Roman Church . . . was the source of the medieval drama, just as the Greek religious rites were the source of the drama of antiquity. Imagine the immense interest in the Latin liturgy his conjectures created among scholars! . . . No close, comparative scrutiny of these texts was made, however . . . because what he had asserted seemed so obvious. (3–6)

After a close study of the liturgy and the mystery plays and their sources, Cargill finds that these in fact differ. The crux of Cargill's argument is that the source of the liturgical material had not been the Gospels, at least not directly, whereas the dramatists seemed to have been "solely occupied with making a harmony for the layman out of the varying Gospel versions" (56). Cargill believes that the biblical text was the immediate source for the plays but not for the liturgy, and therefore church liturgy and medieval drama were unrelated. So not only did the plays not develop from the liturgy, but they had different origins.

Two features of Cargill's argument are of prime interest here. The first is that he is able to point out how inadequate an understanding of the nature of medieval ritual and liturgy Sepet and his followers had. In assuming that the ritual was an enactment performed before the assembled congregation, these scholars had failed to recognize that it had never been mimetic, nor was it performed for the benefit of the congregants. These are Protestant ideas. The congregation was not necessary to the efficacy of the ritual, and in fact, much of its performance could not even be seen by the assembled. The second point of interest is Cargill's case for a dramatist independent of the church who was drafting a play for the benefit of the layperson. As layperson understood only the vernacular, so, Cargill pointed out, would it be illogical to draft plays for them from the Latin liturgy. Cargill imagines the dramatist, with the Bible lying before him, "at pains to reconcile irreconcilable accounts" (58), and therefore drafting a consistent vernacular account of the varying Gospel materials.

Cargill's argument against church ritual as the source of the mysteries is convincing. But just as it would be illogical to use the Latin liturgy as a source, so also would it be to use the Bible. Though vernacular translations did exist, the Bible commonly in use was the Latin Vulgate. If the plays reflect the attempt to reconcile the Bible's inconsistent accounts of sacred history, it is more likely that the dramatist's source was an already smoothed vernacular tradition. Such a tradition existed in the sermons and homilies that were the congregants' primary source of knowledge about the biblical stories, argues G. R. Owst in *Literature and Pulpit in Mediaeval England* (1933, 1961), a study that is generally esteemed but whose argument has not been fully appreciated. In the chapter "Sermon and Drama," Owst explores the vernacular plays' indebtedness to the English sermons and concludes that "it was the preacher who taught the dramatist" (473). Owst was well aware of the nineteenth-century historians' beliefs:

Familiar association of the religious drama in its earliest stages with the Liturgy of the Church hitherto seems to have blinded most scholars to the fact that in the pulpits, for centuries, the sacred episodes had been declaimed with a freedom and dramatic intensity unknown to mere liturgical recitation. To Sir Adolphus Ward, for example, English preaching is virtually non-existent by the close of the thirteenth century, which saw the rise of these same "Mysteries." Neither Sir

Edmund Chambers, nor Professor A. W. Pollard has a word to say upon its activities. Little wonder, therefore, that by others the influence of the pulpit has been so grossly overlooked! . . . Scholarship has been sadly led astray by lack of acquaintance with another and a much despised literature which had already set forth in true and satisfying combination the colloquial, the proverbial, the jovial and the religious. (474–75)

The bulk of this chapter provides evidence that "it was *popular preaching* . . . an activity entirely overlooked by Chambers—that brought about the 'secularization' of the drama" (478). Owst points to the characteristics of the medieval plays—vernacular language, use of Old Testament material, reconciled Gospel accounts, satire and *exempla*, profanities, devils, and humor—and finds their counterpoints in the medieval sermons:

In England, indeed, where the golden age of vernacular religious drama coincides, so far as existing records suggest, with the golden age of vernacular preaching, the parallels between them are far too numerous and arresting to be mistaken for mere coincidences. . . . There remain overwhelming similarities in the actual handling of matter, the details of certain characters and topics, the very texture and language of the two classes of composition. (485–86)

In an age of illiteracy, the source for these plays was not the Bible itself, but the Bible as it was received by the laity, as it had been reworked in church sermons and presented in church art. These included all of the elements that also appeared on the medieval stage: the Fall of Lucifer, the devils and demons, the sacred postbiblical histories of saints, the Harrowing of Hell and Judgment Day. All of the details in these dramatic accounts originated in vernacular sermons:

Students of English literature, at the mercy of the text-books, might well gather the impression that this rollicking, human type of demon, this Mephistopheles of the market-place was a characteristic product of the later religious drama and the antics of human impersonators upon the "scaffold." The truth is, however, that, so far from remaining mere abstract spirits of evil in serious exposition, the leading devils were already known and even mentioned by their nick-names in pulpit manuals from the thirteenth century onwards. (512)

Church liturgy had not inspired the medieval plays, and neither was it the literal Bible that had served as their immediate source. Rather, it was the sermon, which, like church visual art, was the vehicle for the Bible to the assembled congregation. And of course, the preachers of these sermons were clergy, representatives of the church to the laity. The nineteenth-century scholars' criticisms of the medieval plays as having added to the biblical story, incorporated profane material, introduced demons, and otherwise "contaminated [it] with secular admixtures" (Gardiner 1946, 10) reflects their post-Reformation adherence to the literal Bible over the received Bible, and their anachronistic evaluation of the medieval plays according to that standard. The abuses they noted were, in fact, faithfully rendered portions of the extrabiblical but ecclesiastically authorized received story.

All of the nineteenth-century literary historians were at pains to excuse additions that did not fall into the category of abuse. These were chiefly the psychological development of unnamed biblical characters, such as Noah's wife, who appeared in virtually all of the cycles. She was, in these plays, a shrew of sorts who resisted Noah until the end, refusing to get into the boat and having to be carried onto it bodily. "The story of the Ark was saturated with fun arising from the vixenish characteristics which . . . the Miracle dramatists have well-nigh universally agreed in bestowing upon Noah's wife," observes Bates (1921, 171). Yet even these unobjectionable additions had come from church sermons. Shepherds and the lover of the woman taken in adultery were other characters typically developed, usually for some didactic purpose or to relate the religious story to the daily experiences of the audience. Perhaps because these additions did not change the biblical stories substantively, nineteenth-century historians did not view them as abuses. Rather, these historians all comment on the charm or function of these additions:

It is in the treatment of these nameless characters that some of the most dramatic touches are bestowed. They are obviously introduced for the sake of relief . . . welcomed by their spectators as a relief to the extreme tension of feeling which the protracted exhibition of Christ's Passion could not fail to excite. (Pollard 1927, xli)

The other category of abuse cited by the nineteenth-century historians consisted of cases when the plays adhered too closely to the biblical text, such as the rather clear stage direction that prefall Adam and Eve were to appear naked on stage, or the danger to actors from too realistic enactments of the crucifixion or of Judas's hanging. Perhaps the historians also were concerned about other examples of too-faithful adherence to the text. Even Luther had observed that those who were squeamish about obscenity and fornication had better not read the Bible (Blackburn 1971, 28), for clearly there is an abundance of perverse material in the Bible itself. Oddly, though, not much of it appeared in the medieval plays. Lucy Toulmin Smith (1885, 1963) and Lynette Muir (1995) both study the composition of the medieval cycles, outlining the stories they include and in what order. What is particularly notable is the biblical texts not included. A brief list of "perverse" biblical narratives might include the following:

- Noah's drunkenness after the flood and his uncovered genitalia;
- Lot's daughters' seduction of him in order to bear offspring;
- Sodom and Gomorrah and the events leading to their destruction;
- Judah and Tamar;
- Joseph and Potiphar's wife;
- Dinah's rape and its aftermath;
- Esther and Vashti;
- Ruth and Boaz; and
- Abraham's representing Sarah as his sister to Pharaoh.

And of course, there are the Saul–David–Jonathan and Salome–John the Baptist stories. Curiously, none of these topics appeared in the medieval plays. These texts were not part of the Christian story as narrated in church sermons, and they were of no interest to the medieval dramatists. So it is striking that some of these topics were selected by nineteenth- and twentieth-century dramatists.

In 1931, Edward D. Coleman, a librarian at the New York Public Library, compiled a listing of all plays in English treating biblical subjects, arranging them in order of the biblical texts and dividing them into "medieval" and "modern" categories. From the 1870s to the 1920s, the most popular topics, as represented by the number of works, included Joseph and his brothers, Joseph and Potiphar's wife, Jephtha's daughter, Saul, Absalom, David and Bathsheba, Jezebel, Job, Song of Songs, Esther, Judith, Herod (a category of plays based on Josephus's accounts and including Wilde's *Salomé*), John the Baptist, the Prodigal Son, Judas, Magdalene, and Paul. In general, the Old Testament subjects tend to be those suitable to three- to five-act tragedies and focus on a historical figure, either a victim of his or her circumstances or an unlikely hero. (The interest in women seems to derive in part from the movement for women's rights in this period.) The New Testament subjects, apart from those shared with the medieval mysteries—Mary, the nativity, the passion—reflect a similar interest. The medieval dramatic interest was limited to the events of Christian cosmology. After creation, the fall, and the flood, the dramatists' interest in Old Testament subjects was only prefigural, and the bulk of the cycles consists of New Testament material on Mary, the nativity, the passion, and then judgment, plus Lucifer's fall and cosmological involvement. By contrast, the nineteenth-century dramatists—those not involved in reviving the mysteries, but who composed original modern works—exhibited more interest in discrete narratives with tragic potential. The abuses that the nineteenth-century critics of both bodies of works refer to as inevitable and unacceptable in fact differ greatly: vulgar realistic portrayals and devils in the case of the medieval plays, perverse biblical content in the case of modern plays. But all of these cases fit the general rubric of "irreverent" and "holding religion up to ridicule." No wonder the critics never specified what the abuses were; their argument was insupportable from the start.

Perhaps the best source of clarity is public comment. In 1895, when the number of proposals for biblical plays was sharply increasing, one of the plays denied a license was *Joseph and His Brethren*, written by an Australian clergyman, Rev. G. Walters. The play had been rejected summarily by the censor, who by then had a form letter specially designed for this purpose: "Dear Sir,—I have no power as Examiner of Plays to make any exception to the rule that Scriptural plays, or plays founded on or adapted from the Scriptures, are ineligible for licence in Great Britain . . ." (quoted in Elliott 1989, 21). On this particular request for a license, the censor observes curtly: "The episode with Potiphar's wife is the central situation. Quite impossible" (20). Although the play was already ineligible because it was scriptural, the censor takes pains to expressly point out that it focused on a portion of scripture that he found "impossible." Why? The press had gotten wind that the play, which was well known outside of England, had been submitted for a license and reported it, prompting a barrage of letters to the office of the censor. An example is one letter from a Christian who was experiencing "much pain of his moral sense" and considered it shocking if the play, "trafficking in sacred things," was permitted. Specifically, he was concerned about "parading solemn and holy things to be laughed at and ridiculed by worldly minded men and women" and that "such a sacrilegious perversion of Holy Writ being made spectacle to amuse people" was "calculated to bring the Holy Book into contempt" (21). This diatribe expressing real fear of some sort of perversion of scripture was prompted by the rumor that the situation of Joseph and Potiphar's wife had been dramatized and might be performed publicly. What this writer feared was not perversion *of* the Bible, but the public performance of perversion *in* it.

Expressing similar fear to that of the *Spectator* article author, who had warned of the scandal that enacting the "hysterical passion of a Salome" would create, this letter writer seems to have come close to articulating what underlay all of the vaguely but consistently expressed fears: the literary historians' repeated reference to abuses in the medieval plays, the changes and ridicule cited by the defenders of censorship as inevitable by-products of the theater, the need for reverence prescribed by the advocates of the religious stage, and the parading before a worldly audience of solemn things that caused moral pain to Christians who regarded the Bible as the Word of God—namely, the fear of unveiling perversion they knew to be present in the Bible. This seems evident in the horror the writers to the censor and the *Spectator* express at contemplating onstage portrayals of Joseph and Potiphar's wife and Salome and John. For it was not what the dramatists did with this material that worried them, but the idea of this material being enacted. Furthermore, the prospect of introducing the medieval devils onto the modern stage was almost as appalling, for those demons had poked fun at the faith and its believers and held religion up for ridicule, precisely the fear articulated in the public debate about censorship. These seem to be the unarticulated fears of a generation of scholars that constructed a narrative to explain away several centuries of drama, a drama in which they exhibit nevertheless a perhaps prurient interest.

For all the talk of coarseness and primitiveness and making comic the very tragic history in the Bible, in fact there was little of this in the medieval plays and virtually none in the revived or new morality plays at the turn of the twentieth century. The narrative the nineteenth-century literary historians constructed in defense of the otherwise untenable censorship of the Bible on the public stage—church origins, a process of secularization with increasing abuse, and a final demise from natural causes—represented a worldview that remained unchallenged until the second half of the twentieth century. Hardison and Potter had disproved the origins and evolution theory, Gardiner and Wickham the natural demise theory. To claim here that the unspecified abuses the literary historians cited as justification for the plays' demise, and as the natural product of the Bible on stage, were in fact the enactment not of perversions of the biblical material, but of perversions already present in the sacred text, is to challenge the last component of the nineteenth-century narrative. We do not learn much about the medieval mysteries from these literary historians, but we do learn something about the nineteenth-century worldview from the narrative that masked their fears.

The fear underlying and masked by the narrative that the contemporary defenders of censorship employed was that the perversity they knew to be in the Bible would eventually be enacted on the public stage. The only way to prevent this development was to nip all such ideas in the bud. Despite the clearly political origins of the sixteenth-century ban of the medieval plays, the literary historians and defenders of censorship based part of their arguments on the assumption of a seamless three hundred years of historical precedent. Yet it appears that perhaps the sixteenth and nineteenth centuries shared one thing: an unarticulated fear of things Catholic. Nineteenth-century defenders of this precedent invoked the structure of the narrative accounting for the medieval plays to predict the results of allowing the Bible in any form back on stage. As well-intentioned as some dramatists might be, they seem to have argued, abuses would be the inevitable result. The fact that the source of those abuses was likely to be the Bible itself was too troublesome to articulate. Furthermore, for all their confidence in church ritual as the ancient origin of their drama, these historians had overlooked that the "Bible" this was based on was that of church sermon, not that of King James. The nineteenth-century story about how the medieval plays had begun in the church ritual, become commercialized and corrupted with abuses, and collapsed under public pressure was constructed by literary historians who failed to take into account the evidence before them, and it was deployed by defenders of censorship to preclude the public performance of modern biblical plays despite the evidence of the political rather than moral origins of the censorship. The vague but repeated references to abuses in the past and inevitable abuses in a censorless future, and the narrative constructed by literary historians and applied by defenders of stage censorship, represent their concerns and fears far more adequately than they do the history of medieval drama. By examining these references and this narrative, we glimpse a worldview that feared not only perversion of its sacred text, but more interestingly, public confrontation with perversion already present in it.

Oscar Wilde's *Salomé* in 1892 manifested these fears and inspired fifty years of nervous debate. Though a brief biblical passage, the narrative about the death of John the Baptist is integral to the Christian story. Wilde had not chosen an obscure or irrelevant text from the Bible, but one known both to Christians generally and to the several centuries of artists who had explored its theme. Invoking pagan elements, sexuality, and violence, the story of the unnamed daughter of Herodias was bound to fascinate. And the uproar that Wilde's application for a license created is telling. Technically not subject to license because it was written in French,[10] the play was banned immediately as "half biblical, half pornographic." The *Spectator* writer speculating on its horrors had recourse only to the biblical text and his own imagination, yet he could imagine how the play would violate standards of decency. This was because the perversity was not brought to the text by Wilde; rather, Wilde had brought out the perversity in the text. That Wilde had indeed made significant changes to the Bible's brief narrative was unknown to any of these commentators, for the play had been banned and was not published for another year. It did not matter anyway. The really scandalous features of Wilde's play lay in its source, the Bible, and his intention to take it to the public stage sparked the battle that raged between the 1890s and 1910s about the Bible on the stage.

---

10. There were certain exemptions to the general censorship of plays: those written before the 1737 Licensing Act, such as *Everyman*; those that were musical rather than dramatic, as in all of Handel's oratoria; and those written in a foreign language. Wilde's play should have been exempt because it was written and to be performed in French, but the examiner's thoughts on musical and foreign productions had recently changed. This is another example of the capriciousness of the censorship system.

# ACT II

# Interpretive Monologues

## Scene 1
# MANIFESTING FEARS: OSCAR WILDE'S *SALOMÉ*

Much criticism of Oscar Wilde's *Salomé*, both contemporary with it and more recent, suggests that Wilde intended to create a stir with his play, to flout the censor's rules, and had written a work he knew could not be performed. Often read through the lens of events surrounding his trial several years later, Wilde's play has been understood as anticipating his ruin and manifesting the extremity of his views. While this may be the case, this view of the play fails to take into account Wilde's fifteen-year preoccupation with the legend about Salome and John the Baptist, his use of elements of it in his earlier work, and his lifelong, unironic concern for the state of his soul. Richard Ellmann, in his biography of Wilde (1987), points to Wilde's references to the narrative as early as 1875, his exposure to it in Flaubert's *Trois Contes* in 1877, and his allusion to it in several of his early poems. Ellmann furthermore observes that Wilde's interest in the story coincided with his contracting syphilis, and with the disease came the sense of doom that he expresses in this early work. Wilde seems to have had more at stake in *Salomé* than just tweaking the sensibilities of the censor and his cohort. Whether one interprets Wilde's outrage at the censor's banning the performance in 1892 as just so much public posturing, as some critics have suggested, *Salomé* indeed represented the concerns of the censors, manifesting as it did the fears that had been repressed by the censorship.

## SOURCES OF THE SALOME LEGEND

Though there are three biblical accounts of the legend of John the Baptist's beheading at the request of Herod's stepdaughter, the most extensive account is in Mark 6:14–29:

> And King Herod heard of him [Jesus of Nazareth]; (for his name was spread abroad:) and he said, That John the Baptist was risen from the dead, and therefore mighty works do shew forth themselves in him. Others said, That it is Elias. And others said, That it is a prophet, or as one of the prophets. But when Herod heard thereof, he said, It is John, whom I beheaded: he is risen from the dead. For Herod himself had sent forth and laid hold upon John, and bound him in prison for Herodias' sake, his brother Philip's wife: for he had married her. For John had said unto Herod, It is not lawful for thee to have thy brother's wife. Therefore Herodias had a quarrel against him, and would have killed him; but she could not: for Herod feared John, knowing that he was a just man and an holy, and observed him; and when he heard him, he did many things, and heard him gladly. And when a convenient day was come, that Herod on his birthday made a supper to his lords, high captains, and chief estates of Galilee; and when the daughter of the said Herodias came in, and danced, and pleased Herod and them that sat with him, the king said unto the damsel, Ask of me whatsoever thou wilt, and I will give it thee. And he sware unto her, Whatsoever though shalt ask of me, I will give it thee, unto the half of my kingdom. And she went forth, and said unto her mother, What shall I ask? And she said, The head of John the Baptist. And she came in straightway with haste unto the king, and asked, saying, I will that thou give me by and by in a charger the head of John the Baptist. And the king was exceeding sorry; yet for his oath's sake, and for their sakes which sat with him, he would not reject her. And immediately the king sent an executioner, and commanded his head to be brought: and he went and beheaded him in the prison, and brought his head in a charger, and gave it to the damsel: and the damsel gave it to her mother. And when his disciples heard of it, they came and took up his corpse, and laid it in a tomb. (KJV)

In the more condensed account found in Matthew 14:1–12, it was Herod, not Herodias, who had wanted to kill John, but "he feared the multitude, because they counted him as a prophet" (14:5). In Mark, Herod believed John was a holy man and that Jesus was John resurrected; in Matthew, Herod decided that the people who had counted John a prophet were correct and therefore came to believe that Jesus was the prophet returned to life. In the Luke account (3:19–20 and 9:7–9), however, Herod was puzzled by the people who said that John had risen from the dead. "John? I beheaded him. So who is this . . . ?" (9:9, NJB). Here Herod seems to have dismissed altogether the claim that Jesus was the resurrected John. The "biblical source" for the legend about the death of John the Baptist, as it was remembered culturally, seems to have been the account found in Mark.

But Mark's account omits some key details, most noticeably the name of Herodias's daughter who performed the dance before Herod and his guests. For this information, we must consult Josephus, who provides a genealogy of Herod's family in *Antiquities of the Jews* (bk. XVIII, chap. V, no. 4). Here we learn that Herodias had been married to Herod Philip, son of Herod the Great and Mariamne, daughter, of Simeon the high priest, and that she had a daughter, Salome, "after whose birth Herodias took upon her to confound the laws of our country, and divorced herself from her husband while he was still alive, and was married to Herod Antipas, her husband's brother by the father's side; he was tetrarch of Galilee." Salome, in turn, married Philip, the son of Herod, tetrarch of Trachonitis, and as he died childless, she married Aristobolus, the son of Herod, brother of Agrippa. They had three sons, named Herod, Agrippa, and Aristobolus. A translator's note to this page suggests that this great line of Herod went extinct as punishment for the gross incests of which it had been frequently guilty (bk. XVIII, chap. V, no. 4) (446). Amid all of these Herods, the key detail contributed to the legend was the name of the daughter of Herodias, Salome. The details of how Herodias came to have her husband's brother as her second husband were not specified in any of the biblical accounts, nor what law in particular they had violated. In fact, it seems that it was only the names that Josephus had included, and perhaps his evocation of the atmosphere of incest surrounding this family, that were of interest in the development of the legend.

Though the Gospel accounts present Salome as the instrument of her mother Herodias's schemes, from the fourth century Salome herself became the object of denunciations and an example of the evils to which dancing may lead. In a sixth-century illustration of Matthew, for instance, the representation of Salome develops the motif of moral choice (Kuryluk 1987, 195). She also became a popular subject for painters in the Middle Ages and early Renaissance, such as Giotto, Titian, and Donatello, usually shown in a lascivious pose. John the Baptist meanwhile had become the model ascetic for both the early church fathers and later medieval writers, and his words and example were invoked as rebuking the worldly. Biblical drama of the sixteenth century took up the subject of Salome's dance, as illustrated for instance in John Bale's *John Baptist's Preaching* (1985). These late medieval and early Renaissance plays contrast the virtue of John with the vices of Herod, Herodias, and Salome. This is curious, for by this time the ban on biblical plays had been implemented. John Bale was the first Protestant writer of biblical plays, which were clearly anti-Catholic polemic designed to ridicule "popish" faith and ritual and to expedite the reform of the English people. They had been commissioned by the English government from Protestant dramatists as propaganda. Thus by the seventeenth century, the legend of Salome and John the Baptist had developed into polemic against dancing and the Catholic Church, Salome having assumed autonomy as a force of evil and John the role of Puritan ascetic archetype.

Not until the nineteenth century, however, did Salome emerge as a central and popular figure of the literary imagination. Until then, the legend had been maintained chiefly through folklore that centered around the celebration of St. John's Eve, a summer solstice festival that was still active in early-twentieth-century French and Irish villages. Nineteenth-century scholars of folklore, religion, and anthropology studied this festival and its mythology, and James Frazer commented on it in volumes 5 and 6 of his *Golden Bough*.[1] But this tradition usually left out Salome and focused on Herodias (Kuryluk 1987, 189–94). For the Romantics, however, and even for writers well into the early twentieth century, Salome became a compelling subject, featured notably in the work of Flaubert, Heine, Laforgue, Mallarmé, Renan, and Symons. But they transformed the figure presented in the biblical accounts into an archetype of the *femme fatale*. Two paintings of Salome by the symbolist painter Gustave Moreau appear in J-K. Huysmans's novel *Against the Grain (A Rebours)* as belonging to its central

---

1. Wilde's father had been a collector of Irish folklore during his career as a doctor. After his father's death, Wilde had intended to publish this collection, but he turned the project over to his mother, who did so. It is still recognized as a valuable source. Clearly Wilde had multiple opportunities to be exposed to the legend of the death of John the Baptist.

character, Des Esseintes, for whom she is no longer a mere dancing girl, but the symbolic incarnation of lust and hysteria, "an accursed Beauty exalted above all other beauties." Moreau's paintings and Huysmans's novel became central reference points for the aesthetic movements of the turn of the century, appearing, for instance, in Wilde's *Picture of Dorian Gray*. In the nineteenth century, Salome had become something of a cult heroine.

## WILDE'S *SALOMÉ*

Wilde seems to have drawn on the biblical, Josephan, and later traditional accounts of Salome, yet he also made innovations unique to his play. The character Hérode is specifically Herod Antipas,[2] and the daughter of Hérodias is identified as Salomé. For John the Baptist, he follows Flaubert's use of the Greek Iokanaan, alternatively spelled Jokanaan in Wilde's manuscripts and in the English translation. He calls the executioner Naaman, the name of the Old Testament Syrian who consults the prophet Elisha. The play opens with a young Syrian and the Page of Hérodias talking on the veranda outside the banquet hall, where Hérode is entertaining a large, international group of guests. Soldiers are discussing the debates among the Pharisees and Sadducees about the existence of angels. And all of them comment on Iokanaan, who periodically utters biblical-sounding prophecies from the bottom of a cistern where he is imprisoned. Someone makes reference to the imprisonment of Hérode's elder brother in this same cistern for twelve years, until he was finally strangled at Hérode's order.

Salomé enters the veranda to escape the revelry and her stepfather's lustful looks. Hearing Iokanaan in the cistern, she asks the servants and soldiers about him. Looking into the cistern (where her father had been

---

2. In the English translation, at least. Wilde wrote *Salomé* in French and intended that it be performed in London in French. This is one reason he believed it would bypass the censor, for plays in foreign languages until then had been exempt. The play was published the following year, 1893, in French and in English, the translation done by Alfred Douglas. It has been disputed whether Wilde approved of this translation. In any case, it is in the English translation that the character is specified to be Herod Antipas, tetrarch of Judea. In the French, the character is merely Hérode. In the discussion that follows, I am referring to the French text as published in Wise (Symons, ed., 1927), unless it deviates significantly from the manuscript in the University of Texas's Harry Ransom Humanities Research Center. (This I believe is a second draft of the play written while Wilde was still in Paris, for the first half or so is written without correction, as if it was copied, whereas the second part is full of changes and notes.) I use the French spelling of the names when referring to the characters in Wilde's play and the English spellings when referring to the biblical characters. English quotations from the play in this chapter are from Douglas's translation (Aldington and Weintraub, eds., 1981).

imprisoned and murdered, a fact she seems not to know or at least to have forgotten), she observes that it is like a tomb. She persuades the Syrian, by promising intimacies, to bring Iokanaan up out of the cistern, thereby violating Hérode's orders. When Iokanaan appears on the veranda, he spouts a tirade of Revelation-sounding abuse, referring specifically to the whore of Babylon. Salomé is fascinated by him and comments on his terrible voice and his physical beauty: black eyes, white and slender body, black and ringletted hair, and scarlet mouth. Her language to describe him sounds like that of Song of Songs. Still, Iokanaan has nothing but contempt for her attentions, advising her to seek redemption in the desert. The young Syrian, smitten by Salomé, kills himself when he realizes she has interest only in Iokanaan, and the Page of Hérodias grieves for his death, revealing his own love for the young Syrian. So Hérode and the young Syrian are obsessed with Salomé, while she is attracted to the chaste Iokanaan, and the Page is in love with the Syrian. But Hérode, the Syrian, Salomé, and the Page are all rebuffed. A great deal of sexual gazing goes on here.

Hérode enters the veranda, looking for Salomé. Hérodias follows him and chastizes him for his prurient interest in her daughter. Hérode asks Salomé to dance for him, and she declines. He asks her again and promises her gifts, but she still declines. He begs her to dance and offers her whatever she would have, and she relents. Her mother is furious. Salomé performs the dance of the seven veils, which also involves perfume and bare feet, and Hérode is delighted. She then requests the head of Iokanaan on a silver charger, a request applauded by her mother, though Salomé says that it is not her mother's voice that she is heeding. Hérode objects, offering her a long list of sumptuous riches exhaustively described, but Salomé insists on her price. Hérode seems to be paralyzed by the situation, and Hérodias slips the ring of death from his finger to give to Naaman, the executioner. The sound of Iokanaan's head hitting the cistern floor reaches Salomé. When she is presented with the severed head, she addresses it, saying that herewith she has requited her lust for him. But his beautiful eyes are closed, his tongue silenced, his head bodyless, and she is aflame and her lust, alas, unrequited. Salomé kisses Iokanaan's lifeless mouth, and Hérode, observing this, orders her killed.

Wilde's innovations include adding details relevant to his plot and making changes in others. In all of the biblical accounts, the daughter of Herodias dances for Herod and his guests, and they are so delighted that he offers her whatever she desires, but in Wilde's version, Hérode makes his offer before her dance in order to persuade Salomé to perform. The biblical account focuses more attention on the dance itself as provoking the offer, whereas in Wilde's it is Salomé alone who is the object of desire. The dance is described in the biblical account as delightful, but Wilde gives no details except to specify that it is "the dance of the seven veils" ("la danse des sept voiles"). What Wilde intended this dance to be has been the subject of much debate among dramatists and critics, and certainly this is a significant production question, but for the narrative it does not seem to matter. It is Salomé and not her dance that Hérode finds delightful; one feels she could have performed the macarena and he would have been enraptured.

Wilde's Salomé also has fully realized the transformation from an instrument of her evil mother to a *femme fatale* in her own right. She negotiates the deal with Hérode, against her mother's wishes, and then requests the head of Iokanaan as her own idea. That this ultimately pleases her mother is of no consequence to Salomé. It is her frustrated desire for Iokanaan that drives her. Hérodias does, however, reclaim some of her malevolent power when she slips the death ring off the paralyzed Hérode and gives it to the executioner. Hérodias's interests in the death of Iokanaan are consistent with the biblical account, but Salomé's motives are no longer those of the faithful daughter; rather, they are those of the sexual predator.

This attraction of Salomé to Iokanaan is another detail that Wilde added, though the love story version of the legend had already been established by Heine in *AttaTroll* (1843). Influenced by the scholarship published on the folklore, Heine had developed the idea that John was beheaded because of Herodias's love for him. Wilde changed the lover and culprit to Salomé, and the attraction from a love for the Baptist's pure and religious soul to one based upon his physical appearance. Iokanaan, as the object of Salomé's desire, does not have the appearance of the wild man dressed in animal skins and sustaining himself on locusts, as John the Baptist of tradition did—a tradition even the soldiers and others in the play maintain when they discuss what they had heard about Iokanaan. Rather, he is lovely to behold: thin, pale, and passionate.

By adding the details about the circumstances surrounding the marriage of Hérode and Hérodias, that the younger brother had executed the elder, and the transaction effected by sending the death ring from Hérode's finger to the executioner, Wilde raises the question whether Hérode had been as paralyzed then as he was with Iokanaan, thereby raising doubt about who was ultimately responsible for the murder of Hérodias's first husband. Wilde also includes a small but overt homoerotic theme in the Page's grief over the death of the Syrian—the recipient, as it turns out, of his numerous love gifts and attentions. All of the characters in the play, even secondary ones, are suspect, their motives conflicted and unclear—all, that is, except Iokanaan.

Two other material details are the cistern and Salomé's death. In none of the biblical accounts is there any specification of the nature of John the Baptist's prison, but in Wilde's version, it is a cistern that contains Iokanaan and had imprisoned Hérodias's first husband. Ewa Kuryluk (1987) discusses in her chapter "Grotesque Tendencies" the nineteenth-century interest in caves and grottoes as metaphors for the unconscious, a repository for repressed sexual and violent desires. Perhaps this accounts in part for the death of Salomé, which is not reported in the biblical accounts or in Josephus's genealogy, where, in fact, we are told that she married twice and had three sons. Wilde's narrative, however, moves inexorably toward Salomé's demise as the only satisfactory resolution to the issues that the play raises. As Kuryluk points out, in Revelation, which is the source of so much of Iokanaan's language, love equals annihilation. "The message of the apocalypse is accurately repeated in *Salomé* by the saint, for whom there is no other realization of love except through death—the mortification of the flesh and the annihilation of the entire corrupt earth" (220). So also may Salomé's love be realized only in death—or perhaps it is the only fitting end for a *femme fatale* at the *fin de siècle*.

Perhaps just knowing something about the Salome legend, as it had developed in art, literature, and folklore from the biblical accounts, was sufficient to provoke reaction against the performance of a play based on it on the English stage. In the nineteenth-century histories of the medieval plays, scholars accuse them of "abuses" worthy of their ultimately being banned, including irreverent and prurient handling of sacred subjects (Pollard 1927), the vulgar realism of too closely adhering to the text (Kelly 1865), and the introduction of comedy turning what had been illustrated scripture into scandal and buffoonery (Bates 1921). Similarly, those who at the end of the nineteenth century were defending the persistence of the three-hundred-year ban of biblical material from the public stage warned about the dangers of blending solemn history with melodrama, the ridiculing of religion and easy morality that would follow the inevitable irreverence (Farrar, "The Bible and the Stage" 1893), and the mixing up of sacred events with questions of literary taste, criticism, and the appearance of actors (Farrar, "The Bible on the Stage" 1893). These were the articulated fears underlying the nineteenth-century censorship, and it appears that Wilde's *Salomé* manifested them.

Certainly there is prurient handling of the sacred account. Hérode's inappropriate interest in his stepdaughter/niece, the Page's homoerotic affection for the Syrian, who in turn worships the princess, and the virgin Salomé's desire for the chaste Iokanaan all seem to qualify as sexually charged supplementation tending toward prurient treatment. This theme is effected through scopophilia: characters gaze at the objects of their desire, while other characters warn them against this looking. At the play's opening, the young Syrian is in reverie over Salomé, and the Page of Hérodias is looking at the moon.

> THE YOUNG SYRIAN. How beautiful is the Princess Salome tonight!
> THE PAGE OF HERODIAS. You are always looking at her. You look at her too much. It is dangerous to look at people in such fashion. Something terrible may happen.

The Syrian persists, however, and the Page continues to admonish him; his warning, "Something terrible will happen," is prophetic. When the Syrian kills himself, the Page exclaims, "The young Syrian has slain himself! . . . Ah, did he not say that some misfortune would happen? I too said it, and it has come to pass." The young Syrian takes his own life when he realizes that the object of Salomé's looking would only be Iokanaan, and that she is oblivious to his own gaze. When Iokanaan emerges from the cistern, Salomé looks at him "and steps slowly back" in the stage direction. Looking at him further, she observes that he is "wasted," his skin is "like a thin ivory statue," his body "white like the snows," his hair "like clusters of grapes," and his mouth "like a band of scarlet on a tower of ivory" and "like a pomegranate cut in twain with a knife of ivory." When she says to Iokanaan, "I will kiss thy mouth," while the young Syrian is addressing her with "Princess, Princess, thou art like a garden of myrrh, thou who art the dove of all doves, look not at this man, look not at him! Do not speak such words to him. I cannot endure it. . . ." the Syrian is overcome by her failure to look at him, and "he kills himself and falls between Salome and Jokanaan" in the stage direction. Shortly after this, Hérode enters the veranda, looking for Salomé, and Hérodias echoes the Page's words to the

Syrian: "You must not look at her! You are always looking at her!" Looking is how the lines of desire are drawn, an activity that "will provoke 'something terrible' to happen" ("peut arriver un malheur"), and clear evidence of the prurient treatment feared in such a play.

The concern about vulgar realism had been prompted by the attention to detail that the producers of the medieval passion plays gave to, for instance, the crucifixion scene. John Elliott observes that by the nineteenth century, the producers of the Oberammergau Passion Play had eliminated most of the uncomfortable details of such events from the onstage action. The scourging took place behind a curtain, which was then raised to reveal the static pose known in art galleries as *Ecce Homo*. The nailing of Jesus to the cross took place off stage, its sounds covered by a choral dirge, and the curtain was again pulled to show the cross in place and the slumping figure motionless and quiet (1989, 34).

The severing of John the Baptist's head from his body would be a similar moment. The biblical account relates that the executioner beheaded John the Baptist in the prison and then brought his head in a charger to the daughter of Herodias. In Wilde's version of these events, the audience does not observe the beheading, but does hear the muffled thud of the head hitting the cistern floor. Salomé "leans over the cistern and listens." And she comments, "There is no sound. I hear nothing. Why does he not cry out, this man? . . . There is a terrible silence." But then, "Ah! Something has fallen upon the ground. I heard something fall." And then "a huge black arm" rises out of the cistern, supporting the severed and bloody head on the silver platter. This is a difficult effect to create, for if the head does not look real, the scene would be laughable; carried out realistically, it would be awful. Certainly it was Wilde's intent to render precisely this bit of vulgar realism.

But the play goes even further than this too-close adherence to the text, for Salomé makes love verbally to the severed head, and under cover of the darkness of the stage, she kisses its mouth, saying, "Ah! I have kissed thy mouth. . . . There was a bitter taste on my lips. Was it the taste of blood? . . . Nay; but perchance it was the taste of love." Though the writer in the *Spectator* had not seen Wilde's play, he could comment about the implications of this scene: "Who, that had seen Salomé kissing the head of John the Baptist, could hear again the brief and bare statement in which Scripture records the scene of the murder, without interpolating in his imagination all that exciting mimicry of grim death and hysteric passion with which the stage had invested it?" ("The Bible and the Stage" 1893,

155–56). Like Mrs. Howitt-Watt, who had been horrified by the crucifixion scene in the Oberammergau Passion Play, even in its toned-down nineteenth-century performance, and declared that it was "our Lord's Passion stripped of all of its spiritual suffering,—it was the anguish of the flesh—it was the material side of Catholicism" (quoted in Elliott 1989, 34), defenders of censoring the Bible on stage could imagine that scenes like this would focus attention on the physical, fleshly, and carnal and that they would empty the narrative of its spiritual and moral importance.

About the only medieval "abuse" cited by the historians that Wilde's play did not manifest was the introduction of comedy. *Salomé* may have turned scripture into scandal, but it was certainly not Wilde's intention to turn it into buffoonery. That some early audiences did laugh during the play was only because the prop used to represent the severed head was unconvincing.[3] Wilde had included no devils to poke fun at his characters, no episodes to provide comic relief. The play might, however, be accused of melodrama, one of the dangers cited by defenders of the ban of biblical material on stage. Suspenseful, sensational, romantic, histrionic, and exciting, Wilde's plot seems to qualify, particularly if one overlooks that one of the characters is sacred to the Christian story. Hérode and his sister-in-law scheme to murder her husband so that he may assume his brother's throne, her daughter becomes the object of his desire, this desire becomes a source of irritation to her mother, and then the daughter converts this desire into the power to obtain the object of her desire, who is also the tormenter of her mother and the speaker of the truth. This situation plus the sensuous language, the use of symbol, and the sensational behavior all seem to add up to a melodramatic enterprise. Though hardly a happy ending, the death of Salomé at least resolves the play's various tensions and brings about some satisfactory closure. Furthermore, it is the melodramatic elements in the play—the plot, the literary devices—that appear to be its focus, and not the sacred character, the person whose death is the central point of the biblical accounts to many Christians. John the Baptist has become merely an object of desire to one of the central characters. Wilde's play seems to have manifested thoroughly this fear of blending solemn history with melodrama.

---

3. This remained a production problem. Lugné-Poe (1930) reports that the head he borrowed from the Paris wax museum in 1896 fell and smashed into pieces during rehearsals. It was pasted together for the performance. See Tydeman and Price (1996) for a detailed discussion of the play's productions.

The use of biblical-sounding rhetoric for much of the play's dialogue might also be taken as irreverent. Iokanaan's speech makes use of images and themes found primarily in Revelation. Comparing the English translation of Wilde's play with the Authorized King James Version of the Bible makes this readily apparent. When Iokanaan comes out of the cistern, he starts speaking immediately: "Where is he whose cup of abominations is now full? Where is he, who in a robe of silver shall one day die in the face of all the people? Bid him come forth, that he may hear the voice of him who hath cried in the waste places and in the houses of kings." Chapter 17 of Revelation contains some of these images: "decked with gold and precious stones and pearls, having a golden cup in her hand full of abominations and filthiness of her fornication: and upon her forehead was a name written, MYSTERY, BABYLON THE GREAT, THE MOTHER OF HARLOTS AND ABOMINATIONS OF THE EARTH" (vv. 4–5, KJV). The kings of the earth have committed fornication with the great whore, and Iokanaan continues: "Where is she who gave herself unto the Captains of Assyria, who have baldricks on their loins, and crowns of many colours on their heads. . . . Go, bid her rise up from the bed of her abominations, from the bed of her incestuousness, that she may hear the words of him who prepareth the way of the Lord, that she may repent her of her iniquities." Iokanaan's use of Revelation language is, at least, historically consistent, as he is speaking to the agents of Roman authority and talking of it as the Babylon of ancient days just as the author of Revelation did. Herod is one of the kings who has fornicated with the whore of Babylon, Hérodias, and Salomé is the daughter of Babylon. After Salomé introduces herself, saying, "I am Salomé, daughter of Herodias, Princess of Judea," Iokanaan responds: "Come not near the chosen of the Lord. Thy mother hath filled the earth with the wine of her iniquities, and the cry of her sinning hath come up even to the ears of God."

Whereas Wilde provides Iokanaan with rhetoric from Revelation, Salomé speaks in the language of Song of Songs. Kuryluk (1987, 224–26) presents a brief survey of the most obvious correspondences between Salomé's monologues and this ancient biblical poem, including the following (biblical text from the KJV):

| Salome | Song of Songs |
|---|---|
| Suffer me to kiss thy mouth | Let him kiss me with the kisses of his mouth (1:2) |
| Thy hair is like clusters of grapes | Thy hair is as a flock of goats (4:1) |
| Thy mouth is . . . like a pomegranate cut in twain | Thy temples are like a piece of a pomegranate within thy locks (4:3) |
| Thy mouth is like a band of scarlet on a tower of ivory | Thy neck is like the tower of David builded for an armoury (4:4) |
| I am hungry for thy body; and neither wine nor apples can appease my desire | Let my beloved come into his garden, and eat his pleasant fruits (4:16) |
| Neither the floods nor the great waters can quench my passion. . . . I was chaste and thou didst fill my veins with fire. . . . Well I know wouldst have loved me, and the mystery of love is greater than the mystery of death. | For love is strong as death; jealousy is cruel as the grave: the coals thereof are coals of fire, which hath a most vehement flame. Many waters cannot quench love, neither can the floods drown it. (8:6–7) |

Now there has been much debate over the millennia as to what the Song of Songs is really about and how it qualified to be sacred, and the customary orthodox explanation of the place of this intensely sensual and erotic poem in scripture is that it is an allegory for the love between either God and his bride Israel or between Christ and the Church. To have put these words into the mouth of Salomé, the pagan, the daughter of Babylon, the agent of Iokanaan's destruction, may certainly be interpreted as having treated them with irreverence; all the more so that they are made more central, more important than the words of the sacred character. To have borrowed biblical-sounding language in general, rather than having quoted the Bible accurately, might justify accusations of holding religion up to ridicule: what appears and sounds as if it were biblical is in fact not, and rather uses its biblical trappings to tell a quite nonbiblical story about decadence and debauchery centering on a lascivious dance and the meaningless end to a sacred life. So one might argue that Wilde's play manifested such fears, having mixed up sacred events with "literary" concerns to produce a play of interest to and consistent with the aesthetic movements of its time. That he had intended Sarah Bernhardt, the great *histrionne* of tragedy and a rather notorious figure, to play Salomé only confirms that the concern that sacred characters would be confused with the appearance of actors (or in this case, this sinful character with a famous actress) was justified.

So Wilde had invoked a biblical account about the martyrdom of a sacred figure, changed key elements in the narrative, and added material to tell an apparently quite different story about the Herodian family's sex lives in a prurient and vulgar fashion. The pagan princess expresses herself in the language of Song of Songs, which has been understood traditionally as the language of God and Christ, while Iokanaan, expressing himself in the language of Revelation, is ignored and his message of damnation and salvation trivialized. It seems that Wilde had committed nearly every abuse articulated by the nineteenth-century scholars and defenders of censorship. He had fulfilled their expectations and indeed perverted the text. But the intention to perform this play also tapped into their unarticulated fears.

When the public wrote in to the papers to protest the production of *Joseph and His Brethren*, it was not perversion of the biblical text that these writers feared, but the public performance of material they knew to contain perversion already. This is what underlay the articulated fears expressed by the literary historians and defenders of censorship, a real fear repressed by the censorship and all of the rhetoric about inevitable abuses. Furthermore, the suggestion that medieval plays, or modern versions of them, be reintroduced onto the modern stage raised the appalling prospect of resurrecting the vestiges of a Catholicism that in the nineteenth century might have been seen as long gone. As Glynne Wickham explains:

> A country that has first disestablished its Church from Papal hegemony and then fought a Civil War, as much to confirm this disestablishment as for political and economic reasons, is unlikely to seek to preach Roman Catholic dogma from its stages by deliberate revival of pre-Reformation plays—at least until the new order of things has been delivered from all threat of reversal. In other words, not until the nineteenth century was any serious interest again likely to be tolerated in Miracle or Morality plays. (1980, xxiii)

In the nineteenth century, such serious interest again arose, but it was not to be tolerated in a climate in which Catholicism in England was regaining popular interest and converts. One sentiment that the sixteenth and nineteenth centuries shared was an unarticulated fear of things Catholic, and in both periods there was good reason for concern. Whereas sixteenth-century England was engaged in actively suppressing Catholicism and implementing reform in a resistant people, the nineteenth century saw the influence of Cardinal Newman and his numerous converts to Catholicism.[4] Wilde's *Salomé* obviously manifested the fears articulated by the nineteenth-century historians and defenders of censorship, but more importantly, it also manifested these fears repressed by this censorship and its rhetorical defense.

As Kuryluk (1987) points out, a close analysis of the play reveals how much it owes to the sacred writings of Christianity. The combination of the ecstatic, visionary, and hysterical was not Wilde's invention, but derived largely from Revelation. The fact that the mother of the purported author of Revelation, John the Evangelist, also was named Salome had not escaped Wilde, who put the Evangelist's words into the mouth of the Baptist. No one debated that evil forces and people appear in the Bible, nor that biblical narratives are meant to condemn evil. But "the fact that they acquaint us with it, and then, through this very condemnation arouse our sympathy for it," as Kuryluk puts it, creates a real problem (211). For in deriding the evil, it is made familiar. This is the argument used today against violence on television and in film. No one argues that the violence is evil, only whether exposure to it makes it too familiar and makes us too comfortable with it. That the Bible also contains a great deal of sex, and perverse sex at that, is also readily admitted. But again, to portray it, even if ridiculing its perversity, is to make it too familiar. "While goodness is elevated to a distant heaven, evil tends to come right down to earth" (211). The fact that the language of Revelation is fraught with intensely violent and sexual imagery, that indeed the apocalypse is very nearly described entirely in these terms, does not apparently justify publicly airing it on the stage. Contained by the church, its canon and its

---

4. While Wilde was at Oxford, conversions there were numerous, and Wilde himself was tempted to convert, as he was repeatedly throughout his life. But he was prevented from receiving the peace of Catholicism, as he referred to it, by his Protestant father, who threatened to discontinue his financial support and cut off his inheritance if he followed this inclination. Wilde instead became a Mason, joining an order whose mystery, ritual, regalia, and origins in the St. John's Eve festival seem to have fulfilled the same needs for him that Catholicism would have.

sanctuary, the perversity and evil present in the biblical text might be prevented from permeating and corrupting public life, from coming down to
earth. For all the rhetoric about the threat of prurient handling of sacred
texts, the underlying concern was the performance on the public stage of
the sex and violence present in the Bible.

Similarly, the articulated fear of vulgar realism covers for a repressed
fear of the physical, fleshly, and carnal. It also represses the fear expressed
by Mrs. Howitt-Watt of the "material side of Catholicism." Vulgar realism
was not just offensive, but also threatening, for it suggested a return to the
medieval emphasis on physical suffering and, to this nineteenth-century
English Protestant, the distasteful carnality of Catholicism. The physical
would eclipse the spiritual in importance and what might be called "share
of mind"; that is, the physical would receive more attention than the spiritual. The concern about mixing melodrama with sacred history, and mixing the sacred with the artistic, seems actually to have been a fear of
reinterpreting these histories. "What he [Wilde] did in *Salomé*," Kuryluk
claims, "was essentially to dismiss the Christian interpretation of all these
writings, which, though they were filled with sensuality, passion, and
fleshly desire, the Church had transformed into allegories of divine and
spiritual love. . . . His procedure, by and large, resembles Freudian psychoanalysis, laying bare the eroticism behind the poetic figures of imagination or the artistic renderings of nature as well as the manmade world"
(226). But laying bare this eroticism is not to destroy the spiritual value of
these figures, but only to challenge the desexualized readings of these texts
promoted by the church. Hence the articulated fear of public ridicule of
religion might be interpreted as a real fear of exposing what underlies religion, in the sense of received tradition. For what underlay the spiritually
abstract faith of English Protestant Christianity was an ancient history of
very physical, carnal, and violent human life that for many centuries had
been full of religious value. To expose this history was to hold up to
ridicule this arid faith.

## WILDE'S DESIRE AND "RELIGIOUS DRAMA"

Wilde's *Salomé* manifested all the concerns of his contemporaries who
had expressed their fears of the public confrontation with perversity in
the Bible and a return to Catholicism with an increasingly restrictive censorship and the rhetoric to defend it. In a letter to the *Times* of March 2,
1893, after *Salomé* had been banned from performance in London, Wilde

expresses his anticipation of its performance in Paris, the center of the arts, where "religious dramas are frequently performed." Clearly he is including *Salomé* under the rubric of "religious dramas." On what basis might Wilde be justified in claiming that *Salomé* was a religious drama?

One basis might be Wilde's reconnection of the spiritual with the aesthetic and the sexual. Iokanaan is the chief object of desire in *Salomé*, a desire that is both aesthetic and sexual. He is lovely to behold, according to Salomé's description, and he is chaste, a condition that a Freudian would say is more sexual than not. He is also ascetic, noble, pure, and passionately believing. Iokanaan is worthy of all of this desire, and in connecting his aesthetic and sexual appeal with his passionate belief, Iokanaan as an object of desire also may become the agent of spiritual union. Rather than the invisible God whom the Jews in the play are discussing and whom the non-Jews find absurd because he is invisible, Iokanaan is a visible representative of God, and the tragedy of his death is an event that should be cathartic to the audience. Salomé, as the one who desires, matures quickly from youthful innocent intrigued by the curiosity that is Iokanaan to becoming fully aware of her desire to achieve union with him. This daughter of Babylon, product of the heathen and fallen world, desires Iokanaan first aesthetically, then sexually, and finally spiritually—if one is willing to interpret Salomé's kissing the dead Iokanaan as a eucharistic act, one intended to effect union and transcendence. There is meaning in suffering, and there is union in death with the object of desire, for, to quote Song of Songs, *azah kamweth a'havah*: "love is as strong as death" (8:6). That Salomé's language is that of Song of Songs, the purest, most extended, and most poetic expression of desire in the Bible, might be telling. The one who desires speaks the ancient biblical language of desire, and what she desires, the object of that desire, speaks the language of apocalypse and eschaton. If Iokanaan is indeed the object of desire and union, then it is appropriate that he speaks in the language of the biblical book that treats exclusively and poetically how this union will be achieved. Iokanaan symbolizes the object of spiritual desire, and he speaks in the language of the biblical book that poetically describes that object. Salomé symbolizes the one who desires, and she speaks in the language of the biblical book that poetically expresses desire. This poetic language, in both cases, contains sexual and violent imagery and aesthetic appreciation. For Salomé to express her desire for Iokanaan in aesthetic and sexual terms is to have expressed her spiritual desire poetically.

The play also often conflates Iokanaan with the Christ. Critics have mentioned Iokanaan's resemblance to the St. Sebastian of European painting, and this resemblance reflects the play's homoerotic interests. But Iokanaan's likeness to the Christ of the Ravenna mosaics is perhaps more striking and interesting. Wilde had visited Ravenna and seen its mosaics as an Oxford student, and Ellmann (1985) reports that he had been quite impressed by them. In these, Christ is feminized, androgynous, with pale skin, long dark hair, and intense eyes. Art historian Thomas Mathews (1993) suggests that the androgynous features of these Christ figures bore meaning to their fourth-century contemporaries.[5] Pointing out that Christ's sexuality is conspicuously absent from scholarly discussion, Mathews argues that the decidedly feminine aspect of Christ in early Christian art has been overlooked at the cost of understanding these images. Christ's long hair was a style no Roman male would have worn, and even a Roman woman would not have worn her hair loose as he does. But in Greek and Roman art, loose, long hair was a mark of divinity. Christ's youthful, beardless face connects him with Apollo and Dionysus, both associated with fertility and having important androgyne aspects. One such symbol was breasts, and so both Christ and these gods represent a type of adolescent youth, an image that conveys life-giving fecundity. These images, then, comprise numerous symbols of fertility (119–35). Furthermore, Mathews claims, "The reconciliation or unification of the opposite sexes served in early Christianity as a symbol of salvation. . . . The metaphor of a unification of male and female was intended to work on a philosophical level to express unification of the two sides of the human personality" (138). That Wilde had examined these images with great interest suggests that his Iokanaan may embody the features of these Christ figures. Even the Herod of Mark and Matthew had confused Christ with John the Baptist. When Iokanaan suggests that she go into the desert to look for the Son of Man, Salomé asks him, "Is he as beautiful as

---

5. See the chapter in Mathews (1993) titled "Christ Chameleon," in which he treats these androgynous images. His examples include "The Baptism of Christ" in the Arian Baptistery, Ravenna, featuring a naked Christ immersed in water, with genitalia clearly evident, whose beardless face, slender shoulders, girlish breasts, wide hips, and smooth hairless body contrast with the two heavily bearded, broad-chested, robustly masculine figures who flank him (one is John the Baptist himself); the Ravenna sarcophagi, depicting a long-haired, beardless Christ with breasts; and "The Vision of Ezekiel," an apse mosaic in Blessed David, Thessalonica, of a beardless, soft-faced figure with narrow, sloping shoulders and broad hips, lacking any masculine vigor (in fact, some had assumed this was the Virgin).

thou art, Jokanaan?" And indeed, the Christ of Ravenna is as lovely as Wilde's Iokanaan.

In addition to drawing heavily on the words of John the Evangelist in Revelation, Iokanaan's language conflates the scriptural words of John the Baptist, Jesus, and Paul. Described in the English translation of the play as "the Prophet," Iokanaan embodies the prophetic features of all of these figures. He quotes Isaiah, as John the Baptist did, regarding the one who prepares the way for the savior; he repeats some of the Baptist's words, "one mightier than I cometh, the latchet of whose shoes I am not worthy to unloose" (Luke 3:16, KJV); he utters expressions of Jesus' such as "Get thee behind me," "The time is come," and "The day is at hand" (see John 16:32 and 17:1); and he even draws on Paul with "Profane not the temple of the Lord." More striking is his prophecy: "In that day the sun shall become black like sackcloth of hair, and the moon shall become like blood, and the stars of heaven shall fall upon the earth like unripe figs that fall from the fig tree, and the kings of the earth shall be afraid," which echoes Jesus' words: "Immediately after the tribulation of those days shall the sun be darkened, and the moon shall not give her light, and the stars shall fall from heaven, and the powers of the heavens shall be shaken: . . . and then shall all the tribes of the earth mourn" (Matthew 24:29–30, KJV). Wilde's Iokanaan is interested in apocalypse, the nearness of the kingdom, Christ's coming (in the Baptist narrative his first coming, but from the perspective of Revelation his second), and retribution to the nonbeliever. At the end of the nineteenth century, in the context of a materialist culture devoid of aesthetic or spiritual attraction, this Christ-like figure—lovely to behold and speaking of the end of things—seems a figure worthy of reverence. Wilde has revered him, however, in the language and imagery of the *fin de siècle* aesthete.

*Salomé* makes ample use of symbols, as does Revelation. Hérode and Iokanaan are both readers of symbols, but Hérode decides, "It is not wise to find symbols in everything that one sees. It makes life too full of terrors." It renders life impossible especially if what one reads in symbols is one's own destruction, as Hérode does and Wilde might. But Iokanaan sees in the symbols around him the promise of the coming kingdom of God, prompting his exuberant prophesying. Symbols may be worldly expressions that embody otherworldly meanings; that is, they may effect a connection between this world and the one to come and thus transcend mere reality. Symbols also may be signs of the times. In *Salomé*, there is an emphasis on being able to speak and read symbols. Symbols are really the only language that Iokanaan and Salomé have for speaking to each other, he in the symbolic language of Revelation and she in that of Song of Songs. Iokanaan is also quite busy reading the signs he sees around him, symbols and signs that in the play point to the end of the world, to the coming kingdom, to spiritual desire, and to retribution for the wicked. These are all newly meaningful at the *fin de siècle*. The one concerned about the state of his soul must learn to speak and read in symbols to recognize what it is that he truly desires. His search for spiritual union through beauty and passion is urgent, for the end is near. For Wilde, who had contracted syphilis, who desired the peace of Catholicism, who conflated the aesthetic, sexual, and spiritual—hoping that life would imitate art, feeling the call to read the signs of the times, and feeling spiritual hunger—*Salomé* seems an ample expression of religious desire.

For all of the changes he made to the received story, changes that would appear to the guardians of culture as perversions of the biblical account, Wilde had in fact constructed a play true to its source. Not only did it portray the perversity already present in that account—the destruction of the sacred by sexual and political machination—but it also expressed a religious impulse consistent with it. The original narrative, a fairly lengthy one by biblical standards, of the beheading of John the Baptist serves as a precursor to that of the crucifixion of Jesus the Christ. In every Gospel reference to John, it is his role as precursor to Jesus that is emphasized. And he is the announcer that the kingdom is near, that the messiah has arrived, that it is the end of days. Wilde's play brings out these features of the narrative in a way that the legend as it stood alone had never done. The legend had focused on the discrete narrative and its moral implications, rather than on the Gospel context of the narrative and this episode's function in the greater story to advance the Gospel's message. Wilde's play also spoke to its time. It ridiculed the arid religion of nineteenth-century English Protestantism, emptied of but also repressing the sex and violence that were vital parts of the tradition underlying it. He reinterpreted the biblical text, challenging the traditional reading and restoring those vital characteristics to it. The play emphasized the carnality of faith, the aesthetics of spirituality, and the inseparability of the sexual, aesthetic, and spiritual. *Salomé* manifested all of the fears articulated by the guardians of that culture, and also the real fears underlying them and repressed by them. But more radically, *Salomé* expressed a real and powerful religious impulse.

## Scene 2
# PERVERTING THE TEXT: ANDRÉ GIDE'S *SAÜL*

The story of King Saul's rejection by God and the image of the young Saul searching in vain for his father's donkeys preoccupied André Gide and were among several biblical references that recur throughout his works. As a lifelong reader of the Bible, often pursuing a structured daily study of some portion of it, Gide, like Wilde, was thoroughly familiar with its narratives and themes. Yet like Wilde's *Salomé*, Gide's *Saül* differs substantially from the biblical narrative, and some of the changes that he made to it are provocative. Contemporary and more recent critics of the play have emphasized its homoerotic theme, suggesting, for instance, that it was intended to portray a Wilde-like figure and his ruin,[1] or that Gide made use of biblical material in order to legitimate the play's confrontation of the issue of homosexuality.[2] Criticism of Gide's intentions and the nature of his play, whether considered favorably or not, might be neatly summarized by Alice Lerner, the only scholar to conduct a full-length study of *Saül*: "A secular student of the Bible, an avowed homosexual, André Gide seized upon David's tantalizing reference to his powerful love for Jonathan and composed a play at the core of which is Saul's desire for Jonathan's lover" (1980, 34). Gide, therefore, made use of the biblical story

---

1. See, for example, the chapter about *Saül* in Pollard (1991).

2. This is the argument of Lerner, who, in the only comprehensive monograph about Gide's play (1980), points out that this was the first play in modern French literature to confront the issue of homosexuality directly, and she claims that its use of the Bible gave it legitimacy (87).

for his own purposes, and in so doing, he "desacralizes the story of the divinely sanctioned first king of Israel, changing the story of Saul's election, disobedience to God, and death. By introducing homosexuality as a further complication . . . Gide changes the whole thrust of the story . . . making the sacred story profane" (92). As in the case of Wilde's *Salomé*, however, the source for Gide's play was multiple biblical accounts and centuries of interpretation that have done little to solve the problems presented by this difficult story. Likewise, to conclude that Gide "desacralized" the biblical account by perverting it—that is, by making changes to it and by including homoerotic desire as a major theme—is to presume that perversion is, inherently, desacralization.[3] Though Gide indeed may have intended that the play confront the issue of homosexuality, his project may be even more radical than that, for in perverting the biblical account, Gide revealed perversity in the text itself.

## THE "BIBLICAL" ACCOUNT

The narrative in 1 Samuel begins with the miraculous birth of Samuel to his previously barren mother, Hannah; her dedication of him as a *nazir*; his early career in the temple under the priest Eli; and his assumption of leadership of the cult upon the demise of Eli and his corrupt sons. Israel's constant battle with the invading Philistines is introduced as a problem, and the people's demand for a king, when Samuel grew old and his sons became corrupt judges, is a key issue. Samuel and God both interpret this

---

3. In her published dissertation, Lerner refers repeatedly to this theme throughout her discussion of the play (which is in itself otherwise excellent and comprehensive, and the only other extensive consideration of the play in relationship with its biblical source). Lerner dismisses any notion of the play as spiritually motivated on this basis. As a religious reader of the biblical text, interpreting its meaning in quite conventional terms ("Its underlying theme is the question of rightful succession," and it is a "record of divine will, of God's shaping history," on page 12 of her introduction to the biblical text), Lerner cannot see past Gide's introduction of (or in my argument, overcharging of) homoerotic attraction, and therefore also cannot see his spiritual interest in the account. Oddly, Lerner also assumes that Jonathan and David are, in the play, lovers, engaged in homosexual relations. This is no clearer in the play than it is in the biblical account, where she sees no evidence of this at all. Lerner's reaction to Gide's play is a typical one, and one of the two that I will argue in the concluding chapter are common to these perverse midrashim. By fixating on the play's perversion of the biblical narrative, Lerner fails to see the deeper level of meaning in the play, the perversion in the biblical text itself, and thus also its deeper meanings. Though Lerner appreciates Gide's play—well enough to write her dissertation about it—her reaction to it seems a late-twentieth-century version of the late-nineteenth-century mentality (see Act I: Scene 2): offense at this "abuse" of the biblical text, overreaction to Gide's teasing out themes of the biblical text by denying their presence there at all, and dismissing the play as a desacralization.

demand as a rejection of them, and both begrudgingly agree to give the people what they have asked for. Defense of the nation, dynastic corruption, the proper relation between God and his representatives to the people, and getting what was asked for are major themes in this text.[4] The Benjaminite Saul is God's choice for king, a handsome and apparently tall young man whom we first meet while he is out looking for some of his father's straying donkeys. Not only is Saul not seeking the job for which Samuel and God have chosen him, but he does not even seem to know Samuel or anything about the politics of the nation.[5] Samuel anoints Saul twice, first privately and later publicly, and Saul modestly assumes the office under the close guidance or supervision of Samuel. For some years, this arrangement is successful. Though Samuel had thundered against the people for their faithless request for a king, the Israelites have beaten back the Philistines and enjoyed some peace, and the various factions in the nation have become more united under the monarchy.

But Saul is not to enjoy this situation for long. In a series of strange events, Saul exercises poor judgment, and these "sins" apparently warrant his rejection by God as king. In the first situation, he is told by Samuel to go to Gilgal and wait for him there for seven days, when they offer the sacrifices necessary to go into a new battle against the Philistines. During the seven days while Saul waits, the Philistines encamp, and the Israelites lose their nerve and hide themselves in caves. Seeing that the people are slipping away from him, and as Samuel has not yet arrived, Saul goes ahead and offers the sacrifice on his own. As soon as he has finished, Samuel arrives and chastises Saul for taking this initiative on his own:

---

4. Saul's name, *Shaul*, means "asked for," whereas Samuel, *Shemuel*, means "God hears" (*shema-el*). The themes of asking and hearing are significant in this narrative, and thus it is particularly interesting to observe how these names are used. For instance, "when Hannah had conceived and born a son, she called his name Samuel, 'for from YHWH I asked him'" (1 Sam 1:20). In other words, she named him Samuel because she "Saul" him from YHWH. Translations of the biblical text in this chapter are my own.

5. *Shaul* also has the sense of lending, so before her prayer of thanksgiving, Hannah says, "For this boy I prayed and YHWH gave me that which I had asked of him. And so I have lent him to YHWH; all the days that he lives he is lent to YHWH" (1 Sam 1:27–28). Or "YHWH gave me 'Saul' because I 'Saul' him. And so I 'Saul' him to YHWH; all the days that he lives he is 'Saul' to YHWH." Given the tense relationships among Samuel, God, and Saul, this is ironic. All citations from the Hebrew are my own translation, unless noted otherwise. In general, I have tried to render the multivalence and complexities of the text, rather than achieve any stylistic goals. The unpronounceable name of God is rendered in English translation as "YHWH"; in religious tradition, the name of God is not spoken, and where it appears in the text, *adoni*, "the LORD," or *hashem*, "the name," is articulated. I have tried to preserve the sense of the written text by leaving "YHWH" where it appears in the Hebrew, but referring to the character as God.

You were foolish not to keep the command of YHWH your God which he commanded you, for YHWH would now have set your kingship over Israel forever. But now your kingship will not stand; YHWH has sought for himself a man after his heart, and YHWH has ordered him as sovereign over his people, for you did not keep what YHWH commanded you. (1 Sam 13:13–14)[6]

In the second instance, Samuel tells Saul that God has directed him to punish the Amalekites for what they did in opposing the Israelites during their exodus from Egypt. He is to attack and utterly destroy[7] all that they have, to kill every man, woman, child, infant, and animal. Saul and the Israelites defeat the Amalekites and utterly destroy all the people, but they spare King Agag and the best of the livestock and all that is valuable. They utterly destroy what is worthless and spare what is of value, the narrator tells us. "And the word of YHWH came to Samuel saying, I repent that I caused Saul to rule (*malak*) as king for he has turned from behind me and did not establish my word" (15:10–11). When Samuel confronts Saul about this, he asks why Saul did not listen (*shema*) to the voice of God, who had told him to utterly destroy the Amalekite sinners. Saul responds that he did listen to the voice of God and that he brought the Amalekite king and livestock to devote them to destruction as a sacrifice to God at Gilgal. Samuel then thunders, "Does YHWH delight in burnt offerings and sacrifices as to listen to the voice of YHWH? Behold, to listen is better than sacrificing." He quotes a saying, "For a sin of divination is rebellion, and evil and idolatrous is obstinacy," and concludes, "As you rejected the word of YHWH, so he rejects you as king" (22–23). Saul confesses that he has sinned by not doing exactly as he was told,

---

6. There are some subtleties in this passage. Translated here as "keep," *shamar* also means to watch, guard, be careful about, protect, and observe. Translated here as "kingship," *mamlahkah*, from the root *mahlak*, "to be king" or "to reign," and the noun *melek*, "king," also means kingdom, dominion, and royal power. And translated here as as "sovereign," *l'nagid* means chief, leader, prince. This narrative includes several official designations, the distinction among which may be material. Eli had been a *cohen* (priest). Samuel was dedicated as a *nazir* (one set aside), but he seems to have acted as a *shahpat* (judge), a *nabi* (prophet, formerly known as a *roeh*, a seer), and a *cohen*. The people had requested a *melek* to *shahpat* over them; God tells Samuel to cause a *melek* to *mahlak* over them; and when Samuel anoints Saul, he designates him as *nagid*.

7. Translated here as "utterly destroy," the word *herem* means devote to the ban, dedicate to destruction, dedicate to exclusion from profane use and for solely cultic use. A fair amount of scholarship on this word has been written by those trying to understand God's intention and Saul's failure here.

and that he had feared the people and listened to their voice. And then he asks for pardon and to worship God, but Samuel turns to leave him. Saul again confesses his sin, but Samuel turns his back on Saul and hacks the Amalekite king to pieces before God at Gilgal.[8] Both men return to their homes, and the narrator tells us that Samuel does not see Saul again until the day of his death, and that Samuel observes mourning rites over Saul.[9] "And YHWH repented for having caused Saul to rule over Israel" (35b).

The narrative now introduces David, the new anointed one. "And the spirit of YHWH empowered David from that day forward. . . . And the spirit of YHWH departed from Saul, and an evil spirit from YHWH terrified him. And the servants of Saul said to him, Behold how an evil spirit of God is terrifying you" (16:13–15).[10] David comes into Saul's service as a musician to soothe him. "And it was when a spirit of God came to Saul, David would take the lyre and play it in his hand, and it was relieving to Saul and good to him, and the evil spirit would depart from him" (23). In the ensuing narrative, David befriends Saul's son Jonathan, marries Saul's daughter Michal, and becomes a successful and politically savvy warrior in Saul's army. Meanwhile, Saul is afflicted with these spirits of God, tormented by his conflicted feelings about David, and ultimately driven to seek David's life. Samuel dies, while David gathers military strength, spares Saul's life twice, and becomes an apparent but not actual vassal of the Philistines against Saul and the Israelites.

The narrator then reminds us that "Samuel had died" and goes on to report that Saul had expelled all of the mediums and necromancers from the land (28:3). Saul had been asking God what he should do about the gathering Philistines, but God had not answered him, "not by dreams, nor by lots, nor by prophets" (6). So Saul seeks out the medium at Endor to

---

8. Translated here as "hacked to pieces," *shasaf* appears only in 1 Samuel 15:33, so its meaning is really anyone's guess.

9. Usually translated here as "grieved," *abael* means to observe the rites of mourning the dead, not to be sad about a death. To describe Samuel's behavior as treating Saul as if he were dead is quite different from saying that he grieved for Saul. I think the former is more consistent with Samuel's general attitude toward Saul, and it makes more sense given the next line, in which God asks Samuel how much longer he will observe these mourning rites, as if to say, "How long will you keep this up?"

10. Translated here as "spirit," *ruach* means breath, wind, mind; translated here as "empowered," *tzalach* means to be strong, effective, powerful, of use, successful, made prosperous; translated here as "a spirit of God," *ruach-elohim* means literally a spirit of gods—*elohim* refers both to gods and to God—but as a unit is understood to refer to the Creator, as in Genesis.

conjure up the spirit of the dead Samuel. When she does, Saul recognizes the spirit as Samuel[11] and tells him his situation: he is in great distress, the Philistines are warring against him, God (*elohim*) has departed from him and does not respond by prophets or by dreams, so he has called up Samuel that he might tell Saul what to do. The cranky Samuel responds that this request is foolish, that God has departed from Saul and become his enemy; God has done what he said he would, torn the kingdom from Saul's hand and given it to his neighbor David. "Because you did not listen to the voice of YHWH and did not make his wrath against Amalek, thus this thing has YHWH done to you this day" (18). Israel will be defeated by the Philistines this day, and Saul and his sons will join Samuel in death. And this is indeed what happens. On Mount Gilboa, the Philistines overtake Saul and his sons, killing Jonathan and his brothers, but Saul must ultimately take his own life (a rare biblical suicide). When the Philistines come to strip the dead, they find Saul, cut off his head, and fasten his body to a wall for all to see. The body is finally recovered by the Jabesh-gileadites, who burn and bury it appropriately. When the news of the death of Saul and Jonathan reaches David, he sings a great lament over them and then proceeds to consolidate his power over Israel and to assume its kingship.

Physical characteristics and attraction are important in this story. For instance, when Saul is first introduced, he is described as "young and good, and no one among the sons of Israel was better than he, and from the shoulders going up he was taller than all the people" (9:2).[12] Saul's height receives further notice when he is chosen by lots among the people to be king: "and he stood amid the people and he was tall among all the people from his shoulders and going up" (10:23).[13] The Bible is notoriously reticent with physical description, so whenever it includes such details, they are significant. Clearly Saul's physical appearance—his height and

---

11. The medium observes, literally, "I see a god (*elohim*) rising out of the ground" (1 Sam 28:13). Here *elohim* is traditionally rendered "spirit" or "ghost," but it is intriguing to note the actual word she uses.

12. "Young" here translates *bahkur*, referring to a fully grown, vigorous, and still unmarried young man. Rendered here as "good," *tov* is a multipurpose word conveying joyous, pleasing, desirable, advisable, valuable, suitable, lovely, beautiful. It is likely that this description of Saul intends all of these meanings.

13. Rendered here as "tall," *gibah* means high, haughty, tall, a metaphor for majesty; in its verb form, it means to be exalted, high, haughty, and courageous. Again, it is likely that this passage means to convey all of these.

his youthful beauty—is of importance.[14] Underscoring this is God's admonition to Samuel when he sees Eliab, son of Jesse, and concludes that Eliab must be the new anointed: "Do not look at his appearance and his tallness, his height,[15] for I rejected him, for not as man sees, for man sees with eyes and YHWH sees with heart" (16:7).[16] Yet when David appears, the first thing the narrator tells us about him is that he is "ruddy, with beautiful eyes, and good form" (16:12).[17] And God says, "Arise, anoint him, for this is he." Later the narrator says that Saul's children, his daughter Michal and his son Jonathan, love David, Jonathan particularly taking joy or pleasure in him (19:1) and eventually loving him as he loved his own life (20:17).[18] Even Saul is attracted to David, an attraction in conflict with his intentions to kill him, as when he encounters David twice in battle and asks, "Is this your voice, my son?" (24:16; 26:17). Though God claims that physical characteristics are important only to humans, still they serve in the narrative to tell us something about the characters and their relationships.

Responding to the will of his people, God had chosen Saul to be their king, a man whose only qualifications seem to have been height and sincerity. Never very savvy himself, Saul relies on the counsel of others, and his chief counselor is Samuel, the man who had been ostensibly deposed as leader of Israel. With the exception of a few ecstatic moments, Saul does not communicate with God directly, but receives his instructions through Samuel. But Samuel's instructions apparently are not always clear to Saul, so he spends a great deal of time struggling to do the right

---

14. In the biblical account, the Philistines cut off Saul's head and pass it from town to town to proclaim his defeat. There may be an irony here that Saul is above all Israel from the shoulders up, precisely the part severed by his enemies. This is not present in the play, however, where Saül dies quite differently.

15. "Tallness" here is the same word as used with Saul, *gibah*, whereas "height" here translates *komah*, referring specifically to measured height. Recall that *gibah* implies both physical and psychological stature.

16. This is a tricky passage to translate because the text appears to be corrupt. I have rendered it literally.

17. "Ruddy" is the standard translation for *'admoni*, meaning reddish, or perhaps earthy. Adam had been created from *adamah*, the earthen clay; Esau also was *'admoni*. Though scholars have written much on this, not much has been decided. It is really unclear what ruddiness implies about David.

18. *Nephesh*, here rendered "life," means breath, neck, life force, appetite (as distinguished from the Greek idea of soul), selfhood, life, desire, mind, feeling, and will. I point out these various meanings here, as in previous notes, at risk of succumbing to the temptations of "etymologization"—that is, applying meanings of words appearing in one place in the text to other usages. There is a fine line between useful illumination and unwarranted abuse. I hope I tend toward the former.

thing. David, however, seems more concerned with clever strategy. For instance, when he learns about Goliath's challenge and, more important, about Saul's reward to the man who would kill him (the king will make him rich, give him his daughter as wife, and make his father's house free of taxes, 17:25), David inquires, in effect, "Now, tell me again—what exactly will be done for the man who kills this Philistine?" And the people say the same words, confirming the deal. David's brother is angry with him for leaving their father's flocks and growls at him, "I know your pride and the evil in your heart," to which David shrugs, saying, "What have I done? It was only a question." But David is dissimulating, and it is only after he has confirmed the deal that he delivers his rhetoric about the arrogance of one who would defy the armies of the living God and volunteers to take on Goliath. Always working the angles, David is a savvy strategist, and always clever, he is usually able to identify weakness and exploit it. His taking down of the huge and heavily armed Goliath with a stone flung from his sling is only the first of many such well-aimed strategies of David's. Saul, on the other hand, is constantly at the mercy of mediums and of those more clever than he.

God's rejection of Saul is the most troublesome problem in this account. That he chose Saul to be king and then rejected him on the basis of such problematic infractions has perplexed readers for centuries, beginning even in the biblical period. In the 1 Samuel narrative itself, Samuel explains first that God would have established Saul's dynasty over Israel, but Saul lost it by going ahead with the sacrifice at Gilgal without Samuel (13:13–14). Later, however, Samuel tells Saul that God rejected him as king for having failed to comply with God's instructions concerning the utter destruction of the Amalekites. This Samuel tells him twice, first directly after the battle and again when Saul summons him up from the dead. That the narration includes God speaking to Samuel regarding the Amalekites, "I repent that I made Saul king" (15:11), but not the sacrifice (Samuel claims that Saul lost his dynasty by violating God's commandment without any indication that God actually said this), lends further credibility that this was the reason for Saul's rejection by God.

In addition to the account in 1 Samuel, however, another appears in 1 Chronicles, which in the Christian Bible follows the books of Samuel and Kings and seems to function as a politically correct retelling of the ascent and decline of the Davidic monarchy and state of Israel.[19] The narrative

---

19. But in the Hebrew Bible, it appears at the very end, suggesting there its much diminished importance.

about the life and death of Saul here has been reduced to fourteen verses, which begin with the battle on Mount Gilboa and retell almost verbatim how Saul and his sons died. This account also gives a quite different explanation of Saul's rejection. In the last two verses, the Chronicler tells us that "Saul died of his unfaithfulness,[20] that unfaithfulness against YHWH, against the word of YHWH to which he did not listen, and even more for asking a medium for help and not the help of YHWH. And he killed him and turned the kingdom to David son of Jesse" (1 Chr 10:13–14). The title of the Oxford annotation to this passage in the New Revised Standard Version sums up this interpretation: "Saul, the unfaithful predecessor of David."

Though *Antiquities of the Jews*[21] is postbiblical, the Roman Jewish historian Josephus recounts biblical events and was of great interest to nineteenth-century historians and biblical critics. Furthermore, so-called Josephus plays were banned from the public stage as "biblical" by the English censor, and as in the case of the Salome legend, many "biblical" accounts in fact derive from Josephus. His work comprising twenty books provides a comprehensive history of the Jews from the earliest times to the outbreak of the war in 66 C.E. It was completed around 93–94 C.E., while Josephus was living in Rome.[22] But as an *Encylopaedia Britannica* article edited by William Robertson Smith explains:

---

20. *Ma'al*: undutifulness, unfaithfulness, always in relation to God. *Ma'al* is also an adverb meaning above, going up, ascending, as in 1 Samuel 9:2, where Saul is described as young and good (no man in Israel was better than he), and from his shoulders and *ma'al* taller than all the people. Is there a pun here relating Saul's height with his unfaithfulness?

21. I am relying on William Whiston's translation, published in 1895. The Greek text was printed at Basel in the sixteenth century, and critical editions of it appeared in the eighteenth, such as that by Hudson published by Oxford. Dindorf in Paris made emendations to it in 1845–47, which formed the basis for the Becker edition. At the turn of the century, a new edition by Niese based on new manuscript scholarship was expected.

22. Born in Jerusalem during the first year of the reign of Caligula, 37–38 C.E., Josephus was of priestly ancestry, and he reports that as early as fourteen years of age, he was already rendering decisions about the fine points of Jewish law. He studied for three years under an Essene ascetic but was thereafter a Pharisee. In 64 C.E., he went to Rome to intercede for some priests, and when he returned to Judea, revolt against Rome was in the wind. At first he tried to dissuade his fellow Jews from this action, but ultimately he joined them in 66 and for a time governed Galilee. When Rome finally put down the revolt, Josephus was taken prisoner, but he seems to have talked his way into protected status. He left Jerusalem and lived in Rome at the expense and under the protection of the imperial government. Though the exact date of his death is unknown, it is thought that he lived beyond 100 C.E.. All of his literary works were written during his thirty-year residence in Rome as a ward of the empire, and his perspective as both a Jew and a Roman makes for often amusingly conflicted accounts of historical events.

> For the first eleven books, covered by the Scriptural narrative, his exclusive authority seems to have been the Bible itself, especially the LXX. translation. He frequently, however, omits or modifies points which seemed to him likely to give offense; sometimes he supplements with current traditions or uses the works of his predecessors in the same field, Demetrius and Artapanus; and occasionally he gives excerpts from profane writers. (1900b, 13:751)

Because Josephus was so faithful to the biblical narrative, it is particularly interesting to observe where he diverged from it.

As in the 1 Samuel account, Josephus points out the physical appearance of key figures in his narrative, but he makes use of it to comment on their psychologies. For instance, he observes that Saul was "a young man of comely countenance, and of a tall body, but his understanding and his mind were preferable to what was visible in him" (VI.iv.1), and that Samuel had an "innate love of justice, and hatred to [sic] kingly government, for he was very fond of an aristocracy, as what made the men that used it of a divine and happy disposition" (VI.iii.3). Josephus also provides clarifying comments and explanations. In relating the story about Saul waiting at Gilgal for Samuel to prepare the sacrifices, he says, "So he waited, as the prophet sent to him to do, yet did not he, however, observe the command that was given him; but when he saw that the prophet tarried longer than he expected, and that he was deserted by the soldiers, he took the sacrifices and offered them" (VI.vi.2). There is no doubt in Josephus's narrative that Saul did the wrong thing, no consideration of whether Saul's interpretation of their agreement was as valid as Samuel's, as there is in 1 Samuel.

Similarly, in the account about the destruction of the Amalekites, Josephus reports that "Saul promised to do what he was commanded; and supposing that his obedience to God would be shown, not only in making war against the Amalekites, but more fully in the readiness and quickness of his proceedings, he made no delay. . . . He betook himself to slay the women and the children, and thought he did not act therein either barbarously or inhumanly, first because they were enemies whom he thus treated, and, in the next place, because it was done by the command of God, whom it was dangerous not to obey" (VI.vii.2). Josephus makes it clear that Saul intended to do what he had been told. He also seems to feel the need to address the moral problem of God's command to destroy women and children. Then he continues: "He also took Agag, the enemy's king, captive; the beauty and tallness of whose body he admired so much, that he thought him worthy of preservation; yet was not this done, however, according to the will of God, but by giving way to human passions, and suffering himself to be moved with an unseasonable commiseration, in a point where it was not safe for him to indulge it, for God hated the nation of the Amalekites . . . but Saul preserved their king . . . as if he preferred the fine appearance of the enemy to the memory of what God had sent him about" (VI.vii.2). Josephus here has added a fair amount of psychological analysis and speculation to the biblical material, and he then makes explicit a connection that in 1 Samuel is only implied: "God was grieved that the king of the Amalekites was preserved alive, and that the multitude had seized on the cattle for a prey, because these things were done without his permission." Josephus even delves into God's psychology: "For he thought it an intolerable thing, that they should conquer and overcome their enemies by that power which he gave them, and then that he himself should be so grossly despised and disobeyed by them, that a mere man, that was a king, would not bear it." And then he makes the connection: "He therefore told Samuel the prophet, that he repented that he had made Saul king, while he did nothing that he had commanded him, but indulged his own inclination" (VI.vii.4). There are no ambiguities in Josephus's accounts of these sins of Saul's.

Whereas in these two accounts Josephus made connections clearer and added some psychological detail, he did not really change them. In the story about Saul's destruction of the priest Ahimelech, his family, and the city of priests, however, Josephus made a rather substantive modification that goes beyond mere explanation or amplification. In 1 Samuel, when Ahimelech the priest is summoned to Saul to explain why it was reported that he had armed and supplied the renegade David, we know that David had lied to Ahimelech, leading him to believe that David was working under confidential orders from Saul. So Ahimelech, thinking he must maintain this confidentiality and sensing no need to defend David, Saul's servant, fails instead to defend himself against Saul, who never knows that Ahimelech was exhibiting loyalty to him. Saul orders the massacre of Ahimelech and all the priests, and only we can appreciate the full horror of this, because we are privy to all sides. In Josephus's account, however, when Ahimelech is asked by Saul why he gave food and weapons to David, who "was contriving to get the kingdom," he answers, "I did not know that he was thy adversary, but a servant of thine, who was very faithful to thee, and a captain of thy soldiers, and, what is more than these, thy son-in-law and kinsman. . . . Do not thou entertain any ill opinion of me, nor do thou have a suspicion of what I then thought an act of humanity, from what is now told thee of David's attempts against thee, for I did then to him as to thy friend and son-in-law, and captain of a thousand, and not as to thine adversary" (VI.xii.5). Josephus's Ahimelech realizes that there has been a misunderstanding and that David is not what he seems, and so defends himself, unlike in the biblical account. But Saul is not persuaded; "his fear was so prevalent, that he could not give credit to an apology that was very just." So he orders Doeg the Syrian to kill Ahimelech and his family. He also orders the massacre of the city of the priests; he "slew all that were there, without sparing either women or children, or any other age, and burnt it" (VI.xii.6). Whereas in 1 Samuel Saul suffers from insufficient knowledge, in Josephus's narrative it is the enormity of Saul's fear that is responsible for the massacre. The difference here is significant, for at the conclusion of this book on the life and death of Saul, Josephus observes, "To this his sad end did Saul come, according to the prophecy of Samuel, because he disobeyed the commands of God about the Amalekites, and on the account of his destroying the family of Ahimelech himself, and the city of the high priests" (VI.xiv.9).

Josephus's account includes two remarkable digressions on Saul's character. The first occurs directly after Saul's visit to the medium at Endor:

I have a fair occasion offered me to enter on such a discourse, by Saul, king of the Hebrews: for although he knew what was coming upon him, and that he was to die immediately, by the prediction of the prophet, he did not resolve to fly from death, nor so far to indulge the love of life, as to betray his own people to the enemy, or to bring a disgrace on his royal dignity; but exposing himself, as well as all his family and children to dangers, he thought it a brave thing to fall together with them, as he was fighting for his subjects, and that it was better his sons should die thus, showing their courage, than to leave them to their uncertain conduct afterward, while, instead of succession and posterity, they gained commendation and a lasting name. Such a one alone seems to me to be a just, a courageous, and a prudent man; and when any one has arrived at these dispositions, or shall hereafter arrive at them, he is the man that ought to be by all honored with the testimony of a virtuous or courageous man. (VI.xiv.4)

More than twice the length of the portion quoted, this digression is rather intriguing, for in other places Josephus has been so clear in pointing out Saul's failings. It might be significant that before he started writing history, Josephus had himself been a leader of the Jews and a governor of Galilee during the revolution. He had been to Rome and seen the imperial infrastructure, and upon his return, he had tried to persuade the Jews of the foolishness of their rebellion and the impossibility of their success against the imperial armies. Nonetheless, he threw in with the revolutionaries and assumed a leadership position, knowing the rebellion would ultimately fail. Josephus's account of Saul's nobility in the face of certain death seems to echo his own experience as a doomed commander. Similarly, his digression on Saul's arbitrary use of power against Ahimelech seems also to promote a more personal agenda:

> Now this king Saul, by perpetrating so barbarous a crime . . . gives all to understand and consider the disposition of men, that while they are private persons, and in a low condition, because it is not in their power to indulge nature, nor to venture upon what they wished for, they are equitable and moderate, and pursue nothing but what is just, and bend their whole minds and labors that way; then it is that they have this belief about God, that he is present to all the actions of their lives . . . but when once they are advanced into power and authority, then they put off all such notions; and as if they were no other than actors upon a theatre, they lay aside their disguised parts and manners, and take up boldness, insolence, and contempt of both human and divine laws . . . then it is that they become so insolent in their actions, as though God saw them no longer, or were afraid of them because of their power. . . . This reflection is openly confirmed to us from the example of Saul, the son of Kish, who was the first king who reigned after our aristocracy and government under the judges were over. . . . (VI.xii.7)

We can only speculate on whom Josephus had in mind at the time as having assumed power and put aside humility and righteousness, but clearly this reflection on the wickedness of men in great authority, and the danger they are in of rejecting regard for justice and humanity, is intended as a caution that, as the translator observes in a note on this page, "can never be too often perused by kings and great men, nor by those who expect to obtain such elevated dignities among mankind" (159). Josephus interpreted the Saul narrative as speaking to issues about which he was very concerned.

In the "biblical" account, then, is the source for Gide's *Saül*: physical appearance and attraction correlate with Saul's character, as they also are connected with the nature of his sin and the reason for his rejection by God. The narrator of 1 Samuel tells us that he was tall from the shoulders going up, the writer of 1 Chronicles that he was unfaithful, and Josephus that he was comely and therefore of noble spirit. In 1 Samuel, Saul is headstrong and not very smart about using his head (which he ultimately loses[23]); in 1 Chronicles, he seeks a medium's help rather than God's; and in Josephus, he finds Agag's beauty and tallness worthy of preservation. Thus in 1 Samuel, God rejected Saul for disobedience, in 1 Chronicles for unfaithfulness, and in Josephus for "unseasonable commiseration." Among these three accounts, then, no consensus exists on the problem of Saul's sin and God's rejection. Even within 1 Samuel itself, the account that might be presumed to be the original, Samuel's instructions and Saul's failures are unclear. Thus in this, the only place in the Bible where God completely abandons someone—and particularly someone of his own choosing—the "biblical" account is inherently conflicted.

## THE INTERPRETIVE PROBLEM

Readers of 1 Samuel have difficulty distancing themselves from Saul, because what the narrator tells us about the events witnessed is ultimately unsatisfactory. Confronted with complex and problematic characters, we learn about Saul's sin and his punishment, and we cannot help but feel that the punishment is all out of proportion to the sin. We must not understand the gravity of the sin; in fact, we are not entirely sure, despite the narrator, as to the exact nature of the sin. Certainly these were problems with which the Chronicler and Josephus grappled. But so have others since, and we might identify three general interpretive stances—religious, scholarly, and artistic—as three broad lines of interpretive tradition.

In the commentary tradition of both Christian and Jewish thought, the essential question is the nature of Saul's sin: What exactly was it? And how

---

23. The Hebrew *rosh* conveys head, top, and chief. As mentioned in note 6, the 1 Samuel account might also treat the issue of office—*melek, nagid, nazir, cohen, nabi, roeh*, etc. Headship at least seems an issue here.

are we then to behave, or not to behave? For Jewish readers, it is the prophetic content of Samuel that is paramount, summarized generally as the affirmation that it is God who is the author of history. The narrative reinforces this point with the occasional reference to God's activity in the way things work out: the king would be the man of God's choice, God's representative must anoint that king, it was God who decided the success of battles, and so on. In the midrashic tradition, Saul's sin was divination, even though he visited the medium at Endor after he had already been rejected by God; this visit was merely the most overt manifestation of his divinatory activity. This tradition sees his offering the sacrifice himself at Gilgal not as taking power inappropriately into his own hands, but as demonstrating his belief in the supernatural efficacy of the ritual itself. Furthermore, Agag, king of the Amalekites, was the ancestor of Haman, the oppressor of the Jews in the book of Esther. So Saul's sin in not utterly destroying the Amalekites created the horrible situation realized centuries later by Jews suffering under Haman. Thus is God the author of all history.[24]

The Christian Bible is understood to relate the history of the world from its primeval origins to the apocalypse. There is a compelling interest in the nature of kingship, and especially in the Davidic monarchy because of its association with Jesus as the expected Davidic messiah and his message about the kingdom of God. Christian commentaries point out that the books of Samuel tell the story of the transition from tribal confederation to monarchy and emphasize the role of Saul as king. These writings seem to understand generally Saul's sin as having insufficient faith, thereby making him unfit to be king. They often contrast him with David, clearly a great sinner himself, but also a faithful man of God and a really great repenter. Even recent commentaries, with bibliographies citing major recent scholarship, still emphasize the strong personality of David over the weakness of Saul.[25] All of these religious readers seek to determine what Saul's sin was in order to reinforce and inform the content of their faith. What are we to learn from Saul's experience about how to live in right relationship with God? And as a corollary, what behavior should we avoid? By understanding what Saul's sin was, the reader also gains a little distance from him: God seems less arbitrary, Saul more sinful, and

---

24. In *Midrash Shmuel* (not translated), but also in *Esther Rabbah*. See Neusner (1989b).

25. See, for instance, that by Brueggemann (1990, 116–18). The personality of David is a central theme for Brueggemann's commentary.

the whole story becomes an exemplum. This is comfortable: don't seek advice from necromancers, obey God's instructions, and have more faith.

From the nineteenth-century emphasis on historical criticism of the Bible through the present interest in literary methods, biblical scholars focus on why Saul's sin was sinful. The nineteenth-century critics carefully studied the cultural context of the ancient Near East to try to understand both the importance of the cultic activity reported in Samuel and the reason for Saul's behavior. What was the nature and import of the pre-battle sacrifice? Who were the Amalekites? What was the curse tradition in the ancient Near East? And so on. The objective was to understand the cultural context for what was reported in the narrative so as to understand why Saul did what he did, and why God and Samuel were challenging him. This contrasts with more recent scholarship, which assumes the literary unity and coherence of the biblical text and applies the principles of literary criticism to it in order to sort out the problems of the narrative from the material present within the text itself. A question arises in such a context, though: What is the text?

If the text is just the Saul narrative, 1 Samuel 9–31, then it tends to be read as a tragic narrative about a king who did not seek or want the job, tried his best to perform it, but was undermined at every turn by Samuel and God, who never wanted Saul to be successful. Saul's sin is "a theological 'error,' yes; an unwitting 'sin,' perhaps; but a sin of devastating consequence, warranting God's rejection, surely not!" exclaims David Gunn (1980, 54). "The real point of the scene can only be that in some way Saul is already doomed and that any detailed justification for his condemnation is essentially irrelevant" (56). If Saul is a tragic character, then God must be the culpable party. But if the text is the whole of 1 Samuel, rather than just chapters 9–31, then the narrative is read as being about Israel's request for a king and the problem that represents in a theocracy. V. Phillips Long argues that the text presents Saul as always unfit to be king, and he concludes that it is the people of Israel who are at fault: "Everything in the narrative points to the people, and not Yahweh and Samuel as those *ultimately* responsible for the situation" (1989, 240). Gunn would agree with at least part of this conclusion, as he asserts that "Saul is kingship's scapegoat" (1980, 125). Long points to the passage in Hosea, "I gave you a king in my anger, and I took him away in my wrath" (13:11), as a major intertextual interpretive clue. If the problem is the request for a king, then it is the people who are the culpable party.

If the text is both books of Samuel, then the story seems to be about the establishment of an Israelite monarchy, and Saul appears to be a failed first start. The narrative portrays David as not much better, but somehow the reader understands that difficulties present in the kingship of Saul were worked out under the kingship of David. J. P. Fokkelman, after writing a two-thousand-page, four-volume study on the books of Samuel, concludes, "Saul is the victim of a God whose rationality is beyond our ken and, secondarily, whose possible reasons are kept concealed by the narrator, the creator of the character 'God'" (1981, 4:691).

But if the text considered is the whole Deuteronomic history, as Robert Polzin argues, then the narrative is about the problematic establishment of a government and a clergy, and it is likely a criticism of both. In this view, Saul was a victim of Samuel, a poor prophet: "It is rather the narrator's abiding characterization of Samuel as a prophet whose continual lack of insight in the midst of his repeatedly self-serving actions that has largely eluded commentators, ancient and modern alike" (Polzin 1989, 129). Not only are these scholarly critics interested in understanding why Saul's sin was sinful, they also challenge the conventional religious reading of the text, finding some character other than Saul at fault—God, the people, or Samuel.

Though they take a different stance from that of religious readers, the project of these scholarly critics seems ultimately to be the same: to explain, or to explain away, this difficult text. The Saul narrative seems to demand such explanation. Placed in its right, and perhaps no longer relevant, context, it may be understood; uninterpreted, it remains disturbing. Explanation, therefore, serves the purpose of creating distance between the reader and the text. If we can determine what precisely Saul *did* to deserve the severest punishment—separation from God—then we may take care not to do the same thing. Or if we can determine why such behavior was considered sinful to that community in that time, then we may contextualize the sin—that is, place it in a context not our own. In either case, it seems that the object is to explain away any identification we might otherwise have with the hapless Saul.

It may be that there is a clue here in the need to find fault, to explain, to create distance between the reader and the text. The artistic community tends to take a quite different approach to reading the text and has asked different questions. Typically reading the text as expressing the human condition, artists have asked how it feels to be rejected by God. How is rejection by God experienced? Paintings from Rembrandt to Kokoschka, music from Handel to Sargon, the poetry of Alfieri, Browning, Lasker-Schüler, and

Tchernichowski, and the drama of Werfel, Shimkin, and Gide exhibit a general acceptance of the situation as described in the narrative and a portrayal of the human response to it. These artists make no attempt to explain the situation; rather, they protest against its injustice. Saul is portrayed as tortured, old, burdened by his regalia; David as young and beautiful; and Samuel as thundering and awesome. Artists considering this subject have approached the narrative as a given and explored the experiences of its characters, often relating them to modern or personal experience. They are interested not in the nature of Saul's sin, nor why it was sinful, but in Saul's experience as rejected by God.

## GIDE'S PERVERSIONS

The nature of the sin that separated Saul from God is so unimportant to Gide that his play opens its action immediately after his rejection,[26] thereby focusing on the psychological disintegration of Saül under the pressures of seeking and not finding reunion with God, being plagued by the *ruach raah* God had sent to torment him, and his conflicting desire for and fear of David, the agent of his ultimate destruction. Like the account in 1 Samuel, Gide's drama offers no comfortable answers to the problem of Saul's rejection by God, no explanations, and no clearly culpable party. Rather, it is the experience of Saul's separation from God that Gide explores.

When the play opens,[27] Saül has spent another sleepless night praying as the demons arrive at the palace and discuss him. Specifically, they refer to

---

26. And therefore do I disagree with a major strain of interpretation of this play as Gide's condemnation of succumbing to temptation. This strain sees *Saül* as an "antidote" to his earlier *Les Nourritures terrestres*; see, for instance, Thomas (1950, 99) or even Gide himself, who writes to a Catholic critic on November 27, 1927: "The danger presented by the doctrine [expressed in *Les Nourritures terrestres*] appeared so clearly to me that I immediately composed *Saül* as an antidote." But he writes to a Protestant minister on March 15, 1928: "The disintegration of the personality to which too passive an openness [*accueil*] leads is the subject of *Saül*." Another observation by Gide seems more apt: "Its subject is the ruin of the soul, the fall from grace [*déchéance*] and the powerlessness [*évanouissement*] which lack of resistance to temptations entails" (quoted in Pollard 1991, 335). These temptations, personified in the play by demons, are the result of God's rejection, not its cause.

27. References to the text are from the 1953 translation by Dorothy Bussy of the 1922 Editions de la Nouvelle revue française collection of Gide's plays. Bussy was Gide's principal translator into English. This edition identifies the actors who performed the play in the June 16, 1922, production at the Vieux-Colombier. This was the world premier of the play, as Gide had not been able to have it produced directly after its writing in 1898 as he had anticipated, so it was first published in 1903 as dramatic literature. Though they do not differ much, the 1922 edition has the advantage over the 1903 of being a performed text.

his having had their "masters" killed, all of them except "the witch of Endor." The demons identify themselves with various temptations or sins: "fury, lust, fear, doubt, power, vanity, legion." But why did Saül kill all of the "sorcerers" "Clever fellow! He'll be the only person left now to know the future."[28] He has determined from his astrological research that his son Jonathan will not succeed him on the throne, a fact he wants no one else to know and that he hopes to change. He has not, however, learned who will succeed him, and this question drives much of his behavior in the first half of the play. In succeeding scenes, palace servants discuss Saül's recent drunkenness and sleeplessness, and we realize that there is a conspiracy to spy on him for the High Priest and the Queen. From the Queen, we learn that Jonathan "dropped from me before his time, like an unripe fruit which decays without every ripening," and that she hates Saül. The proximity of the Philistines and Goliath's challenge surface in their conversation. Saül's barber, another conspirator, and the Queen try to persuade Saül that a harp player will soothe him in his moments of distress, while Saül mutters, "The woman detests me," and "I hate her." David arrives in the company of the High Priest from the camp where he has volunteered to battle Goliath, and the Queen introduces the brave David to the weak Jonathan, who enjoy an instant rapport. Another group of men discuss Saül's secret, and one of them reveals that before Samuel's death, he anointed David just as he had Saül. David defeats Goliath, and the Queen tries to enlist his assistance in her conspiracy against Saül, but Saül has been observing them from behind a drapery. When David escapes the Queen, Saül confronts and kills her.

Several lengthy scenes treat the development and relations of the major characters. Saül is tormented by the demons and finally cries out in anguish, "God of David! Help me!" Saül tries to teach Jonathan the kingly art, but this gives Jonathan a headache. Saül leaves as David arrives and hides again behind a drapery to observe them together. Jonathan dresses David in the royal regalia, and it suits him, which both father and son observe and admire. Meanwhile, David notes Jonathan's slender beauty now apparent, covered by just his tunic. They exchange affectionate remarks. Saül has his beard shaved by the barber to appear younger and more handsome. From the barber, he learns that one sorcerer still lives, so he determines to see her now that he has been rendered unrecognizable

---

28. This and the following quotations from Gide's *Saül* are from the 1953 translation by Dorothy Bussy.

by this change in his appearance. "This time my passion serves my interest." The sorcerer does recognize Saül, however, and pities him, eventually agreeing to summon the dead Samuel. Samuel asks Saül why he has disturbed him when "the Lord God has withdrawn from thee and become thy enemy?" Saül replies that he has no one to guide him, to tell him what to do. Samuel admonishes, "Why dost thou always lie in the face of thy Lord? Thou knowest that from the depths of thy heart another thought arises. It is not the Philistines that disquiet thee, and it is not for that that thou hast come to question me." Furthermore, it is too late. "It is now thine enemy that the Lord protects. Before he was conceived in his mother's womb, the Lord had already chosen him. It is to make ready for that that thou dost harbour him." Saül asks the key question: "What then was my fault?" to which Samuel answers, "To harbour him." So Saül is guilty of doing exactly what God intended him to do—in fact, predestined him to do: to welcome that which would destroy him. When Saül realizes that the sorcerer now knows his secret, he kills her, though not before she warns him: "King so deplorably given to welcoming, shut your door! . . . Shut your door! Close your eyes! Stop your ears, and let not love's perfume . . . find a way into your heart. All that is delightful to you is your enemy. Free yourself!" Returning to the palace, Saül not only welcomes David, but after an extensive scene together, in which Saül is tormented by his desire for his harp player while recalling the sorcerer's words of warning, he makes verbal love to David:

David! David! Shall we combine together against God? David, supposing it was I who gave you the crown? Ha! Ha! Ha! You see that a beardless king is still able to laugh. . . . The crown! David! You want the crown! Ha! Ha! Fie! And Jonathan? Have you forgotten poor, dear Jonathan? . . . Just play! For that matter, your singing disturbs my thoughts. . . . I too once praised the Lord, David! I sang songs to Him; there was a time when my mouth was always open in His praise, and my tongue never ceased to speak in His honour. But my lips now are afraid to open and are closed down over my secret; and my secret, alive within me, cries aloud with all its strength. . . . Horror! Horror! Horror! They want to know my secret and I don't know it myself! . . . David! My soul is in unparalleled tourments! . . . My lips, what name are you uttering? Shut tight, oh! Lips of Saul! Wrap close your royal mantle, Saul! You are besieged by all that lies around you! Stop your ears against his voice! All that comes near me is hostile to me! . . . To wander with him in the ardour of the desert, as once, alas! Long ago, seeking for my she-asses. In the heat of the air, I should burn! And then I should feel my soul less burning—my soul which this music stirs—and which rushes from my lips—towards you, Daoud, delicious.

David flees, exclaiming, "Farewell, Saul! No longer for you alone will your secret be intolerable!" And in the scenes following, David and Jonathan exchange vows of loyalty and words of devotion—"Jonathan, my brother! My soul is sobbing with love. . . . Good-bye! Remember! More than my soul. . . . Ah! Jonathan! More than my soul"—while Saül sinks into the torment of his demons.

The Philistines gather, David's army is encamped on Mount Gilboa, and Saül's army has gone out to meet them. Saül enters a grotto, accompanied by a demon, and there he overhears a meeting between David and Jonathan. While David is praying, Jonathan observes that Saül is in the grotto, thinks he is sleeping, and interrupts David's prayer. David then tells Jonathan of his plan to alert him when he will invade with the Philistines so that Jonathan might save Saül and himself. Jonathan replies that Saül will never believe that this is David's plan or agree to escape, and so David argues that Jonathan must persuade his father. David says he will cut off a piece of Saül's robe to make the point to him that he could have killed him, which he does, not realizing that Saül has overheard the whole conversation. In the remaining scenes, Saül spends more and more time with his demons while the battle rages around him. David alerts Jonathan of his impending invasion, and Jonathan tries to persuade Saül to leave his tent and escape. But Saül will not leave his demons, and Jonathan cannot leave without him, so both are killed, David ending the play with "I did what I could, Jonathan! I did what I could, Jonathan, my brother!" and instructions to carry the bodies of the king and the prince back to the palace for a royal funeral.

It is immediately apparent that Gide took great liberties with the biblical narrative as the source of his play. He has made significant changes in its plot and characters, omitted material, and added new characters and themes. A key difference between the biblical and Gidean accounts is in the characterizations of the central figures. Whereas in 1 Samuel, Saul's son Jonathan is a worthy warrior, in Gide's play he is effeminate and weak, an unworthy successor to the throne. He is a disgrace to his parents, who have fought the obvious—the Queen weaning him early and turning him over to live solely with warriors, and Saül forcing him to wear the royal regalia and to observe the activities of his court—and he is a reluctant heir apparent, quite willing to cede his throne to the clearly more competent David. But everyone, including David, also recognizes that there is grace and beauty in Jonathan, that his weakness has aesthetic value. While the biblical David is a complex character, ambitious and canny, in Gide's play he is a two-dimensional figure, a very devout servant of the monarchy and of God. He claims he does not want the crown of Israel, and in a prayer reminiscent of the soon-to-be-crucified Christ, he asks that "this crown be taken from me." Neither Jonathan nor David wants the throne, then, and for the same reason: it is too burdensome. Saül had not wanted the throne either, and thus there is an odd tragedy in Gide's play in which these three characters are embroiled in a battle for succession to a throne none of them wants. Rather, each is sadly playing out the destiny allotted to him. But Saül is also fighting destiny, attempting to change his son and the future, trying to recover control over his kingdom and his life, longing for his youth when he innocently searched for his father's donkeys and was strong and attractive like David, and seeking reunion with the God who no longer speaks to him and without whom he is bereft of guidance.

The ambitious and scheming character in Gide's play is the Queen, a character who does not appear in the biblical account.[29] It is she, the Queen tells us, who has been running the kingdom through the High Priest, the primary counsel to Saül. Gide attributes to this new character some of the characteristics of the biblical David, but Saül's relationship with her is quite straightforward: they hate each other, he suspects her of conspiracy, and she is guilty of it. The biblical Saul was never that clear in his relationship with David. The introduction of the High Priest as a fairly large character in the play suggests that there is a mediation or interpretation problem. He is the cultic authority and, after Samuel's death, God's representative to Saül. Yet he is involved in the Queen's conspiracy and, without the murdered *sorcières*, incapable of advising Saül anyway. The *ruach raah*, the evil spirits from God that we are told in 1 Samuel plague

---

29. The text alludes to her, however, such as when Saul burns with anger against Jonathan and calls him "son of a perverse rebellious woman," which is not so far from an adequate description of Gide's Queen. In the next line, he burns even hotter, saying, "You have chosen the son of Jesse to your shame and to the shame of your mother's nakedness," an extremely vulgar statement (see 1 Sam 20:30).

Saul, are in Gide's play personified vices. Portrayed by children in the 1922 production, these demons persuade Saül of their affection and then tease and torment him at every turn. Samuel, Saül's primary connection with God, is dead; the High Priest, the cult's authority, is corrupt; the Queen has never been an ally, and now she is an enemy. The only characters exhibiting concern for Saül and agency for God are the demons God sent to torment Saül. Saül seems to have been abandoned in every significant way, ultimately even by his own reason and sense of self-preservation.

All of the characters around Saül help bring about his tragic disintegration. The two-dimensionality of Jonathan, David, the Queen, and the High Priest represents Saül's point of view of them; that is, these characters are portrayed as Saül sees them. Jonathan is weak, nothing like Saül, unworthy to succeed him, and an inadequate defense against any pretender to the throne—and Jonathan behaves consistently with Saül's estimation throughout the play. David exhibits many of the traits of the youthful Saül—natural beauty, love of the goatherd's life, resistance to leadership, skill in war, and faith—traits that Saül has now lost. David is also kind and respectful of Saul, cutting off a piece of Saül's robe to warn him, enlisting Jonathan in an elaborate plan to rescue him and his father from the Philistine attack, and treating their dead bodies with the reverence due their station—all remarkable changes from the biblical story and character, but serving to portray David as Saül sees him: sincere, pious, good. The Queen, on the other hand, is an enemy, and Saül does not trust her—"If she proposes anything, it must be something that will do me harm"—and with good reason. And the High Priest is a false medium who is unable to speak to or for God and is part of the Queen's conspiracy. That all of the characters are portrayed as from Saül's point of view is further underscored by the portrayal of the *ruach raah* as demons personifying vices, with whom we can observe Saül in developing relationship. None of the other characters even know these demons are with them on stage. Thus Gide's changes of characterization and addition of new characters serve to point to Saül's experience as the focus of the play and to his character as the tragic hero.

The greatest torment to Saül in Gide's play is the paradoxical situation of his both desiring and fearing David. Characters constantly comment on this throughout the play: "All that is delightful to you is your enemy," the sorcerer at Endor cautions Saül, and "Thou hast other enemies to overcome than the Philistines; but that which hurteth thee, thou dost harbour," Samuel admonishes him. As Patrick Pollard (1991) observes, "Gide's chief invention is to develop the notion that Saül has a 'secret'": that he is intensely attracted to David, that he loves his naturally noble beauty and lusts after his youthful purity (328). This secret intersects with the question of succession, both coming together in David, the object of Saül's desire and the threat to his dynasty. As Pollard puts it, "David is the answer to both questions, and Saül is thereby shown to be destroyed by what he finds most desirable" (329). As in the biblical account, Saül's son Jonathan loves David in a way that "surpasses the love of women." In Gide's play, then, both father and son love David, who is the agent of their destruction. Saül's secret and this love triangle—and the paradoxes inherent in them—form the central theme of Gide's play.

To realize this theme, Gide needed to make changes in the biblical narrative. The slaying of the sorcerers, for instance, occurs at a different point in the story and for a different reason: whereas in the biblical account Saul ordered the massacre of the priests as retribution for Ahimelech's assisting the renegade David, in Gide's play the massacre precedes Saül's even meeting David and is motivated by his desire to destroy everyone who might know the future. But Gide did preserve the Chronicler's and Josephus's explanations that Saul's consulting a medium and destroying the priests were the reasons for God's rejection of him: Saül complains that God no longer speaks to him directly, nor through sorcerers or *prêtres*, the former destroyed by him and the latter represented by the inadequate High Priest. Implied in the play is the idea that Saül cut himself off from any communication with God.

From the triangle of homoerotic physical attraction, critics have tried to glean some sort of Gidean statement on inappropriate homosexual behavior or succumbing to temptation. These attempts are problematic, however, in that whereas Saül's desire for David effects his destruction, the attraction between David and Jonathan does not bear the same connotation of sin. Thus critics have been successful in finding in the play only a condemnation of pederasty, of desire on the part of an older man for a younger, a rather uncomfortable conclusion given Gide's personal preferences and his thoughts on homosexuality as expressed in *Corydon*. Rather, it seems that, like Wilde's *Salomé*, *Saül* is not about a particular kind of sexual desire, in this case homoerotic, as much as the play makes use of this desire for some other purpose: as a metaphor for spiritual desire. That it is homoerotic desire that serves as the metaphor makes the equation of the sexual and the spiritual all the more provocative.

Desire in Gide's play is manifested in several ways: as physical attraction, as seeking and not finding, and as yearning for communion with God. The theme of physical beauty and attraction is a strong one in the play, as it was in the biblical account and Josephus's retelling of it. Gide has not really introduced a new theme here, but has developed one clearly present in his source. Physical characteristics are significant in 1 Samuel in conveying something about the characters, and they are in Gide's play as well. What Gide has done, however, is nuance the physical attraction with modern features, such as Jonathan's graceful weakness, a value of *fin de siècle* aesthetic culture. In Josephus's account of the destruction of the Amalekites, Saul's attraction to the physical beauty of Agag prevents him from killing his enemy; in the 1 Samuel account, David's appearance attracts Saul's daughter Michal, his son Jonathan, and Saul himself; in Gide's play, Saül's desire for David is overcharged. Though Saül increasingly succumbs to the temptations proffered by his demons, his desire for David seems more a desire for his own past youth and the relationship David clearly enjoys with God. This is evident in the scene in which Saül reveals to David his feelings for him. They have been seated together, David playing the harp and singing psalms to Saül. Saül is anxious to engage him in conversation and asks him, "What do you think the most remarkable thing about me?" David replies, "Your royalty." Saül interests David only as the king, but Saül wants David to notice his appearance without his beard. When David observes merely, "I like the king better," Saül explains that he had it cut for David because it had made him look older. David is embarrassed and makes a move to leave, but Saül tries to converse with him again, asking if David prays to God. When David replies that he does, Saül asks him why, as "He never grants one's prayers." But David asks him what a king could possibly pray for that was never granted. Saül also changes the subject and asks David what he prays for. David, in some confusion, replies, "Never to become king." Saül is enraged and suggests that they unite against God, telling David that he used to praise God but now he must keep silent because of his secret, the secret that lives within him, and cries aloud with all its strength: "Silence is wearing me away. Since I have stopped speaking, my soul is being consumed; its secret is eating it away day and night like an ever wakeful fire." And it is here that Saül reveals to David his secret: that he desires David, but also that he still desires God. Because David enjoys God's presence, Saül's desire for reunion with God manifests itself in his desire for David, who rejects him with repugnance just as God had. Whereas in the biblical account Saul often refers to God as Samuel's, in the play he is David's God.

Gide's Saül might be characterized by the theme of seeking and not finding. The play makes two allusions to Saül's search for his father's lost donkeys, the innocence of that earlier search contrasting with the obsession of Saül's later search of the skies and underworld for information. In neither instance, however, does Saül find what he is searching for. In the earlier, he stumbles across the kingship, and in the later, he discovers the object of his desire, and both the kingship and David are responsible for his demise. No one else in the play is seeking and desiring as Saül is. Jonathan does not desire David as much as he commits himself to him, and he seeks nothing until the final scene, when he tries to persuade his father to escape with him. David does not appear to desire anyone; rather, he is totally devoted to God. The Queen and the High Priest seek to know Saül's secret, but for political purposes only. Like Saül, the Queen recognizes David as an object of desire—both of them try to persuade him to let them call him Daoud, the Moabite affectionate diminutive, a privilege he allows only his family and Jonathan—but it may be that the Queen sees in David, as Saül does, the young Saül, the husband of her youth. In both the biblical and Gidean accounts, Saul seeks David's life, and in both, when David meets him in the field, he succumbs to his affections for David and his guilt over seeking his life. Hence, yet again, Saül seeks and does not find the object of his search. But what is the real object of the search?

As other critics have pointed out, Gide uses some standard metaphors for spiritual thirst, with the desert chief among them, symbolizing first sensual ardor but also aspirations transcending the satisfaction of the senses.[30] This appears in *El Hadj*, *L'Immoralistes*, *La Retour de l'enfant prodigue*, and *Saül*. Gide had traveled in the desert as a young man, and his experiences there left a decidedly important impression on him.[31] Saül tries and fails every night to slake this spiritual thirst with drink, and in fact, a rather significant character in the play is the youthful cupbearer

---

30. See, for instance, Thomas (1950).

31. The desert is also where he met Oscar Wilde for the first time, who was to introduce him to the sensual pleasures available there. It is interesting that Wilde started writing *Salomé* directly upon his return to Paris after this encounter with Gide. Gide was quite clear in identifying the encounter as pivotal in his own life.

Saki, who observes that his king drinks through the night without becoming drunk. Critics have pointed to the relationship between Saül and his cupbearer as another homoerotic and pederastic moment in the play. Likewise, after Saul's confrontation with David, when David flees to the Philistines and makes a pact with Jonathan, Saül is in the desert with a demon. Clearly he is losing his mind. "What did I come here to look for? Ah! My asses!" In the ensuing dialogue with the demon, who taunts him about leaving his crown, robe, and scepter with David, the demon says that he recognized Saül because of his beauty, almost that of the young Saül, and then reminds him that he has been here in the desert before, looking for the donkeys. Saül in turn notices the demon's dark beauty, and then they have the following exchange:

DEMON: I haven't seen you look like that for many a long year! My young Saul! You've been here already, do you remember? You were looking for some asses.
SAUL: Ah! My she-asses!
DEMON: King Saul, where did you leave your she-asses?
SAUL: Do you know where, eh? Do *you* know?
DEMON (*pulling him by his cloak*): Come on then! We'll look for them together, shall we? (*They go off behind the sandhill. The Demon's voice is heard.*) Oh, King Saul, I'm so tired! Carry me.
SAUL (*in a caressing voice, off*): Poor little thing! Poor little thing!

Critics have cited this scene as the final evidence that Saül succumbs to his prurient and pederastic desires. Given all the symbolic markers of spiritual thirst in these two scenes, however, these seem to be superficial readings. Rather, seeking what he cannot find because God has rejected him, and thirsting for his soul's satisfaction, Gide's Saül, like the Bible's, turns to whomever he thinks may be able to serve as intermediary: Samuel, Saki, the demon, David.

Gide's interpretation of this biblical narrative clearly perverts it, but for all the changes Gide made in the text, in the end the play seems to be about the same problem as in its biblical source: Saul's experience of rejection by God. What does it feel like to be rejected by God? You can trust no one; everyone around you is in league against you and serves to bring about your destruction. You struggle against an unchangeable reality, and your efforts bring about nothing but your disintegration; you come apart. Saül's "fault" is in welcoming what destroys him, and what destroys him is the object of his desire, that object being sent by God to destroy him. Saül plays out the tragic role assigned him by God. This is how Gide has portrayed Saül's experience, and I believe that the changes that he made to the biblical text serve that purpose. That Gide made changes to it for his play is not to say that he has changed what it is about, for Gide's play is about the experience of divine abandonment, unrequited spiritual thirst, and the desire for spiritual union.

Gide's use of repression to portray Saül's tormented experience is particularly interesting. As Germaine Brée (1963) points out, Saül gradually realizes a fact that he has been repressing and combatting, his desire for David, and he discovers within himself a hidden self that is stronger for being repressed and that might come to light at any moment. She calls it a Sartrean moment of decision when an irrevocable act manifests the hidden inner direction, the undisclosed self that appears in the guise of another. Saul's obsession with the future, she concludes, is really a regret for a past self when he was young and handsome like David, when he was the beloved of God (116–22). And it seems that, like the biblical Saul, who is constantly pursuing reconciliation with God through Samuel, this Saül is constantly desiring such union with David—the image and embodiment of God's anointed.

Just as Wilde employed the sexual language of Song of Songs to express spiritual desire, so Gide also used the metaphor of sexual desire as an analogue to the spiritual. The Hebrew Bible makes frequent use of a similar metaphor to express such spiritual desire: Israel as the bride, as God's beloved. In fact, a standard allegorical reading of Song of Songs is that the lover is God and the beloved is Israel. "Israel" refers to the people of God, including Jacob, whom God had given that name, and his descendants, "the sons of Israel." Throughout the Bible, Israel and God seek reunion, and the language to express that search or desire is typically sexual, with Israel feminized as the object of God's desire and with the deity anthropomorphized. Despite the creation of both male and female in God's image, and despite several exceptional references, God as a male character predominates in the biblical narrative. Hence Israel, originally a male character and later a people comprising men, and God, also a male character, desire union with each other. The Bible has other echoes of this homoerotic relation. God's creation of Adam out of the ground, for instance, is one example of the absence of the female, and this in the original procreative act. Similarly, Jesus, the son of God, has no divine mother. In both cases, the feminine is earthy, material, mortal. Furthermore, the description of the love between David and Jonathan as "surpassing the love of women" suggests that in fact there is such a greater love. Without deviating into a discussion already well outlined by feminist scholars,[32] it is enough to note that at the very least, it is a peculiarity of the Bible that the metaphor used to express its central theme—the love and desire for union between man and God—is a sexual one, and indeed a homosexual one. Gide's play exposes this perverse truth.

The fear that Saül repressed is not unlike the fears repressed by centuries of censorship of the Bible on stage: fear of the hidden, ancient self in primitive relation with a God who is as capable of inexplicable rejection as he is of inexplicable favor; and fear of a sacred text that treats this, defying centuries of explanations and interpretations that create distance between it and the reader. Gide prefers spiritual thirst to the watered-down religion of his day, and he portrays this thirst in the most provocative of ways, as homoerotic desire whose ultimate object is reunion with the God who has inexplicably disappeared. And this might be the greatest and most repressed fear of all: that God, in the materialist age, has disappeared,[33] and that we are caught in a permanent longing for reunion with him. If Song of Songs is an allegory for that longing, then it is also an allegory for God as a fickle lover, just as Saül might be a figure for man's yearning for his youth when he was the beloved of God. Gide's *Saül*, like Wilde's *Salomé*, perverts the biblical text and in so doing reveals perversion already present in it—unrequited desire for a rejecting God—thereby manifesting the fears articulated by the guardians of *fin de siècle* European culture, and more provocatively, the real fears underlying and repressed by them.

---

32. See, for instance, Sedgwick (1985), Trible (1978), and almost anything by Rosemary Radford Ruether.

33. Friedman (1996) discusses this disappearance in Western literature, beginning with the Bible.

# Epilogue
# "PERVERSE MIDRASHIM"

## OVERCOMING ADVERSITY

Despite the three-hundred-year proscription of biblical drama, biblical
plays proliferated in the twentieth century. Most of them, however, are of
a very different kind from Wilde's *Salomé* and Gide's *Saül*. John R. Elliott
(1989) takes up the issue of the "sword and sandal" plays that followed the
English Drama Society's attempted revival of the medieval mystery and
morality plays.[1] Elliott divides religious plays of this period into two categories: religious spectaculars and psychological studies of the effects of
religion on characters in modern times. In the first category are plays such
as *Quo Vadis* and *Ben Hur*, "catering to the popular taste, then as now, for
a mixture of religion, spectacle and sex. . . . Under the guise of romantic
melodrama, these plays tried to bring back at least some hint of the supernatural into a theatre dominated by realism, although in most of them the

---

1. In his chapter "Mysteries Revived," Elliott treats the difficulties with the Lord Chamberlain's
censorship. Elliott's interest in the films and plays mentioned here comes from their influence on the
revival of the medieval plays: "During the next forty years a great many religious plays found their
way onto the English stage, and the subjects that they treated, as well as the manner in which they
presented them, were to profoundly influence the methods by which the mystery plays would be
staged when the time for their revival finally came in the 1950s. For that reason it will be useful to
look briefly at some typical examples of religious drama written during these years, and in particular
to record some of the ways that playwrights found to skirt the restrictions placed by the Lord
Chamberlain on their trade" (48).

miracles of religion took second place to the miracles of modern set-design and lighting" (48). Elliott observes that the future of these religious spectaculars lay largely in films, whereas the more modest psychological studies turned out to be more suitable to the stage.

Between 1910 and 1950, hundreds of these "modern passion plays" were written in England and performed under restrictions by the Lord Chamberlain. One of the chief restrictions was that the figure of Christ had to be veiled from the eyes of the audience. Examples of these plays include *The Upper Room* (R. H. Benson, 1915), which introduced the "Christ-less Passion Play," in which the disciples observe and report the trial, the scourging, and so forth from the upper room;[2] *A Man's House* (John Drinkwater, 1934), which made great use of the "leading question" and description of events seen at a distance;[3] *The Cup of Salvation* (Raymond Birt, 1950), which was saved from blasphemy by ingenious lighting;[4] *Christ Crucified: A Passion Play in Six Scenes* (Margaret Cropper, 1932), in which an angel appears in place of Christ; *The Way of the Cross* (Henri Gheon, 1932), a frequently produced play about St. Helen's search for the true cross, in which she purifies herself by reenacting the stations of the cross in mime; and *Good Friday* (John Masefield, 1917), which actually was not about Jesus at all, but about Pilate (Elliott 1989, 49–54).[5] Elliott observes that Pilate plays in particular were useful as a weapon against Bolshevism and represent one class of twentieth-century drama that was politically inspired. May Creagh-Henry, for example, "specialized in a type of biblical drama that was designed to strengthen the conservative convictions of her audience" (54). It seems, in fact, that all of these plays served this purpose, for they were essentially conservative projects advancing a nationalistic and romantic brand of Christianity. That they were able to get past the censor merely by keeping Jesus off stage demonstrates how culturally reinforcing they must have been.

Marie Philomène de los Reyes was interested in the plays of this era, beginning in the 1920s, when she considered "the biblical theme in

---

2. Others making use of this device: *Good Friday* (John Masefield, 1917), *Greater Love Hath No Man* (May Creagh-Henry, 1920), *Passover in Jersalem: A Passion Play* (Donald Dugard, 1939), and *The Housetop: A Play on the Passion of Our Lord Jesus Christ* (Cecil Tugman, 1964).

3. Others in this category are *The Victory of the Cross: A Passion Play* (May Creagh-Henry, 1920) and *The Room of the Last Supper* (Alan Wilkin, 1969).

4. Lighting also redeemed *The Dark Hours* (Don Marquis, 1926).

5. Pilate plays became quite popular; others include *Caesar's Friend* (Campbell Dixon and Dermot Morrah, 1933) and *The Day's Beginning* (Willis Hall, 1963). Elliott provides a comprehensive listing of these plays in his chapter "Mysteries Revived."

modern drama" in her 1978 book of that title. She falls prey to the now dismissed view that the medieval mysteries "were nourished in the liturgy taking place in cathedrals, enacted by clerics themselves, until the guilds took over, and scriptural drama went out to the towns in the form of cycles." As a result, the "natural development" of these plays gradually dimmed the halos of scriptural figures and led to their eventual and inevitable proscription (1–2). She also was happy to leave behind those plays that "spent their force painting the scriptural heroes black and whitewashing the villains" for the "greater seriousness in appraisal [that] was once more creeping in biblical drama" (6). Dividing the later modern biblical plays into two types, those that consider the audience to be skeptical of biblical material and those that assume a common belief in the truth of the Bible, Philomène is more interested in the latter. This "creeping in" was initiated by the Religious Drama Society, and the seriousness was epitomized in the works of writers such as Christopher Fry and Paul Claudel. She cites Wilde's *Salomé* as representative of plays that blacken scriptural heroes and Archibald MacLeish's *J. B.* and Jean Giraudoux's *Judith* as two plays in the category of those skeptical of biblical material (48–50). Philomène, however, is merely restating, and watering down, what Murray Roston claims in his 1968 study of biblical drama in England.

Arguing that biblical plays attract dramatists in inverse proportion to the current reverence for the Bible,[6] Roston points to the period and the example of Wilde's *Salomé* as "iconoclastic." He also comments that the sudden diminishing of biblical reverence during the first half of this century produced an impressive list of dramatists interested in biblical material, including Shaw, Yeats, D. H. Lawrence, Housman, Frost, and MacLeish. Because Lawrence's *The Man Who Died* (1931)[7]—which is not a play at all, but a novella—treats the Christ of flesh and blood, it was greeted with a storm of protest for its suggestion that he could indulge in carnal love. As Roston observes, "The dramatist was free to interpret the Old Testament as liberally as he wished, but public opinion was too strong to allow similar liberties to be taken with the Gospels themselves. Once again, therefore, the resurgence of biblical drama was restricted almost exclusively to the stories of the Old Testament" (240). Thus Lawrence's play *David* (1926) fits this vogue of sorts, though it expresses his "crusade

---

6. Roston uses the term *sanctity* rather than *reverence*. The phenomenon he describes, however, might better be described as untouchability or "taboo-ness": when the Bible is taboo, would-be adulteraters arise to challenge its untouchability.

7. Published originally in 1928 as *The Escaped Cock*.

against hypocrisy" and may have contributed to his becoming "the embodiment of the anti-Christ" to churchgoers (274). Like those of Wilde and Gide, Lawrence's religion was not a traditional Christianity; rather, he sought a return to the original meaning of the biblical text "unspoilt by the formal church" (275). *David* exemplified this kind of rereading,[8] though it remains less provocative than *The Man Who Died*, and much less so than, say, Laurence Housman's *Samuel the Kingmaker*, which presents an extreme indictment of the biblical prophet as indulging in a sham of divine inspiration. Here the rejection of Saul results from Samuel's spiteful revenge.[9] Roston says that Housman had an "obsessive desire to vilify the biblical account" and calls such vilifiers "iconoclasts," because they pull down heroes from their pedestals and conduct moral reassessments that condemn the innocent and acquit the guilty in the process of rewriting biblical stories.

Roston prefers the plays betokening "the inception of a less aggressive approach to the Bible, of a desire less to ridicule and distort the scriptural canon than to examine it with some reverence and even with some humility as a sacred body of literature which still possessed important lessons for mankind" (289). Though Roston seems to understand and appreciate Lawrence, quoting Lawrence extensively and analyzing his childhood in order to account for his work, in the end Roston is more impressed with less "aggressive" writers, such as MacLeish or Robert Frost, for "ultimately Frost's sympathies are with the Bible, and his tendency, as [T. S.] Eliot put it, to 'tease the orthodox Christian believer' never leads him into a direct denial of faith" (310). It seems that the issue is one of aggression versus teasing. Though like Lawrence, and like Wilde and Gide, Frost and MacLeish were "searching in the Bible for the essential validity of its message, probing, scrutinizing, and cutting away what seemed extraneous in the conviction that within these ancient tales was concealed some almost ineffable truth" (313), these latter also exhibited "the new sensitivity among biblical playwrights of the mid-century," who "speak hesitantly from the midst of their own doubts and perplexities— perplexities which by their very awareness that religion offers no easy path

---

8. Roston reports that the manuscript's title *David* is crossed through and the name *Saul* substituted (277). The play's focus, however, seems to be on rethinking Samuel.

9. The focus on Samuel by Lawrence and Housman is intriguing, perhaps reflecting an interest in the relationship between representatives of the religious institution and the faithful. This has been a vein of thought pursued by recent biblical scholars, such as Polzin (1989).

to the intelligent believer are all the more persuasive" (320). Rather than sensitively tease the orthodox into considering the doubtful grounds of their faith, as Roston seems to advocate, Housman and Lawrence—and Wilde and Gide—force that confrontation in their biblical plays, and that fact leads him to qualify them as "iconoclastic."

But is that an adequate description of these authors' intentions in these plays? Early-twentieth-century biblical drama includes, according to Elliott, Philomène, and Roston, revived mystery and morality plays; "sword and sandal" dramas comprising religious spectaculars and modern passion plays; Pilate plays; skeptical plays that blacken scriptural heroes' serious plays that assume belief in the truth of the Bible; aggressively iconoclastic plays; and sensitive works that hesitantly explore perplexities. None of these categories describes Wilde's and Gide's work sufficiently. Rather, it seems that while *Salomé* and *Saül* manifested repressed fears, they also effected a period of "aphasia," represented by the "sword and sandal" and sensitive works. In the context of *fin de siècle* and early-twentieth-century biblical drama, Wilde's *Salomé* and Gide's *Saül* are exceptional and outside the generic categories of biblical drama.

## A SUBVERSIVE GENRE

Oscar Wilde's *Salomé* and André Gide's *Saül* manifested the fears of the *fin de siècle* defenders of censorship of the Bible on stage, both the fears they had articulated and, more significantly, those they had repressed. Wilde's play created a furor without having been performed, and that fact alone called into question all of the assumptions made by those guardians of culture. That Wilde's trial followed so closely after this furor largely obscured the original issues in the debate; the play came to symbolize little more than Wilde's fall from grace. Gide's play also failed to be performed until well into the twentieth century and had come to be associated by then with Gide's increasingly well-known thoughts on homosexuality. Both plays, however, clearly participated in the discourses of their time that advocated new ways of reading the Bible, called for theatre reform, and debated stage censorship. In fact, these plays form a nexus of those discourses, embodying the hopes and fears that motivated them. These plays, then, are products of a culture that in effect called them into being. For more than three hundred years, this culture had repressed its fears by enforcing an increasingly restrictive censorship, which ultimately produced these works.

Overtly biblical and clearly perverse, these plays were retellings of some sort, but what sort? A sort that has not received definition; a sort that might be called "perverse midrashim."[10] The Hebrew word *midrash*, deriving from the verb *dahrash*, to inquire about or to care about, is a noun meaning merely study or writing.[11] Beginning in the biblical period itself, and continuing through the rabbinic, medieval, and early modern periods of Jewish scholarship, midrashic retelling developed into a lively narrative tradition of much interest today.[12] Jacob Neusner, one of the most prolific writers on the topic, defines it in his introductory book on midrash (1989a) as an investigation of the meaning in scripture that treats biblical narratives as portions of a comprehensive and meaningful whole. Michael Fishbane (1993) describes midrash as a form of interpretive expression that is concerned with the creation of meaning, rather than its investigation, and claims that it is not a genre of exegesis. David Stern (1991) calls midrash exegesis that makes the Torah livable. Judah Goldin (1988) regards it as a form of translation. More recent literary theorists also are treating midrash, most notably Geoffrey Hartman (1986), who defines midrash as a genre of biblical exegesis designed to keep the Bible from becoming literature (that is, static), and an effort reflecting a need both to create and to revere a fixed text simultaneously. James Kugel (1990), Neusner's nemesis,[13] sees midrash as an interpretive stance or a way of reading sacred texts that seeks to smooth textual difficulties. Harold Bloom (1975) looks at it as a stance toward ancestors and a heuristic way to think about reading. Jeffrey Perl describes midrash as an effort to unify the disunified Bible, calling it a very conservative project tending toward a "golden mediocrity."[14]

---

10. The plural of midrash.

11. Perl has called a *drash* a "riff" as in jazz parlance.

12. The tradition of narrative midrash grows out of the *aggadah*, from *hagahdah*, meaning legend or saying, which is an explication of those texts that deals with contemporary problems and forms part of a synagogue meeting homily. See the articles titled "Nature of Aggadah," by Heinemann, and "Two Introductions to Midrash," by Kugel, in Hartman and Budick (1986), in the section titled "Midrash and Aggadah." Different from the *halakhah*, which provided rules and decisions on specific issues, the aggadah was a way of thinking. Biblical aggadah expands and elaborates on biblical narrative. For instance, the biblical David, heroic fighter, little resembles the wise and pious David of aggadah, who studies torah night and day. The discussion that follows refers to aggadic rather than to halakhic midrash.

13. Neusner has written hundreds of books on traditional Jewish writing, and dozens on midrash in particular. In these, he rarely resists the opportunity to argue against the view of midrash expounded and represented by Kugel.

14. For these characterizations of midrash and those to follow, see Neusner (1989a), Fishbane (1993), Stern (1991), Eichler and Tigay (1988), Kugel (1990), Hartman and Budick (1986), and Bloom (1975). Perl's observations cited here are from personal conversations.

Midrash, then, is characterized by narrative, an imaginative recasting of scripture that makes new and urgent points through a retelling that focuses not on isolated verses, but on an entire composition or theme (Neusner 1989a, vii, 185). It is a way of dramatizing a message that gives a dominant role to the narrator, who often tells what the characters are thinking, and that unfolds from a condition of tension or conflict to one of resolution (212). It is a narrative of exegesis that begins with a text-based crisis that is followed by the effort to salvage the text—not only its meaning, but also its value in the life of the reader (Stern 1991, 44). It is also an expanded narrative, comprising extras that are essentially exegetical because they are based on something actually in the biblical text. Generally, midrashic motifs arise from a single problem in the text, usually a troubling word or a textual peculiarity, and the expansions seek to explain these anomalies; they interpret without the appearance of interpretation (Kugel 1990, 4). Midrash arises in moments of cultural and intellectual crisis, and it calls for attention to a text that appears to have lost its significative function. The interpretation helps the text regain meaning, relevance, and applicability (David Tracy quoted in Fishbane 1993, 9). Midrash has a joking quality, however, that is caused by a dissonance between religion and the book from which it is derived (Kugel quoted in Hartman and Budick 1986, 80). Yet "midrash somehow engages in ever-new revelations of an originary text, while the question of origins is displaced into the living tradition of writing . . . affirm[ing] the integrity and authority of the text even while fragmenting and sowing it endlessly" (Hartman and Budick 1986, xiii).

These qualities of midrash also seem to characterize *Salomé* and *Saül*. Clearly both are imaginative recastings of entire biblical narratives that unfold from conditions of tension and conflict to resolution (albeit tragic); that expand on something present in the biblical text, a textual anomaly or a motif arising from a single site of focus; and that make some new and urgent points. The plays seek to regain the significative function of the biblical texts that they retell, to salvage the text from its problems, and to affirm the textual authority even as they fragment it. Thus it seems fair to call these plays a variety of midrashim. But in classical literary theory, a situation of conflict that is resolved is called a comedy. Is it really fair then to call tragedy a resolution of conflict? The joking quality that Kugel identifies seems somehow disconsonant with the perversity and tragedy of *Salomé* and *Saül*. Is expanding on a textual problem the same thing as perverting the text in order to reveal its perversity? And while midrash is often playful and occasionally challenging, it is essentially a conservative project, to recall Perl's description. Is it likely that Wilde and Gide were pursuing the conservative aims of traditional midrash? Not if the urgent point they highlight is the dissonance between religion and the text from which it is derived. Rather, *Salomé* and *Saül* are perverse midrashim: they do not smooth textual anomalies so much as they highlight what was elided by orthodoxy, and their aims are hardly conservative.

That which is perverse is not only contrary to accepted practice, but also directed away from what is right or good, obstinately persisting in an error, predisposed to oppose and contradict. Perversity also commonly refers to "abnormal" sexual activity, and the abuses that the nineteenth-century defenders of censorship feared were of this kind. But the plays revealed greater perversities also present in the biblical text: the destruction of the sacred by the profane, and a morally relativist god who had disappeared from human experience. Related to *perversion* are *inversion* and *subversion*. To invert is to reverse the normal order, and in the late nineteenth century, the noun *invert* had become common nomenclature for the homosexual, precisely because he reversed the normal order.[15] These plays also invert, in effect calling the sexual spiritual and publicly representing deviant attraction as stageworthy. To subvert is to destroy completely, to undermine, to overthrow. The normal order of things always, virtually by definition, fears subversion. These plays were subversive, for they challenged the arid spirituality of their day, undermining traditional understandings of these biblical narratives and seeking to overthrow the normal order of things.

Harold Bloom (1975) talks about the history of poetic influence as one of anxiety, distortion ("misreading"), and perversion, of willful revisionism. To Bloom, strong poets are perverse, meaning turned the wrong way in relation to the precursor. The stronger the dependence, the greater the anxiety it generates. While the strongest of precursors for Bloom is Shakespeare, the Bible surely is stronger still. In Bloom's first revisionary ratio, *clinamen*, the poet misreads the precursor as an act of creative correction. The result appears to be an imitation of the precursor, but in fact it reflects a swerve (not a bad synonym for perversity in one sense) that functions as a corrective to it. Bloom's theory of influence in general is one of inversion in which the work of the precursor is overturned, particularly

---

15. This was also Freud's term, and it was retained in psychological jargon until quite recently.

in his second revisionary ratio, *tessera*. Here the poet completes the precursor by retaining the terms of the parent poem but meaning them in another sense. This is an antithetical move that precedes *kenosis*, the movement toward discontinuity with the precursor. Bloom's theory seems to capture something of what is going on with Wilde's and Gide's biblical plays, and it offers another way of thinking about perversity. But a further twist in all of this is that both of these plays in fact return us to the biblical text. Unlike Bloom's theory, in which the poet ultimately succeeds in destroying the poetic father, the readings that Wilde and Gide offer of the precursor texts serve ultimately to return to them to recover something that has been lost and restore it to modernity. To echo Tracy's observation quoted in Fishbane (1993) regarding midrash, these plays arose in a moment of cultural and intellectual crisis, called for attention to texts that seemed to have lost their significative function, and reread them so as to help them regain their meaning, relevance, and applicability. They were new revelations about the texts, affirming the Bible's authority. As midrashim, these plays subvert modern notions of poetic influence; as perverse and tragic rereadings of biblical narrative, they pervert conventional notions of midrash.

These perverse midrashim retell a biblical account, taking up a textual problem as a site for focus and creative expansion. But in changing or perverting the text, perverse midrashim highlight perversity in it. By making these changes, perverse midrashim reveal a culture's repressed fears; their shocking quality derives from something culturally perverse or taboo, something elided by orthodoxy. The objective or purpose is to return us to origins, to recover something that has been lost by ecclesiastical retelling, and to restore it to the text. Perverse midrashim, then, are highly unorthodox reinterpretations of scripture that, in the process of perversion, seek to conserve or, perhaps more accurately, to restore something in the text that orthodoxy has elided, obscured, or even hidden. For perverse midrashim to be effective, they must aggressively confront cultural fears, and thus the medium is significant. *Salomé* and *Saül* were composed for the public stage, the most powerful and therefore controversial medium at the *fin de siècle*, when censorship was more restrictive than ever. Lawrence's *The Man Who Died*, however, was a novella never intended for public performance, but only for private reading. Though certainly the power to ban books is meaningful, still it is the public quality of the experience, the revealing of repressed fears for all to see, that lends particular piquancy to these perverse midrashim.

## REVERTING TO WILDE AND GIDE

While *Salomé* and *Saül* manifested the fears repressed by censorship by revealing perversities present in the biblical texts, these plays also returned to those texts something that had been lost and restored it for the experience of modern audiences. In bringing together the essentially irreconcilable movements of biblical criticism and theatre reform, however, the plays also embodied an ambivalence that deepened the anxiety. It is not new to claim that Wilde's and Gide's plays participated in the avant-garde theatre movements of their time. Wilde's play has been described as consciously *symboliste*,[16] and Gide had hoped that his would be performed by one of the most innovative theatre companies in Paris. Both Wilde and Gide had attended Mallarmé's *mardis*,[17] and both were attracted to what they saw as the aestheticism of the Roman Catholic Church and the medieval emphasis on symbol and mystical experience as best exemplified by the eucharist, itself perhaps as much a dramatic as a religious experience. But Wilde's and Gide's plays were just as much implicated in the project of the biblical critics, who looked back to the period of the Hebrew prophets as the time when revelation began and to the life of Christ as the time when it was embodied. These critics sought to recover the prophetic experience of being present to revelation as it was occurring in the person of a prophet or of Christ.

Whereas many dramatists, particularly those in Wilde's and Gide's circles, looked back to ancient Greek ritual drama and medieval mystery plays as examples of drama serving its original function of a spiritual expression and as a site of spiritual experience, Wilde and Gide selected narratives from these two periods of biblical revelation and made them over into dramas of spiritual desire. They effected the experience of transcendence occurring in the individual through the agency of drama by making the connection between a symbol, in both cases sexual desire, and its platonically pure origin, spiritual desire. By making over into drama the encounter with revelation in history, Wilde and Gide accomplished what both the biblical critics and the avant-garde dramatists had sought, a direct and individual experience with the divine in the real. To conflate

---

16. See, for instance, Donohue (1994) and Quigley (1994), a pair of articles appearing in *Modern Drama.*

17. Mallarmé's famous Tuesday evening salons were where major writers and artists convened. To be *seen* there was prestigious, for it seems Mallarmé did all the talking.

Matthew Arnold's and Jeffrey Perl's terminology, these plays effected a Hebraist *nostos* and a Hellenist *shavah* at the same time.

This was not, however, a comfortable reconciliation. Whereas Richard Green Moulton (1895) theorizes that prophecy was the philosophy of history erected into drama, and that it served for the ancient Israelites the role that drama had in classical literature, to equate Hebrew prophecy with classical ritual drama as genres remains different from combining them in actual practice. It is perhaps not unlike the ambivalence that both Wilde and Gide felt of being half Protestant and half Catholic, an experience both found to be profoundly unsettling. One of the most apparent difficulties is in the artificial nature of the drama, particularly as Gide had argued for it, which was to be the venue for the real prophetic experience. Not only were these plays reenacting biblical events, an activity inherently mimetic and artificial, but they also had modified these events and perverted these accounts. The plays then would seem to be light-years away from any originary prophetic experience. Yet drama was to make the transition from the merely mimetic to the symbolic invocation of direct spiritual experience.

This was Gide's point in his essay *L'Evolution de la théâtre* (1904), in which he asks what happened to the classical mask. If it migrated to the audience, as he argues it did in his time, then it would serve to mask life, but if it were returned to the stage, as it should rightfully be and has been in ages of brilliant drama, then it would separate the audience from the stage. This separation focuses tragedy on character rather than on situation, and it maintains the sense of strangeness that an artist seeks to produce by putting his characters at a distance from the audience rather than pursuing an illusion of realism, of episodism and particularity. In her 1984 study of masks in modern drama, Susan Valeria Harris Smith explains that while the mask liberates man off the stage, as anthropologists have observed, on the stage it suggests restricted activity and determines the audience's relationship to the action (2). The use of the mask separates the presentational stage from the representational stage of realism and naturalism and elevates it to the level of ritual. This idea is based on two common assumptions: that the theatre began as a masked religious ritual and that masks implemented the magnification of stage action, removing it from the merely human realm to a superhuman or spiritual one. "The human experience is intensified and reduced to essentials; the human face is transformed by the mask into a symbol, into a huge image, an icon" (50). Smith summarizes the use of masks based on these assumptions as characteristic of modern drama:

This new ritualistic, hieratic, symbolic, aesthetic theater would appeal to the unconscious mind, would speak in images. The masker in primitive cultures was a visible vehicle of communal religious expression when he danced; the imitation of an ordered universe reaffirmed and maintained that cosmic order. The idea that a modern community might also experience such ritual prompted Max Reinhardt, Antonin Artaud, William Butler Yeats, and others to employ the devices of an esoteric, aesthetic, and intellectual theater. The mask figured prominently in this attempt to revive communal theater. (3)

The heroic mask of the drama of myth and ritual symbolized aggrandized and ennobled humankind, and the spectator witnessing the actions of masked heroes shared the experiences of the godlike. The hero, effecting the union with the god, acted out the struggle on behalf of the entire community, and the antique mask created an "objective reality" for the audience, an "altered dimension," as its most important function (51). The mask then serves to identify the hero on stage, the totem in a community ritual designed to expiate sin. It is critical for producing distance, a sense of strangeness: drama as drama, as ritual, as art, as artificial and not pursuing the illusion of reality. This was Gide's argument, that drama is the community ritual that effects direct spiritual experience in the audience, rather than merely portraying someone else's experience. The mask was his metaphor for this theory. So Wilde and Gide invoked in their plays an ancient totemic ritual[18] of the Semites and the Greeks that went far

---

18. Though he does not specifically say so, Gide draws on a line of thought prevalent in his generation. Sigmund Freud (1913; 1946) cites heavily the 1889 (1995) work of Robertson Smith on the ritual practices of the ancient Semitic peoples. Freud was particularly interested in Robertson Smith's discussion of the "totem meal" as an originary communal ceremony in which a sacred animal was sacrificed and eaten. Building on Robertson Smith's hypothesis that the sacramental killing and communal eating of the totem animal was an important feature of totemic religion, Freud's psychoanalysis of this event reveals that the totem animal was in reality a substitute for the primal father, who had driven the younger men out of the tribe because they competed with him for women. United, they had the courage to do what each could not have done on his own. "The totem meal, which is perhaps mankind's earliest festival, would thus be a repetition and a commemoration of this memorable and criminal deed, which was the beginning of so many things—of social organization, of moral restrictions and of religion" (501). Robertson Smith shows that the meaning of this act was sanctification through participation in a common meal, allaying the sense of guilt by the solidarity of all the participants. At some time, the concept of God emerged and took control, and Freud concludes, "At bottom God is nothing other than an exalted father" (504). Thus "after a long lapse of time their bitterness against their father, which had driven them to their deed, grew less, and their longing for him increased; and it became possible for an ideal to emerge which embodied the unlimited power of the primal father against whom they had once fought as well as their readiness to submit to him. . . .

beyond mere mimesis.[19]

Though Gide refers to the mask as an abstract principle of drama designed to create artificiality and strangeness, he actually used masks in his 1922 premier of *Saül*. The stage setting was simple and only vaguely suggested the scenes with drapery, a throne, and a couple of stools. The central characters were costumed in exaggerated and symbolic dress, though not masked.[20] Saül wore a very long and dark beard, an enormous crown, and a full-length, long-sleeved velvet gown belted by a wide jeweled girdle; David was practically naked, dressed only in an animal skin; the Queen, the barber, and the various men of the people all appeared in

---

The elevation of the father who had once been murdered into a god from whom the clan claimed descent was a far more serious attempt at atonement than had been the ancient covenant with the totem" (505). This is for Freud the beginning of both society and the sense of guilt. In Robertson Smith's interpretation, these ceremonies in which the ancient Semites celebrated the death of the deity were the commemoration of a mythical tragedy. "'The mourning,' he declares, 'is not a spontaneous expression of sympathy with the divine tragedy, but obligatory and enforced by fear of supernatural anger. And a chief object of the mourners is to disclaim responsibility for the god's death'" (507). In later developments, the son's senses of guilt and rebelliousness became more operative, the son putting himself in the place of the father-god while at the same time feeling the need to atone for the originary crime, murder, which can be expiated only by the sacrifice of another life. In the sacrifice of the son, he both offers the greatest possible atonement to the father and becomes the god in place of the father. "Thus we can trace through the ages the identity of the totem meal with animal sacrifice, with the anthropic human sacrifice and with the Christian eucharist" (509).

19. In the history of Greek art, Freud continues, we come upon a situation strikingly similar to the scene of the totem meal identified by Robertson Smith. In Greek tragedy, a company of individuals surround a single figure; they are the chorus and he the impersonator of the hero. The hero of the tragedy must suffer, bearing the burden of "tragic guilt," which, Freud observes, "is not always easy to find, for in the light of our everyday life it is often no guilt at all. As a rule it lay in rebellion against some divine or human authority" (509). Why does the hero have to suffer? In short, "because he was the primal father, the Hero of the great primaeval tragedy which was being re-enacted with a tendentious twist; and the tragic guilt was the guilt which he had to take on himself in order to relieve the Chorus from theirs. . . . In the remote reality it had actually been the members of the Chorus who caused the Hero's suffering; now, however, they exhausted themselves with sympathy and regret and it was the Hero himself who was responsible for his own sufferings. The crime which was thrown onto his shoulders, presumptuousness and rebelliousness against a great authority, was precisely the crime for which the members of the Chorus, the company of brothers, were responsible. Thus the tragic Hero became, though it might be against his will, the redeemer of the Chorus. That being so, it is easy to understand how drama, which had become extinct, was kindled into fresh life in the Middle Ages around the Passion of Christ" (509–10). Here Freud has come to the same conclusion the nineteenth-century literary scholars advanced—that secular drama had developed from religious ritual—and the dramatists implicitly espoused this same thesis in their attempts to return to these religious and dramatic origins. "The Church," writes Max Reinhardt, "especially the Catholic Church, is the very cradle of our modern theatre" (quoted in Smith 1984, 62).

20. Smith (1984) points out that in many cases the hero was not masked; the heroic mask in modern ritual drama was often the human face, surrounded by masked faces, attesting to the ritual quality of the action and the heroic dimensions of the protagonist's struggle. Here the masks supply the context, not the main point of focus (88). This is the case with *Saül*.

vaguely Middle Eastern dress; the Sorcerer at Endor wore only a long, moplike wig and rags; and the ghost of Samuel appeared robed, with only his white-bearded face visible. The demons were all masked and dressed in abstractly painted bodysuits. The masks seemed quite primitive,[21] with exaggerated facial features and woolly hair. It was not apparent from their costumes which demon represented what vice; rather, they all were bizarre and somewhat frightening. As the review of the production in the July 1922 *Le Théâtre* expresses it, "The set and costuming of *Saul* imagined by the Vieux-Colombier [. . .] placed it in the category of work in which there is no pretension to historical truth."[22] Regarding the demons in particular, the review reports that in the first scene, when they took over the palace, "this 'infamous menagerie' who had appeared in the frontispiece to *Flowers of Evil*, were a poetic work of true dramatic invention."[23] On the actors' portrayal of the demons, the reviewer concludes, "Praises for the manner in which they played, at once simple and picturesque, stirring and 'drunken,' as had written Charles Baudelaire."[24] Clearly this was no realistic enactment of biblical narrative, but a highly contrived and artistic rendering designed to exploit the artificial and strange. Gide's production of his play was consistent with his drama theory, specifically with reference to the mask.

So also was Gide's play consistent with Freud's description of Greek tragedy. Saül is clearly the hero who must suffer, the source of whose tragic guilt is indeed difficult, if not impossible, to discern but is clearly related to his rebellion against divine and human authority. He suffers because he is the surrogate for the primal father, and he takes on a guilt for which it is hard to find him really responsible so as to relieve others of their responsibility and guilt. In Wilde's play, meanwhile, Iokanaan assumes the hero-son-Christ role of sacrifice, supplanting the primal father as god and atoning for his mythical murder. Thus did these plays, together, enact the ancient psychological drama, one that Freud had

---

21. They also look remarkably like Picasso's masks, such as in *Les Desmoiselles d'Avignon*. As Smith (1984) points out, masks of many kinds fascinated various artists at the *fin de siècle* and into the twentieth century.

22. Translated from "La mise en scène de *Saül* et les costumes imaginés par le Vieux-Colombier [Jacques Copeau's theatre, where it was performed] situent la pièce dans le cadre qui lui est propre et sans nuire aucunement à de prétendues vérités historiques." Translations in this chapter are my own.

23. Translated from "c'est la 'ménagerie infâme' dont il est question au frontispice des *Fleurs du Mal*, et ces confidents-là sont, à la fois, une trouvaille de poète et une véritable invention dramatique."

24. Translated from "Des éloges pour la manière à la fois simple et pittoresque dont ils jouent, agissent et 'ribotent' comme eût écrit Charles Baudelaire."

pointed out was a Christian, classical, and even more ancient theme. It is the peculiar nature of tragic drama that while its artificiality creates distance between the audience and the stage, that distance is eclipsed by the audience's experience. Whereas centuries of interpreters of the Saul narrative in the Bible seem to have explained it in order to create distance between Saul's situation and the reader, Gide truncated that distance by refusing to seek explanation and instead exploring Saül's experience in such a way that the audience participated in his tragedy. Wilde had accomplished the same thing in his play by implicating the entire Gospel context and message rather than treating John the Baptist's death at the hands of Herodias's daughter as a discrete narrative. Key to both of these projects was their use of tragedy, or really the resurrection of the ancient ritual of atonement underlying the Christian eucharist.

For, in a period of dueling dualisms—when romanticism and classicism were still contending for the tradition, when *symbolisme* and realism struggled both to describe and to improve life, when Catholicism and Protestantism were confronting modernity and each other all over again, and when spiritualism and materialism seemed hopelessly opposed— atonement was needed. Yet Wilde and Gide defied the strategies that would merely polarize, synthesize, or anesthetize these movements, embracing instead the ambivalence that underlay the surface of *fin de siècle* culture. Returning to the original drama of the human and divine relationship, they uncovered the ancient anxieties attending the experience of separation and abandonment, of desire for union with God, of the plight of humanity in this modern as in that ancient age, joining the psalmist and Jesus in their plaint, "Eloi, Eloi, lemah sabachthani?"[25] Art, drama, affects that union. Art, the symbol is true; history is cultural mythmaking, false. As perverse midrashim, *Salomé* and *Saül* exposed the secret that Western culture's most sacred document does not sustain its myths and values, that the referent for so-called blasphemy is the cultural myth and not the text itself, and that the Bible, in its perplexities and perversities, is in fact a subversive challenge to that culture's most cherished beliefs.

---

25. Mark 15:34; Matt 27:46. In Ps 22:1, "Eli, Eli, lama 'asabthani?"

# WORKS CITED

## PRIMARY WORKS

### *SALOMÉ* AND *SAÜL* TEXTS

Aldington, Richard, and Stanley Weintraub, eds. 1981. *The Portable Oscar Wilde*. New York: Viking Penguin. Standard English text.
Gide, André. 1922. *Saül*. Paris: Editions de la Nouvelle revue française.
"Salomé." N.d. Geneva: Bodmer Library.
"Salomé." N.d. Philadelphia: Rosenbach Foundation Museum.
"Salomé." N.d. University of Texas at Austin: Humanities Research Center.
Symons, Arthur, ed. 1927. *The Complete Works of Oscar Wilde: Salome and Other Plays*. New York: Wm. H. Wise & Co. Standard French text.

### LITERARY AND DRAMATIC WORKS

Bale, John. 1985. *Complete Plays of John Bale*. Ed. Peter Happ. Cambridge: Cambridge University Press. Includes *On the Threefold Law of God* and *John Baptist's Preaching*.
Baudelaire, Charles. 1973. *Correspondances*. Paris: Gallimard.
Flaubert, Gustave. 1944. *Trois Contes*. Montreal: Les Editions Variétés.
Gide, André. 1932–39. *Ouevres Complêts d'André Gide*. Paris: Nouvelle revue française.
———. 1953. *The Return of the Prodigal: Preceded by Five Other Treatises with "Saul: A Drama in Five Acts."* Trans. Dorothy Bussy. London: Seeker & Warburg. "Saul," 151–304.
Heine, Heinrick. "AttaTroll," *Zeitung für die Elegante Welt*. Ed. H. Laube. 1843.
Huysmans, J-K. 1922. *A Rebours*. Paris: G. Crés.
Lawrence, D. H. 1926. *David*. New York: Knopf.
———. 1973. *The Escaped Cock*. Los Angeles: Black Sparrow Press.
———. 1994. *The Man Who Died*. Princeton, NJ: Ecco Press.
Mallarmé, Stéphane. 1945. *Ouevres Complêts*. Ed. Henri Mondo and G. Jean-Aubry. Paris: Gallimard.
Milton, John. 1892. *Paradise Lost*. New York: Crowell.

———. 1977. *Samson Agonistes*. New York: Cambridge.

Poe, Edgar Allan. 1959. *Philosophy of Composition*. New York: Pageant.

Racine, Jean. 1856. *Chef d'oeuvres de Jean Racine*. Ed. Louis Fasquelle. New York: Ivison.

Ward, Mrs. Humphry. 1909. *Robert Elsmere*. Boston: Houghton Mifflin.

———. 1911. *The Writings of Mrs. Humphry Ward*. Boston: Houghton Mifflin. Includes *The History of David Grieve, Helbeck of Bannisdale, Eleanor, The Case of Richard Meynell,* and *Robert Elsmere*.

Wilde, Oscar. 1927. *The Complete Works of Oscar Wilde: Salome and Other Plays*. Intro. Arthur Symons. Vol. IX. New York: William H. Wise. "Salome," 1–53.

———. 1985. *The Picture of Dorian Gray*. Ed. Peter Ackroyd. Middlesex, England: Penguin.

———. 1996. *Salome*. New York: Random House.

## SCHOLARSHIP AND CRITICISM

Antoine, André. 1964. *Mes Souvenirs sur le Théâtre Libre*. Trans. Marvin A. Carolson, ed. H. D. Albright. Coral Gables, FL: University of Florida Press. Reprint 1994. New Haven, CT: Yale University Press.

Arnold, Matthew. 1869. *Culture and Anarchy*. London. Reprint 1903. London: Macmillan.

———. 1873. *Literature and Dogma: An Essay Towards a Better Apprehension of the Bible*. London.

Aubignac, Abbé D'. 1968. *Projet pour le rétablissement du théâtre*. New York: Blom Bates, Ernest Sutherland, ed. 1936. *The Bible Designed to Be Read as Living Literature: The Old and the New Testaments in the King James Version*. New York: Simon & Schuster.

Bates, Katharine Lee. 1893. *The English Religious Drama*. London: Macmillan. Reprint 1921.

"The Bible and the Stage." 1893. *Spectator* (February 4): 155–56.

"The Bible on the Stage." 1893. *New Review* (February): vol. 8, 183–89.

"Books of the Week." 1893. *Times* (February 23): 8.

Chambers, E. K. 1903. *The Mediaeval Stage*. Oxford: Clarendon Press.

Copeau, Jacques. 1990. *Copeau: Texts on Theatre*. Trans. and ed. Rudlin, John, and Norman H. Paul. New York: Routledge.

Drummond, Prof. 1885. "Contributions of Science to Christianity." *Expositor* (February).

Dumas, Alexandre, F. W. Farrar, and Henry Arthur Jones. 1893. "The Bible on the Stage." *New Review* (February): 183–89.

Farrar, Frederic W. 1872. *Witness of History to Christ*. London: Macmillan.

———. 1874a. *Life of Christ*. London: Cassell, Petter, and Galpin.

———. 1874b. *Silence and the Voices of God*. London: Macmillan.

———. 1876. *Fall of Man*. London: Macmillan.

———. 1878a. *Eternal Hope*. London: Macmillan.

———. 1878b. *St. Paul at Athens: Spiritual Christianity in Relation to Some Aspects of Modern Thought*. New York: Charles Scribner.

———. 1878c. *Theism and Christianity*. London: Christian Evidence Committee.

———. 1879. *Life and Work of St Paul*. London: Cassell, Petter, and Galpin.

———. 1880. *Solomon: His Life and Times*. London: Anson DF Randolph

———. 1882. *Early Days of Christianity*. London: Cassell, Petter, and Galpin.

———. 1885a. *Inspiration: A Clerical Symposium on "In What Sense and within What Limits Is the Bible the Word of God?"* New York: Thomas Whittaker.

———. 1885b. *Messages of the Books*. London: Macmillan.

———. 1886. *History of Interpretation: Eight Lectures Preached before the University of Oxford in the Year 1885*. New York: E. P. Dutton.

———. 1889. *Life of the Fathers*. Edinburgh: A&C Black.

———. 1890a. *Minor Prophets*. New York: Fleming H. Revell Co.

———. 1890b. *The Passion Play at Oberammergau 1890*. London.

———. 1891. *Social and Present Day Questions*. Boston: Bradley and Woodruff.

———. 1892. *The Voice from Sinai, the Eternal Bases of the Moral Law*. London: Isbister.

———. 1893a. *The Gospel According to Luke with Maps*. London: Cambridge University Press.

———. 1893b. *Lord's Prayer*. London: Isbister.

———. 1893–94. *First and Second Book of Kings*. London: Hodder and Stoughton.

———. 1895. *The Book of Daniel*. London: Hodder and Stoughton.

———. 1897a. *The Bible: Its Meaning and Supremacy*. London: Longmans, Green, and Co.

———. 1897b. *Sin and Its Conquerors*. New York: Revell.

————. 1898a. *Great Books*. New York: Ty Crowell and Co.

————. 1898b. *Herods*. New York: E. R. Herrick.

————. 1898c. *Seekers after God*. London: Macmillan.

————. 1899a. *Texts Explained*. New York: Dodd, Mead.

————. 1899b. *True Religion*. London: Freemantle.

————. 1902. *The Epistle of Paul the Apostle to the Hebrews*. London.

Findon, B. W. 1905. "A Plea for the Religious Drama." *Fortnightly Review* 84:708–15.

Fowell, Frank, and Frank Palmer. 1970. *Censorship in England*. New York: Burt Franklin. (Orig. pub. 1913.)

Frayne, John P., and Colton Johnson, eds. 1970. *Uncollected Prose by W. B. Yeats*. New York: Columbia University Press.

Frazer, J. G. 1963. *The Golden Bough: A Study in Magic and Religion*. New York: Simon & Schuster. (Orig. pub. 1922.)

————. 1909. *Passages of the Bible Chosen for Their Literary Beauty and Interest*. London: A&C Black.

Freud, Sigmund. 1946. *Totem and Taboo: Resemblances between the Psychic Lives of Savages and Neurotics*. Trans. A. A. Brill. New York: Vintage.

G. M. G. 1908. *The Stage Censor, An Historical Sketch: 1544–1907*. London: Sampson, Marston, & Co.

Gide, André. 1904. *L'Evolution de la théâtre*. Brussels: Société de la Libre Esthétique.

Greville, Robert Kaye. 1830. *The Drama Brought to the Test of Scripture and Found Wanting*. Edinburgh: William Oliphant.

Hone, William. 1823. *Ancient Mysteries Described, Especially the English Miracle Plays, Founded on Apocryphal New Testament Story, Extant among the Unpublished Manuscripts in the British Museum*. London: William Hone.

Jones, Henry Arthur. 1909. *The Censorship Muddle and a Way Out of It: A Letter Addressed to the Right Honourable Herbert Samuel*. London: Chiswick Press.

Julleville, L. Petit de. 1880. *Les Mystères*. Paris: Librairie Hachette.

Jusserand, J. J. 1885. *A Literary History of the English People from the Origins to the Renaissance*. London: T. Fisher Unwin.

Kelly, William. 1865. *Notices Illustrative of the Drama, and Other Popular Amusements, Chiefly in the Sixteenth and Seventeenth Centuries, Incidentally Illustrating Shakespeare and His Cotemporaries [sic]; Extracted from the Chamberlains' Accounts and Other Manuscripts of the Borough of Leicester*. London: John Russell Smith.

Lemaître, Jules. 1891–96. *Impressions du théâtre*. Paris: Société Française.

————. 1892. *Annales du théâtre*. Paris: Société Française.

Lugné-Poè, Aurélien François. 1930. *La Parade: souvenirs et impressions du théâtre—Le Sot du Tremplin*. Paris: Librairie Gallimard.

Marie, Gisèle. 1973. *Le Théâtre Symboliste: Ses origines, ses sources, pionniers et réalisateurs*. Paris: A-G Nizet.

Michaud, Guy. 1947. *La Doctrine Symboliste: Documents*. Paris: Librairie Nizet.

Moulton, Richard. 1895. *The Literary Study of the Bible: Account of the Leading Forms of Literature Represented in the Sacred Writings; Intended for English Readers*. London: Macmillan.

————. 1899. *The Bible as Literature*. London: Macmillan.

————. 1901. *A Short Introduction to the Literature of the Bible*. Boston: D. C. Heath.

————. 1907. *The Modern Reader's Bible*. 21 vols. New York: Macmillan. (Orig. pub. 1895.)

Palmer, John. 1913. *The Censor and the Theatres*. New York: Mitchell Kennerley.

Pollard, Alfred W. 1927. *English Miracle Plays, Moralities, and Interludes: Specimens of the Pre-Elizabethan Drama*. Oxford: Clarendon. (Orig. pub. 1890.)

Sarcey, Francisque. 1900–1902. *Quarante Ans de théâtre*. Paris: Biblioteque des annales politiques et littéraires.

Sepet, Marius. 1867. *Les Prophétes du Christ: études sur les origines du théâtre du moyen âge*. Paris: P. Letnielleux.

Shaw, George Bernard. 1931. *Our Theatres in the Nineties: Criticisms Contributed Week by Week to the* Saturday Review *from January 1895 to May 1898*. New York: Wm. H. Wise & Co.

Smith, Lucy Toulmin. 1963. *York Plays: The Plays Performed by the Crafts or Mysteries of York on the Day of Corpus Christi in the 14th, 15th, and 16th Centuries*. New York: Russell & Russell. (Orig. pub. 1885.)

Smith, William Robertson. 1876. "The Progress of Old Testament Studies." *British and Foreign Evangelical Review* 25:471–93.

————. 1900a. "Bible." *Encyclopaedia Britannica*. 9th ed.

————. 1900b. "Josephus." *Encyclopaedia Britannica*. 9th ed.

————. 1900c. "Prophet." *Encyclopaedia Britannica*. 9th ed.

————. 1908. *The Old Testament in the Jewish Church: A Course of Lectures on Biblical Criticism*. London: A&C Black.

————. 1912. *Lectures and Essays of William Robertson Smith.* Ed. John Sutherland Black and George Chrystal. London: A&C Black.

————. 1919. *The Prophets of Israel and Their Place in History to the Close of the Eighth Century BC.* London: A&C Black.

————. 1995. *Lectures on the Religion of the Semites, Second and Third Series, of William Robertson Smith.* Ed. John Day. Sheffield, England: JSOT.

"Théâtre du Vieux-Colombier: *Saul*." 1922. *Le Théâtre* (July): 11–13.

Unsigned review. 1893. *Pall Mall Gazette* (February 27): 3.

Ward, Adolphus William. 1899. *A History of English Dramatic Literature to the Death of Queen Anne.* London: Macmillan. (Orig. pub. 1875.)

Ward, Mrs. Humphry. 1911. *The Writings of Mrs. Humphry Ward.* Boston: Houghton Mifflin. Includes articles "Mr Renan's Autobiography," "The Literature of Introspection: Amiel's *Journal Intime*," "Review of *Marius the Epicurean* by Walter Pater," "The New Reformation: A Dialogue," "A New Book on the Gospels," and "The Apostles' Creed: A Translation and Introduction"; and pamphlets *A Morning in the Bodleian* and *Unbelief and Sin.*

————. 1917. *Towards the Goal.* London: Murray.

————. 1918. *A Writer's Recollections.* London: Collins.

Warton, Thomas. 1737. *History of English Poetry.* London.

Whiston, William, ed. and trans. 1895. *The Complete Works of Flavius Josephus, The Celebrated Jewish Historian.* Philadelphia: John E. Potter.

Wilde, Oscar. 1893. Letter to the *Times*. (March 2).

Winstanley, L., ed. *Shelley's Defence of Poetry.* 1911. London: D. C. Heath.

Yeats, W. B. 1961. *Essays and Introductions.* London: Macmillan.

## SECONDARY WORKS

Alter, Robert. 1981. *The Art of Biblical Narrative.* San Francisco: Basic Books.

————. 1992. *The World of Biblical Literature.* San Francisco: Basic Books.

Balakian, Anna E. 1977. *The Symbolist Movement: A Critical Appraisal.* New York: New York University Press.

————. 1982. *The Symbolist Movement in the Literature of European Languages.* Budapest: Akademiai Kiado.

Bird, Alan. 1977. *The Plays of Oscar Wilde.* New York: Barnes & Noble.

Blackburn, Ruth H. 1971. *Biblical Drama under the Tudors.* The Hague: Mouton.

Block, Haskell. 1963. *Mallarmé and the Symbolist Drama*. Detroit: Wayne State University Press.

Bloom, Harold. 1975. *Kabbalah and Criticism*. New York: Seabury Press.

Brée, Germaine. 1963. *Gide*. New Brunswick, NJ: Rutgers University Press.

Brueggemann, Walter. 1990. *First and Second Samuel, Interpretation*. A Bible Commentary for Teaching and Preaching. Louisville, KY: John Knox Press.

Butterfield, Herbert. 1965. *The Whig Interpretation of History*. New York: Norton.

Cargill, Oscar. 1969. *Drama and Liturgy*. New York: Octagon Books. (Orig. pub. 1930.)

Claude, Jean. 1992. *André Gide et le théâtre*. Paris: Gallimard.

Cohen, Philip K. 1978. *The Moral Vision of Oscar Wilde*. Madison, NJ: Fairleigh Dickinson University Press.

Coleman, Edward D. 1931. *The Bible in English Drama: An Annotated List of Plays Including Translations from Other Languages from the Beginnings to 1931*. New York: New York Public Library.

Deak, Frantisek. 1993. *Symbolist Theater: The Formation of an Avant-Garde*. Baltimore: PAJ/Johns Hopkins Press.

Dollimore, Jonathan. 1991. *Sexual Dissidence: Augustine to Wilde, Freud to Foucault*. Oxford: Clarendon Press.

Donohue, Joseph. 1994. "*Salome* and the Wildean Art of Symbolist Theatre." *Modern Drama* 37:84–103.

Ehrman, Bart D. 1993. *The Orthodox Corruption of Scripture: The Effect of Early Christological Controversies on the Text of the New Testament*. New York: Oxford University Press.

Eichler, Barry L., and Jeffrey H. Tigay, eds. 1988. *Judah Goldin: Studies in Midrash and Related Literature*. Philadelphia: Jewish Publication Society.

Elliott, John R. 1989. *Playing God: Medieval Mysteries on the Modern Stage*. Toronto: University of Toronto Press.

Ellmann, Richard. 1985. "Overtures to *Salome*." In *Modern Critical Views: Oscar Wilde*, ed. Harold Bloom, 77–90. New York: Chelsea House Publishers.

———. 1987. *Oscar Wilde*. New York: Vintage Books.

Eltis, Sos. 1996. *Revising Wilde: Society and Subversion in the Plays of Oscar Wilde*. Oxford: Clarendon Press.

Fiorenza, Elisabeth Schüssler. 1983. *In Memory of Her: A Feminist Theological Reconstruction of Christian Origins*. New York: Crossroads.

Fishbane, Michael, ed. 1993. *The Midrashic Imagination: Jewish Exegesis, Thought and History*. Albany: SUNY.

Fokkelman, J. P. 1981. *Narrative Art and Poetry in the Books of Samuel: A Full Interpretation Based on Stylistic and Structural Analyses.* 4 vols. Netherlands: Van Gorcum, Assen.

Friedman, Richard Elliott. 1996. *The Disappearance of God: A Divine Mystery.* New York: Little, Brown.

Fryer, Jonathan. 1997. *André and Oscar.* London: Constable.

Gardiner, Harold C. 1946. *Mysteries' End: An Investigation of the Last Days of the Medieval Religious Stage.* New Haven, CT: Yale University Press.

Goldin, Judah. 1988. *Judah Goldin: Studies in Midrash and Related Liturature.* Ed. Barry L. Eichler, Jeffrey H. Tigay. Philadelphia: JPS.

Gunn, David M. 1980. *The Fate of King Saul: An Interpretation of a Biblical Story.* Sheffield: Scholars Press.

Gunn, David M., and Danna Nolan Fewell. 1993. *Narrative in the Hebrew Bible.* New York: Oxford University Press.

Hardison, O. B. 1965. *Christian Rite and Christian Drama in the Middle Ages: Essays in the Origin and Early History of Modern Drama.* Baltimore: Johns Hopkins University Press.

Harris, John Wesley. 1992. *Medieval Theatre in Context: An Introduction.* New York: Routledge.

Hartman, Geoffrey H., and Sanford Budick, eds. 1986. *Midrash and Literature.* New Haven, CT: Yale University Press.

Henderson, John A. 1971. *The First Avant-Garde, 1887–1894: Sources of the Modern French Theatre.* London: George G. Harrap & Co.

Hoare, Philip. 1997. *Wilde's Last Stand: Decadence, Conspiracy, and the First World War.* London: Duckworth.

Hytier, Jean. 1962. *André Gide.* Trans. Richard Howard. New York: Doubleday.

Jasper, Gertrude. 1947. *Adventure in the Theatre: Lugné-Poe and the Théâtre de l'Oeuvre to 1899.* New Brunswick, NJ: Rutgers University Press.

Kermode, Frank. 1979. *The Genesis of Secrecy: On the Interpretation of Narrative.* Cambridge, MA: Harvard University Press.

Knowles, Dorothy. 1967. *French Drama of the Inter-war Years, 1918–39.* London: George G. Harrap & Co.

Kohl, Norbert. 1989. *Oscar Wilde: The Works of a Conformist Rebel.* Trans. David Henry Wilson. Cambridge: Cambridge University Press.

Kugel, James L. 1990. *In Potiphar's House: The Interpretive Life of Biblical Texts.* San Francisco: Harper.

Kuryluk, Ewa. 1987. *Salome and Judas in the Cave of Sex: The Grotesque—Origins, Iconography, Techniques.* Evanston, IL: Northwestern University Press.

Lancaster, Henry Carrington. 1936. *A History of French Dramatic Literature in the Seventeenth Century.* Baltimore: Johns Hopkins Press.

Lerner, Alice Lapidus. 1980. *Passing the Love of Women: A Study of Gide's Saül and Its Biblical Roots.* Lanham, MD: University Press of America.

Long, V. Phillips. 1989. *The Reign and Rejection of King Saul: A Case for Literary and Theological Coherence.* Atlanta: Scholars Press.

Margerie, Bertrand de, ed. 1993. *An Introduction to the History of Exegesis.* Vol. 1. Petersham, MA: St. Bede's Publishing.

Mathews, Thomas. 1993. *The Clash of Gods: A Reinterpretation of Early Christian Art.* Princeton, NJ: Princeton University Press.

McLaren, James C. 1953. *The Theatre of André Gide: Evolution of a Moral Philosopher.* Baltimore: Johns Hopkins Press.

Moore, Will G. 1971. *The Classical Drama of France.* New York: Oxford University Press.

Muir, Lynette R. 1995. *The Biblical Drama of Medieval Europe.* Cambridge: Cambridge University Press.

Nassaar, Christopher S. 1974. *Into the Demon Universe: A Literary Exploration of Oscar Wilde.* New Haven, CT: Yale University Press.

Neusner, Jacob. 1989a. *Invitation to Midrash: The Workings of Rabbinic Biblical Interpretation: A Teaching Book.* San Francisco: Harper.

————. 1989b. *The Midrash Compilations for the Sixth and Seventh Centuries: An Introduction to the Rhetorical, Logical, and Topical Program.* Atlanta: Scholars Press.

Norton, David. 1993. *A History of the Bible as Literature.* Vol. 2. London: Cambridge University Press, 1993.

Owst, G. R. 1961. *Literature and Pulpit in Medieval England: A Neglected Chapter in the History of English Letters and of the English People.* Oxford: Blackwell. (Orig. pub. 1933.)

Pagels, Elaine. 1995. *The Origin of Satan.* New York: Vintage Books.

Perl, Jeffrey M. 1984. *The Tradition of Return: The Implicit History of Modern Literature.* Princeton, NJ: Princeton University Press.

————. 1985. Stéphane Mallarmé. In *European Writers: The Romantic Century,* ed. Jacques Barzun and George Stade, 1567–95. New York: Charles Scribner's Sons.

Peterson, William S. 1976. *Victorian Heretic: Mrs. Humphry Ward's Robert Elsmere.* Great Britain: Leicester University Press.

Phillips, Henry. 1980. *The Theatre and Its Critics in Seventeenth-Century France*. Cambridge: Oxford University Press.

Philomène de los Reyes, Marie. 1978. *The Biblical Theme in Modern Drama*. Quezon City, Philippines: University of the Philippines Press.

Pollard, Patrick. 1991. *André Gide: Homosexual Moralist*. New Haven, CT: Yale University Press.

Polzin, Robert. 1989. *Samuel and the Deuteronomist: A Literary Study of the Deuteronomic History*. New York: Harper & Row.

Potter, Robert. 1975. *The English Morality Play: Origins, History, and Influence of a Dramatic Tradition*. London: Routledge.

Powell, Kerry. 1990. *Oscar Wilde and the Theatre of the 1890s*. Cambridge: Cambridge University Press.

Quigley, Austin E. 1994. "Realism and Symbolism in Oscar Wilde's *Salomé*." *Modern Drama* 37:104–19.

Rhoads, David, and Donald Michie. 1982. *Mark as Story: An Introduction to the Narrative of a Gospel*. Philadelphia: Fortress.

Rogerson, J. W. 1990. *The Bible and Criticism in Victorian Britain: Profiles of F. D. Maurice and William Robertson Smith*. London: JSOT.

Roston, Murray. 1968. *Biblical Drama in England: From the Middle Ages to the Present Day*. Evanston, IL: Northwestern University Press.

Scott, Bernard Brandon. 1989. *Hear Then the Parable: A Commentary on the Parables of Jesus*. Minneapolis: Fortress.

Sedgwick, Eve. 1985. *Between Men: English Literature and Male Homosocial Desire*. New York: Columbia University Press.

Smith, Susan Valeria Harris. 1984. *Masks in Modern Drama*. Berkeley: University of California Press.

Spong, John Shelby. 1992. *Born of a Woman: A Bishop Rethinks the Birth of Jesus*. San Francisco: Harper.

Stern, David. 1991. *Parables in Midrash: Narrative and Exegesis in Rabbinic Literature*. Cambridge, MA: Harvard University Press.

Sternberg, Meir. 1985. *The Poetics of Biblical Narrative: Ideological Literature and the Drama of Reading*. Bloomington: Indiana University Press.

Stevens, Martin. 1990. "Misconceptions," *Approaches to Teaching Medieval English Literature*. New York: MLA.

Thomas, Lawrence. 1950. *André Gide: The Ethic of the Artist*. London: Secker & Warburg.

Trible, Phyllis. 1978. *God and the Rhetoric of Sexuality*. Philadelphia: Fortress.

Tydeman, William, and Steven Price. 1996. *Wilde: Salome.* Cambridge: Cambridge University Press.

Wickham, Glynne. 1980. *Early English Stages, 1300–1660.* Vol. 1, *1300–1576.* New York: Columbia University Press. (Orig. pub. 1959.)

Yoshii, Akio. 1992. *André Gide: Le Retour de l'enfant prodigue.* Fukuoka: Presses Universitaires du Kyushu.

# INDEX